शिवसंहिता।

Shiva Samhita

A Classical Text on Yoga and Tantra

(English Translation of Sanskrit Verses
with Their Roman Transliteration)

Translated into English by
Swami Vishnuswaroop

Divine Yoga Institute
Kathmandu, Nepal

ALSO BY THE AUTHOR

Yoga Kundalini Upanishad (in English)

Yoga Darshana Upanishad (in English)

Minor Yoga Upanishads (in English)

HathaYoga Pradipika (in English)

Two Yoga Samhitas (in English)

Triyoga Upanishad (in English)

Gheranda Samhita (in English)

Goraksha Samhita (in English)

Surya Namskara (in Nepali)

Shiva Samhita (in Nepali)

Durga Strotram (in Nepali)

Vagalamukhi Stotram (in Nepali)

Amogha Shivakavacham (in Nepali)

ISBN: 9781521738757

DEDICATION

Tasmai Shri Gurave Namah!

To My Guru Swami Satyananda Saraswati,
Founder of Bihar School of Yoga,
Munger, India.

GRATITUDE

First of all, I would like to express my heartfelt salutations to Adinatha (the Primordial Master) and my Guru Swami Satyananda Saraswati for their inspiration and guidance I have received for my work. I realize that my unwavering faith and belief in God and Guru is a motivational gift for me in completing this work. I could never have done it without their blessings.

I am always thankful to Ms. Bhawani Uprety for her untiring support she has provided me during the preparation of various classical texts on yoga. My many thanks go to her forever.

May God and Guru inspire us to tread the path of yoga in order to achieve the ultimate goal of human life!

- Swami Vishnuswaroop

CONTENTS

INTRODUCTION

Śiva Samhitā is an unparalleled and unique Sanskrit text on classical yoga. It explains the concept of yoga, its philosophy and practice in detail. Lord *Śiva*, the expounder of yoga, has declared this science of yoga for the welfare of all creatures in all three worlds. The discourse and teachings in all five chapters in this text are primarily focused on the philosophy of creation and dissolution of the universe, bondage and liberation, the right knowledge of the reality and the ultimate aim of human life – *mokṣa* or the liberation.

It elaborates the ways of attaining perfections through the practice of various forms and techniques of yoga and finally, awakening the *Kuṇḍalinī*, the *Śakti*. It also discusses the human body - the microcosm as the replica of macrocosm, the principles and importance of yogic way of life and the importance of the practice of *āsana, prānāyāma, mudrā, bandha, pratyāhāra, dhāranā and dhyāna* as the fundamental step by step means to achieve *sāmādhi*, the ultimate goal of yoga.

One of the distinct features of the present text is that it includes all *mudrās* on the *tāntric* sexual acts from the original manuscript in Chapter Four. A few commentators of *Śiva Samhitā* have excluded them from their texts as they marked that such *tāntric* performance was "an obscene practice indulged in by low-class *Tāntrists.*"

It is an important treatise on the subject of yoga for a precise understanding of its philosophy and practice for both teacher and student of yoga.

In this text, the original Sanskrit verses are in Devanagari along with their Roman transliteration so that any reader of English could directly read the original verses or their transliteration and translation in English.

It is hoped that this text would be beneficial to the yoga scholars, students and interested readers of the subject.

Publisher

प्रथमः पटलः

Prathamaḥ Paṭalaḥ

Chapter One

Discourse on Dissolution

Existence of One Reality Only

एकं ज्ञानं नित्यमाद्यन्तशुन्यं नान्यत् किञ्चिद्वर्तते वस्तु सत्यम् ।
यद्भेदोऽस्मिन्निन्द्रियोपाधिना वै ज्ञानस्यायं भासते नान्यथैव ॥१॥

ekaṃ jñānaṃ nityamādyantaśunnyaṃ
nānyat kiñcidvartate vastu satyam /
yadbhedo'sminnindriyopādhinā vai
jñānasyāyaṃ bhāsate nānnyathaiva /1/

The *Jñāna* (knowledge of the *Brahman*) alone is eternal. It is without beginning and end. There does not exist anything real. What-so-ever diversities are seen in the world, are but the attributes of the senses. They are reflections of that *Jñāna* (knowledge of the *Brahman*) which remains alone and nothing else. –1.

अथ भक्तानुरक्तोऽहं वक्ति योगानुशासनम् ।
ईश्वरः सर्वभूतानामात्ममुक्तिप्रदायकः ॥२॥

atha bhaktānurakto'haṃ vakti yogānuśāsanam /
īśvaraḥ sarvabhūtānāmātmamuktipradāyakaḥ /2/

त्यक्त्वा विवादशिलानां मतं दुर्ज्ञानहेतुकम् ।
आत्माज्ञानाय भूतानामनन्यगतिचेतसाम् ॥३॥

tyaktvā vivādaśīlānāṃ mataṃ durjñānahetukam /
ātmajnānāya bhūtānāmananyagaticetasām /3/

Being affectionate towards my devotees, I now explain the discipline of yoga. I am *Īśvara* (the Eternal Being); I am the true Self of all living beings, and the giver of liberation to all. The views of the disputants that are the causes of false knowledge are given up here. It is for gaining the knowledge of the Self by those people whose minds are focused on that ultimate shelter alone. –2-3.

Difference in the Scriptural Opinions

सत्यं केचित्प्रशंसन्ति तपः शौचं तथापरे ।
क्षमां केचित्प्रशंसन्ति तथैव सममार्ज्जवम् ॥४॥

satyaṃ kecitpraśamsanti tapahaḥ śaucaṃ tathāpare /
kṣamāṃ kecitpraśamsanti tathaiva samamārjjavam /4/

Some admire truth, others austerity and purity; some praise forgiveness, others equanimity and sincerity. –4.

केचिद्दानं प्रशंसन्ति पितृकर्म तथापरे ।
केचिद्कर्म प्रशंसन्ति केचिद्वैराग्यपमुत्तमम् ॥५॥

keciddānaṃ praśamsanti pitṛkarma tathāpare /
kecitkarma praśamsanti kecidvairāgyamuttamam /5/

Some praise donation, others praise obsequial rites (offering oblation to forefathers); some speak highly of karma and some regard non-attachment as the best quality. –5.

केचिद्गृहस्थकर्माणि प्रशंसन्ति विचक्षणाः ।
अग्निहोत्रादिकं कर्म तथा केचित्परं विदुः ॥६॥

kecidgṛhasthakarmāni praśamsanti vicakṣaṇāḥ /
agnihotrādikaṃ karma tathā kecitparaṃ viduḥ /6/

Some wise people praise the duties of family life, while others consider fire-sacrifice etc. as the highest importance. –6.

मन्त्रयोगं प्रशंसन्ति केचित्तीर्थानुसेवनम् ।

एवं बहूनुपायांस्तु प्रवदन्ति हि मुक्तये ॥७॥

mantrayogaṃ praśamsanti kecittīrthānusevanam /

evaṃ bahūnupāyāṃstu pravadanti hi muktaye /7/

Similarly, some praise *Mantra Yoga* (union with the *Paramātman* through the repetition of a *mantra*); some believe making pilgrimages is the highest good. In this manner, numerous ways are declared for attaining liberation. –7.

एवं व्यवसिता लोके कृत्याकृत्यविदो जनाः ।

व्यामोहमेव गच्छन्ति विमुक्ताः पापकर्मभिः ॥८॥

evaṃ vyavasitā loke kṛtyākṛtyavido janāḥ /

vyāmohameva gacchanti vimuktāḥ pāpakarmabhiḥ /8/

Even with the knowledge of which actions are good and which are evil, being free from sinful acts, people are thus diversely engaged in this world, and are subject to bewilderment. –8.

एतन्मतावलम्बी यो लब्ध्वा दुरितपुण्यके ।

भ्रमतीत्यवशः सोऽत्र जन्ममृत्युपरम्पराम् ॥९॥

etanmatāvalambī yo labdhvā duritapunyake /

bhramatītyavaśaḥ so'tra janmamṛtyuparamparām /9/

Those people who follow these various doctrines, continually receiving the fruits of their good and bad actions, constantly wander through the cycle of birth and death in this world. –9.

अन्यैर्मतिमतां श्रेष्ठैर्गुप्तालोकनतत्परैः ।

आत्मानो बहवः प्रोक्ता नित्याः सर्वगतास्तथा ॥१०॥

anyairmatimatāṃ śresṭhairguptālokanatatparaiḥ /

ātmāno bahavaḥ proktā nityāḥ sarvagatāstathā /10/

Others, wisest among the many, are eager to investigate the mystical science. They describe that the Self is manifested as many, is eternal and is all pervading. –10.

यद्यत्प्रत्यक्षविषयं तदन्यन्नास्ति चक्षते ।

कुतः स्वर्गादयः सन्तित्यन्ये निश्चितमानसाः ॥११॥

yaddyatpratyakṣaviṣayaṃ tadannyannāsti cakṣate /

kutaḥ svargādayaḥ santīttyanye niścitamānasāḥ /11/

Others say that only those things that are perceived by the senses do exist. They confidently question with their firm mind, 'where is the heaven and where is the hell?' –11.

ज्ञान प्रवाह इत्यन्ये शून्यं केचित्परं विदुः ।

द्वावेव तत्वं मन्यन्तेऽपरे प्रकृतिपूरुषौ ॥१२॥

jñāna pravāha ityanye śūnyaṃ kecitparam viduḥ /

dvāveva tatvaṃ manyante'pare prakṛtipūruśau /12/

Others are in the opinion that the world is the current of conscious knowledge. Some say that void is the fundamental aspect. Similarly, some others believe that there exist two fundamental essences– *Prakṛti* (the Cosmic Energy) and *Puruṣa* (the Cosmic Conscious- ness). –12.

अत्यन्तभिन्नमतयः परमार्थपराङ्मुखाः ।

एवमन्ये तु संचिन्त्य यथामति यथाश्रुतम् ॥१३॥

निरीश्वरमिदं प्राहुः सेश्वरञ्च तथापरे ।

वदन्ति विविधैर्भेदैः सुयुक्त्या स्थितिकातराः ॥१४॥

atyantabhinnamatayaḥ paramārthaparāṅmukhāḥ /

evamanye tu sañcintya yathāmati yathāśrutam /13/

nirīśvaramidaṃ prāhuḥ seśvarañca tathāpare

vadanti vividhaibhedaiḥ suyuktyā sthitikātarāḥ /14/

In this way, believing in entirely different views and opinions, turning their faces away from the supreme spiritual goal by virtue of their intellectual understanding thinking and hearing, they declare that there is no God in this world. Others believe and declare that there is a God. Based on their differing irrefutable logics (coming from their scriptures and texts), they are eager to express and establish their opinions regarding the existence of God. –13-14.

एते चान्ये च मुनयः संज्ञाभेदा पृथग्विधाः ।
शास्त्रेषु कथिता ह्यते लोकव्यामोहकारकाः ॥१५॥
एतद्विवादशीलानां मतं वक्तुं न शक्यते ।
भ्रमन्त्यस्मिञ्जनाः सर्वे मुक्तिमार्गबहिष्कृताः ॥१६॥

ete cānye ca munayaḥ sañjñābhedā pṛthagvidhāḥ /
śāstreṣu kathitā hyete lokavyāmohakārakāḥ /15/
etadvivādaśīlānāṃ mataṃ vaktuṃ na śakyate /
bhramantyasmiñjanāh sarve muktimārgabahiṣkṛtāḥ /16/

These and many other sages in various traditions and sects have declared their various opinions in *Śāstras* (the scriptures) and these are the root cause of creating delusion in the human mind. It is impossible to describe fully the opinions and views of those people who seem so much interested in quarrels and disputes. As a result, people wander in this world being driven away from the path of liberation. –15-16.

Yoga Alone True Doctrine

आलोक्य सर्वशास्त्राणि विचार्य च पुनः पुनः ।
इदमेकं सुनिष्पन्नं योगशास्त्रं परं मतम् ॥१७॥

ālokya sarvaśāstrāṇi vicāryaṃ ca punaḥ punaḥ /
idamekaṃ suniṣpannaṃ yogaśāstraṃ paraṃ matam /17/

Having gone through all the *Śāstras* (scriptures) and having thought over them again and again, it has been well found that the views of *Yogaśāstra* (the Science of Yoga) alone are supreme. –17.

यस्मिन ज्ञाते सर्वमिदं ज्ञातं भवति निश्चितम् ।

तस्मिन्परिश्रमः कार्यः किमन्यच्छास्त्रभाषितम् ॥१८॥

yasmin jñāte sarvamidaṃ jñātaṃ bhavati niścitam /

tasmin pariśramaḥ kāryaḥ kimanyacchāstrabhāṣitam /18/

Since by knowing this *Yogaśāstra* (the Science of Yoga), everything is known with certainty. Therefore, one should make every effort to acquire it. What is the need of learning any other *Śāstras* (the scriptures) then? –18.

योगशास्त्रमिदं गोप्यमस्माभिः परिभाषितम् ।

सुभुक्ताय प्रदातव्यं त्रैलोक्ये च महात्मने ॥१६॥

yogaśāstramidaṃ gopyamasmābhiḥ paribhāṣitam /

subhaktāya pradātabyaṃ trailokye ca mahātmane /19/

This *Yogaśāstra* (the Science of Yoga) described by us is very secret. It should be imparted to the most devoted ones, and the great souls in all the three worlds. –19.

The Rituals and Rites

कर्मकाण्डं ज्ञानकाण्डमिति वेदो द्विधा मतः ।

भवति द्विविधो भेदो ज्ञानकाण्डस्य कर्मणः ॥२०॥

karmakāṇḍaṃ jñānakāṇḍamiti vedo dvidhā mataḥ /

bhavati dvividho bhedo jyānakāṇḍasya karmaṇaḥ /20/

There are two types of systems established in the *Vedas*: – *Karmakāṇda* (the branch of ceremonial acts and sacrificial rites) and *Jñānakāṇda* (the branch of knowledge of the Supreme Self). Each of these two systems is further divided into two parts. –20.

द्विविधः कर्मकाण्डः स्यान्निषेधविधिपूर्वकः ॥२१॥

dvividhaḥ karmakāṇdaḥ syānniṣedhavidhipūrvakaḥ /21/

Injunctions and prohibitions are the twofold divisions of *Karmakāṇda* (the rituals and rites). –21.

निषिद्धकर्मकरणे पापं भवति निश्चितम् ।

विधिना कर्मकरणे पुण्यं भवति निश्चितम् ॥२२॥

niṣiddhakarmakaraṇe pāpaṃ bhavati niścitam /

vidhinā karmakarāṇepuṇya ṃ bhavati niścitam /22/

Prohibited actions will certainly result in sin; actions performed according to rule (religious law) will certainly bring forth *puṇya* (virtue). –22.

त्रिविधो विधिकूटः स्यान्नित्यनैमित्तकाम्यतः ।

नित्येऽकृते किल्बिषं स्यात्काम्ये नैमित्तिके फलम् ॥२३॥

trivido vidhikūṭaḥ syānnityanaimityakāmyataḥ /

nitye'kṛte kilbiṣaṃ syātkāmyenaimittike phalam /23/

There are three types of injunctions – *nitya* (regular), *naimittika* (periodical) and *kāmya* (optional to be done as desired). If regular actions are not performed, this brings forth sin; if the periodical and optional actions are performed, this results in merits. –23.

द्विविधन्तु फलं ज्ञेयं स्वर्गो नरक एवं च ।

स्वर्गो नानाविधिश्चैव नरकोऽपि तथा भवेत् ॥२४॥

dvividhantu phalaṃ jñeyaṃ svargo narakameva ca /

svargo nānāvidham caiva narako'pi tathā bhavet /24/

The fruits of actions are of two types – heaven or hell. There are various kinds of heavens as well as hells. –24.

Pious Actions – Heaven and Sinful Acts – Hell

पुण्यकर्माणि वै स्वर्गो नरकः पापकर्माणि ।

कर्मबंधमयी सृष्टिर्नान्यथा भवति ध्रुवम् ॥२५॥

puṇyakarmāni vai svargo narakaḥ pāpakarmāni /

karmabandhamayī sṛṣṭirnānyathā bhavati dhruvam /25/

Pious actions lead to heaven; sinful acts lead to hell. This creation is certainly bound by actions and their results, and surely, it is not otherwise. –25.

जन्तुभिश्चानुभूयन्ते स्वर्गे नानासुखानि च ।

नानाविधानि दुःखानि नरके दुःसहानि वै ॥२६॥

jantubhiścānubhūyante svarge nānāsukhāni ca /

nānāvidhāni duḥkhāni narake duḥsahāni vai /26/

All creatures enjoy and experience various pleasures and happiness in heaven whereas they suffer various unbearable pains in hell. –26.

पापकर्मवशाद्दुःखं पुण्यकर्मवशाद्सुखम् ।

तस्मात्सुखार्थी विविधं पुण्यं प्रकुरुते ध्रुवम् ॥२७॥

pāpakarmavaśādduḥkhaṃ puṇyakarmavaśātsukham /

tasmātsukhārthī vividhaṃ puṇyaṃ prakurute dhruvam /27/

Pain results from sinful acts and happiness results from pious acts. Hence, people desirous of happiness always certainly carry out meritorious actions. –27.

पापभोगावसाने तु पुनर्जन्म भवेत्खलु ।

पुण्यभोगावसाने तु नान्यथा भवति ध्रुवम् ॥२८॥

pāpabhogāvasāne tu punarjanma bhavetkhalu /

puṇyabhogāvasāne tu nānyathā bhavati dhruvam /28/

When the resultant sufferings of the sinful acts are over, then certainly rebirths take place again. Similarly, when the fruits of meritorious acts are enjoyed through, certainly after that also the result is the same and not otherwise. –28.

Experience of Pain Even in Heaven

स्वर्गेऽपि दुःखसंभोगः परश्रीदर्शनादिषु ।
ततो दुःखमिदं सर्व भवेन्नास्त्यत्र संशयः ॥२६॥

svarge'pi duḥkhasambhogaḥ paraśrīdarśanādiṣū /
tato duḥkhamidaṃ sarvaṃ bhavennāstyatra samśayaḥ /29/

There is experiencing of pain even in heaven while seeing the supremacy and grandeur of others; truly, this whole world is full of sorrow and there is no doubt in it. –29.

तत्कर्मकल्पकैः प्रोक्तं पुण्यं पापमिति द्विधा ।
पुण्यपापमयो बन्धो देहिनां भवति क्रमात् ॥३०॥

tatkarmakalpakaiḥ proktaṃ puṇyaṃ pāpamiti dvidhā /
puṇyapāpamayo bandho dehināṃ bhavati kramāt /30/

The authors of ritualism have classified karma in two parts– meritorious and sinful acts; both are absolute bondages, and each in its turn causes the cycle of deaths and births of the beings. –30.

Yoga - The Path of Spiritual Knowledge

इहामुत्र फलद्वेषी सकलं कर्म संत्यजेत् ।
नित्यनैमित्तिकं संज्ञं त्यक्त्वा योगे प्रवर्तते ॥३१॥

ihāmutra phaladveṣī sakalaṃ karma santyajet /
nityanaimittikaṃ sañjñaṃ tyaktvā yoge pravartate /31/

Those who do not want to enjoy the fruits of their actions here is this world, or in next, should renounce all actions that are done with the hope of getting fruits, and in the same way, having discarded attachment to *nitya* and *naimittika* karmas (the regular and periodical acts) should engage in the practice of yoga. –31.

कर्मकाण्डस्य महात्म्यं ज्ञात्वा यागी त्यजेत्सुधीः ।
पुण्यपापद्वयं त्यक्त्वा ज्ञानकाण्डे प्रवर्तते ॥३२॥

karmakāndasya māhātmyaṃ jñātvā yogī tyajetsudhīḥ /
puṇyapāpamdvayaṃ tyaktvā jñānakāṇḍe pravartate /32/

After knowing the merits of *Karmakāṇda* (the ritual acts), the wise yogi should give up them; and having renounced both virtue and evil, he should engage *in Jñānakāṇda* (the path of gaining the knowledge of the Ultimate Self) through the practice of yoga. –32.

आत्मा वाऽरेतु द्रष्टव्यः श्रोतव्येत्यादि यच्छुतिः ।

सा सेव्या तत्प्रयत्नैन मुक्तिदा हेतुदायिनी ॥३३॥

ātmā vā'retu draṣṭabyaḥ śrotavyetyādi yaccrūti /

sā sevyā tatprayatnena muktidā hetudāyinī /33/

Śrutis (the *Vedic* texts) say: – '*Ātmā* (the Self) alone is worthy to be seen' and 'One should hear about it.' It is the cause of everything and gives liberation to every being. Therefore, It should be served (experienced) with great care and effort. –33.

Integral Unity of Self and the Universal Self

दुरितेषु च पुण्येषु यो धीर्वृत्तिं प्रचोदयात् ।

सोऽहं प्रवर्तते मत्तो जगत्सर्व चराचरम् ॥३४॥

सर्व च दृश्यते मत्तंः सर्व च मयि लीयते ।

न तद्भिन्नोऽहमस्मीह मद्भिन्नो न तु किंचन ॥३५॥

duriteṣu ca puṇyeṣu yo dhīrvṛttiṃ pracodayāt /

so'haṃ pravartate matto jagatsarvaṃ carācaram /34/

sarvaṃ ca dṛśyate mattaḥ sarvaṃ ca mayi līyate /

na tadbhinno'hamasmīha madbhinno na tu kiñcana /35/

That *Intelligence* which directs the propensity of mind towards virtue and evil is Me. The whole universe movable and unmovable is born from Me. All things are seen (stood) in Me and they are all merged in Me. All beings are inseparable from Me and I am not separate from any beings. Therefore, there exists nothing except integral unity between all beings and Me. –34-35.

जलपूर्णेष्वसख्येषु शरावेषु यथा भवेत् ।

एकस्य भात्यसंख्यत्वं तद्भेदोऽत्र न दृश्यते ॥३६॥

उपाधिषु शरावेषु या संख्या वर्तते परा ।

सा संख्या भवति यथा रवौ चात्मनि तत्तथा ॥३७॥

jalapūrṇeṣvasaṅkhyeṣu śarāveṣu yathā bhavet /

ekasya bhātyasaṅkhyatvaṃ tadbhedo'tra na dṛśyate /36/

upādhiṣū śarāveṣū yā saṅkhyā vartate parā /

sā saṅkhyā bhavati yathā ravau cātmani tattathā /37/

In innumerable clay pots full of water, many reflections of the sun are seen, but in reality there is one sun and not many; similarly the one Self (*Ātmā*) alone is manifested in various forms in innumerable beings, just like the same sun in innumerable water pots. –36-37.

The Veil of Māyā – Cause of Wrong Knowledge

यथैकः कल्पकः स्वप्ने नानाविधतयेष्यते ।

जागरेऽपि तथाप्येकस्तथेव बहुधा जगत् ॥३८॥

yathaikaḥ kalpakaḥ svapne nānāvidhatayeṣyate /

jāgare'pi tathāpyekastathaiva bahudhā jagat /38/

In a dream, one *Jīvātmā* (embodied Self) creates many objects and events, but upon awakening, everything disappears except the dreamer. Similarly, this whole universe appears so diversified and differentiated due to the veil of *Māyā* (illusion). –38.

सर्पबुद्धिर्यथा रज्जौ शुक्तौ वा रतजभ्रमः ।

तद्वदेवमिदं विश्वं विवृतं परमात्मनि ॥३९॥

sarpabuddhiryathā rajjau śuktau vā rajatabhramaḥ /

tadvadevamidaṃ viśvaṃ vivṛtaṃ paramātmani /39/

As in an illusion in which a rope seems like a snake or a pearl shell like silver, this whole universe is superimposed in *Paramātmā* (the Ultimate Self). –39.

रज्जुज्ञानाद्यथा सर्पो मिथ्यारुपो निवर्तते ।

आत्माज्ञानात्तथा याति मिथ्याभूतमिदं जगत् ॥४०॥

rajjujñānādyathā sarpo mithyārūpo nivartate /

ātmājñānāttathā yāti mithyābhūtvamidaṃ jagat /40/

As a right knowledge of the rope dispels the illusion of the snake; similarly, when the right knowledge of the Self arises, this illusory world disappears. –40.

रौप्यभ्रान्तिरियं याति शुक्तिज्ञानाद्यथा खलु ।

जगतभ्रान्तिरियं याति चात्मज्ञानात् सदा तथा ॥४१॥

raupyabhrāntiriyaṃ yāti śuktijñānādyathā khalu /

jagatbhrāntiriyaṃ yāti cātmajñānādyadā tathā /41/

Just as the illusion of the silver disappears when the knowledge of the pearl oyster is gained; similarly, by the realization of the self, the illusion of the world disappears. –41.

यथा वंशो रगभ्रान्तिर्भवेदभेकवसाञ्जनात् ।

तथा जगदिदं भ्रातिरभ्यासकल्पनाञ्जनात् ॥४२॥

yathā vamso ragabhrāntirbhavedbhekavasāñjanāt /

tathā jagadidaṃ bhrāntirabhyāsakalpanāñjanāt /42/

Just as when a man applies collyrium (a salve for the eyes) made of fat of frog on his eyes, a bamboo appears like a snake for him, so the world appears a delusion due to the pigment of habitual practice and imagination. –42.

आत्माज्ञानाद्यथा नास्ति रज्जुज्ञानादभुजङ्गमः ।

यथादोषवशाच्छुक्लः पीतो भवति नान्यथा ।

अज्ञानदोषादात्मपि जगदुभवति दुस्त्यजम् ॥४३॥

ātmājñānādyathā nāsti rajjujñānādbhujaṅgama /

yathādoṣavaśāccuklaḥ pīto bhavati nānyathā /

ajñānadoṣādātmāpi jagatbhavati dustyajam /43/

As by the knowledge of the rope the snake disappears, in the same way all illusion disappears with the knowledge of the self. With jaundiced eyes, white appears yellow; likewise, due to ignorance, the world appears superimposed in the *Paramātmā* (Universal Self) – a delusion very difficult to be removed. –43.

दोषनाशे यथा शुक्लो गृह्यते रोगिणा स्वयम् ।

शुक्लज्ञानात्तथाऽज्ञाननाशादात्मा तथा कृतः ॥४४॥

doṣanāśe yathā śuklo gṛihate rogiṇā svayam /

śuklajñānāttathā'jñānanāśādātma tathā kṛtaḥ /44/

As when the jaundice is cured, the patient himself sees white as it is; in the same way, when the erroneous ignorance is destroyed the true knowledge of the *Ātmā* (the Self) is realized. –44.

कालत्रयेऽपि न यथा रज्जुः सर्पो भवेदिति ।

तथात्मा न भवेद्विश्वं गुणातीतो निरञ्जनः ॥४५॥

kālatraye'pi na yathā rajjuḥ sarpo bhavediti /

tathātmā na bhavetviśvam gunātīto nirañjanaḥ /45/

Just as the rope can never become a snake in the past, present or future; similarly, *Ātmā* that is pure and beyond all qualities can never become the world. –45.

आगमाऽपायिनोऽनित्यानाश्यत्वेनेश्वरादयः ।

आत्मबोधेन केनापि शास्त्रादेतद्विनिश्चितम् ॥४६॥

āgamā'pāino'nityanāsyatvenesvarādayaḥ /

ātmābodhena kenāpi śāstrādetadviniścitam /46/

Wise men with deep knowledge of the Self and the *Vedic* texts have concluded that gods like *Indra* and others are not eternal, but are subject to death, birth, and destruction. –46.

यथा वातवशात्सिन्धावुत्पन्नाः फेनबुद्बुदाः ।

तथात्मनि समुद्भतं संसार क्षणभंगुरम् ॥४७॥

yathā vatavaśātsindhāvutpannāḥ phenbudbudāḥ /

tathātmani samudbhutaṃ samsāraṃ kṣaṇabhaṅguram /47/

Like bubbles and foams that arise in the sea by the wind; this transient world appears from *Ātmā* (the Self). –47.

Integral Unity of the Self in Diversity

अभेदो भासते नित्यं वस्तुभेदो न भासते ।

द्विधात्रिधादिभेदोऽयं भ्रमत्वे पर्यवस्यति ॥४८॥

abhedo bhāsate nityaṃ vastubhedo na bhāsate /

dvidhātridhādibhedo'yaṃ bhramatve paryavasyati /48/

The eternal unity is always expressed, and diversity (in the universe) does not exist. Twofold, threefold and manifolds diversifications appear only through delusion. –48.

यद्भूतं यच्च भव्यं वै मूर्तामूर्त तथैव च ।

सर्वमेव जगदिदं विवृतं परमात्मनि ॥४९॥

yadbhutaṃ yacca bhāvyaṃ vai mūrtāmūrtaṃ tathaiva ca /

sarvameva jagadidaṃ vivṛtaṃ paramātmani /49/

Whatever was in the past, whatever is in the present and whatever will be in the future, either formed or formless, everything in this universe rests on *Paramātmā* (the Universal Self). –49.

कल्पकैः कल्पिताविद्या मिथ्या जाता मृषात्मिका ।

एवन्मूलं जगदिदं कथं सत्यं भविष्यति ॥५०॥

kalpakaiḥ kalpitāvidyā mithyā jātā mṛṣātmikā /

evanmūlaṃ jagadidaṃ kathaṃ satyaṃ bhaviṣyati /50/

This world is created out of *avidyā* (the ignorance or false knowledge), which is born out of untruth and whose very base is unreal. How can this universe be true with such a foundation? –50.

Omnipresence of Ātmā - the Universal Self

चैतन्यात्सर्वमुत्पन्नं जगदेतच्चराचरम् ।

तस्मात्सवं परित्यज्य चैतन्यं तु समाश्रयेत् ॥५१॥

caitanyātsarvamutpannaṃ jagadetaccarācaram /

tasmātsarvaṃ parityajya caitanyaṃ tu samāśrayet /51/

The whole universe, movable or immovable, has come out of *Caitanya* (the Intelligence). Therefore, giving up everything, one should take shelter in it. –51.

घटस्याभ्यन्तरे बाह्ये यथाकाशं प्रवर्तते ।

तथात्माभ्यन्तरे बाह्ये कार्यवर्गेषु नित्यशः ॥५२॥

ghaṭāsyābyantare bāhye yathākāśaṃ pravartate /

tathātmābyantare bāhye kāryavargeṣu nityaśaḥ /52/

As space pervades a pot in and out, similarly the Universal Self permeates in and out of this ever-changing universe. –52.

असंलग्नं यथाकाशं मिथ्याभूतेषु पंचसु ।

असंलग्नंस्तथात्मा तु कार्यवर्गेषु नान्यथा ॥५३॥

asamlagnaṃ yathākāśaṃ mithyābhuteṣu pañcasu /

asamlagnastathātmā tu kāryavargeṣu nānyathā /53/

Just as space covering the five elements is not attached to them, similarly the Universal Self remains unattached to this ever-changing universe and it is never otherwise. –53.

ईश्वरादिजगत्सर्वमात्मव्याप्तं समन्ततः ।

एकोऽस्ति सच्चिदानंदः पूर्णो द्वैतविवर्जितः ॥५४॥

īśvarādijagatsarvamātmavyāptaṃ samantataḥ /

eko'sti saccidānandaḥ pūrṇo dvaitavivarjitaḥ /54/

From God to this material universe *Ātmā* (the Self) pervades all everywhere. It is one *Saccidānanda* (the Truth, Intelligence and Bliss), perfect and without duality. –54.

यस्मात्प्रकाशको नास्ति स्वप्रकाशो भवेत्ततः ।

स्वप्रकाशो यतस्तस्मादात्मा ज्योतिः स्वरूपकः ॥५५॥

yasmātprakaśako nāsti svaprakāśo bhavettataḥ /

svaprakāśo yatastasmādātmā jyotiḥ svarūpakaḥ /55/

Therefore, it receives light from nothing and it is self-luminous. Because of its self-luminosity, the Self takes the form of light. –55.

अवछिन्नो यतो नास्ति देशकालस्वरूपतः ।

आत्मनः सर्वथा तस्मादात्मा पूर्णो भवेत्खलु ॥५६॥

avachinno yato nāsti deśakālasvarūpataḥ /

ātmanaḥ sarvathā tasmādātmā pūrṇo bhavetkhalu /56/

The Self by its true nature is not limited by time and space, so it is infinite, omnipresent and fully complete in itself. –56.

यस्मान्न विद्यते नाशः पंचभूतैर्वृथात्मकैः ।

तस्मादात्मा भवेन्नित्यस्तन्नाशो न भवेत्खेलु ॥५७॥

yasmānna vidyate nāśaḥ pañcabhūtairvṛthātmakaiḥ /

tasmādātmā bhavennityastannāśo na bhavetkhalu /57/

The Self is not like this universe that is made of five elements that are illusory (false) and subject to destruction. Therefore, the Self is eternal and certainly never destroyed. –57.

यस्मात्तदन्यो नास्तीह तस्मादेकोऽस्ति सर्वदा ।

यस्मात्तदन्यो मिथ्या स्यादात्मा सत्यो भवेत् खलु ॥५८॥

yasmāttadanyo nāstīha tasmādeko'sti sarvadā

yasmāttadanyo mithyā syādātmā satyo bhavet khalu /58/

Besides and beyond it there exists nothing else. The Self alone always exists, and everything else other than it is unreal. Therefore, the Self alone certainly remains true. –58.

अविद्याभूतसंसारे दुःखनाशे सुखं यतः ।

ज्ञानादाद्यंतशून्यं स्यात्तस्मादात्मा भवेत्सुखम् ॥५६॥

avidyābhūtasansāre duhkhanāse sukhaṃ yataḥ /

jñānādādyantaśūnyaṃ syāttasmādātmā bhavetsukham /59/

Here in this world created by the ignorance, happiness is gained by the destruction of sorrow. However, through *jñāna* (the knowledge or wisdom) there is actually no beginning and the end of sorrow. Therefore, *Ātmā* (the Universal Self) is (supreme) happiness. –59.

यस्मान्नाशितमज्ञानं ज्ञानेन विश्वकारणम् ।

तस्मादात्मा भवेज्ज्ञानं ज्ञानं तस्मात्सनातनम् ॥६०॥

yasmānnāśitamajñānaṃ jñānena viśvakāranam /

tasmādātmā bhavejjñānaṃ jñānaṃ tasmātsanātanam /60/

Because *Avidyā* (the ignorance) is the cause of the universe, it is destroyed through *jñāna* (the knowledge). Therefore, *Ātmā* (the Self) becomes *jñāna* (the knowledge) and *jñāna* is eternal. –60.

कालतो विविधं विश्वं यदा चैव भवेदिदम् ।

तदेकोऽस्ति स एवात्मा कल्पनापथवर्जितः ॥६१॥

kālato vividhaṃ visvaṃ yadā caiva bhavedidam /

tadeko'sti sa evātmā kalpanāpathavarjitaḥ /61/

When this world with various forms and modifications is created by the time, then certainly there exists one who is *Ātmā* (the Self) that is never changing; for which there is no possibility of imagination, for *Ātmā* (the Self) is Truth and It is not imagined. –61.

बाह्यानि सर्वभूतानि विनाशं यान्ति कालतः ।

यतो वाचो निवर्त्तन्ते आत्मा द्वैतविवर्जितः ॥६२॥

bāhyāni sarvabhūtāni vināśaṃ yānti kālataḥ

yato vāco nivartante ātmā dvaitavivarjitaḥ /62/

Kāla (the time) destroys all the external materials and beings, but the Self always exists without duality, which cannot be described by words (human words return back being unable to express it). –62.

न खं वायुर्न चाग्निश्च न जलं पृथिवी न च ।

नैतत्कार्यं नेश्वरादि पूर्णैकात्मा भवेत्खलु ॥६३॥

na khaṃ vāyurna cāgniśca na jalaṃ pṛthivi na ca /

naitatkāryaṃ neśvarādi pūrṇaikātmā bhavetkhalu /63/

Neither ether, air, fire, water, earth nor their integrated action, nor the heavenly Gods are complete; *Ātmā* (Self) alone is surely so. –63.

Yoga and Māyā (Illusion)

आत्मानमात्मनो योगी पश्यत्यामनि निश्चितम् ।

सर्वसंकल्पसंन्यासी त्यक्तमिथ्याभवग्रहः ॥६४॥

ātmānamātmāno yogī paśyatyātmani niścitam

sarvasaṅkalpasannyāsī tyaktamithyābhavagrahaḥ /64/

After giving up all worldly false desires and renouncing all mundane attachments, the yogi certainly sees in his Self the Universal Self by his own Self. –64.

आत्मानात्मनि चात्मानं दृष्ट्वानन्तं सुखात्मकम् ।

विस्मृत्य विश्वं रमते समाधेस्तीव्रतस्तथा ॥६५॥

ātmānātmāni cātmānam dṛṣṭvānantaṃ sukhātmakam /

vismṛtya visvaṃ ramate samādhestīvratastathā /65/

Having seen the Universal Self with infinite happiness in his own Self by his own Self, he (the yogi) forgets this world and enjoys a deep blissful state of *Samādhi* (a super- conscious state of mind). – 65.

मायैव विश्वजननी नान्या तत्त्वधियापरा ।

यदा नाशं समायाति विश्वं नास्ति तदा खलु ॥६६॥

māyaiva visvajananī nānyā tattvadhiyāparā /

yadā nāśaṃ samāyāti visvaṃ nāsti tadā khalu /66/

Māyā (the illusion) is the mother of this world. It is not created from any other element. When the *Māyā* comes to an end, then certainly the world does not exist at all. –66.

हेयं सर्वमिदं यस्य मायाविलसितं यतः ।

ततो न प्रीतिविषयस्तनुवित्तसुखात्मकः ॥६७॥

heyaṃ sarvamidaṃ yasya māyāvilasitaṃ yataḥ /

tato na prītiviṣayastanuvittasukhātmakaḥ /67/

For those that this world is a playground of *Māyā,* everything becomes avoidable and valueless; they cannot find and enjoy happiness in body, wealth, pleasures. –67.

अरिर्मित्रमुदासीनस्त्रिविधं स्यादिदं जगत् ।

व्यवहारेषु नियतं दृश्यते नान्यथा पुनः ।

प्रियाप्रियादिभेदस्तु वस्तुषु नियतः स्फुटम् ॥६८॥

arirmitramudāsīnastrividhaṃ syādidaṃ jagat /

vyavahāreṣū niyataṃ dṛśyate nānyathā punaḥ /

priyāpriyādibhedastu vastuṣu niyataḥ sphuṭam /68/

This world has three aspects in relation to people - inimical, friendly or indifferent; it is always seen that the worldly behaviors fall into these groups. Certainly, there is also definite distinction in all worldly things between the good, bad and indifferent. –68.

आत्मोपाधिवशादेवं भवेत्पुत्रादि नान्यथा ।

मायाविलसितं विश्वं ज्ञात्वैवं श्रुतियुक्तितः ॥

अध्यारोपापवादाम्यां लयं कुर्वन्ति योगिनः ॥६९॥

ātmopādhivaśādevaṃ bhavetputrādi nānyathā /

māyāvilasitaṃ viśvaṃ jñātvaivam śrutiyuktitaḥ /

adhyāropāpavādābhyāṃ layaṃ kurvanti yogīnaḥ /69/

Because of the differentiation of the same and one Self, there are relations like son, father, etc. The *Śrutis* (*Vedic* texts) have explained that the world is the playground of *Māyā* (the illusion). The yogis destroy this world by knowing that it is the result of the false knowledge – *adhyāropa* (superimposition) and through *Apavāda* (refutation of wrong belief). –69.

निखिलोपाधिहिनो वै यदा भवति पूरुषः ।

तदा विवक्षतेऽखंडज्ञानरूपी निरंजन ॥७०॥

nikhilopādhihino vai yadā bhavati pūruṣaḥ /

tadā vivakṣate'khaṇḍajñānarūpī nirañjanaḥ /70/

When a person becomes entirely free from all worldly conditions, then he can express that he is *Akhaṇḍa Jñānarūpī Nirañjanaḥ* (the Indivisible Intelligence and Pure Being). –70.

Creation of Māyic (Illusive) World

सो कामयतः पुरुषः सृजते च प्रजाः स्वयम् ।

अविद्या भासते यस्मात्तस्मान्मिथ्या स्वभावतः ॥७१॥

so kāmayataḥ puruṣaḥ sṛjate ca prajāḥ svayam /

avidyā bhāsate yasmāttasmānmithyā svabhāvataḥ /71/

The *Paramātman* (Universal Self) voluntarily desired to create his beings. From his desire to create, *avidyā* (the ignorance) emerged. Therefore, this universe by nature is false because it came out of *avidyā*. –71.

शुद्ध ब्रह्मत्व संबद्धो विद्यया सहितो भवेत् ।

ब्रह्मतेनसती याति तत आभासते नभः ॥७२॥

suddha brahmatva sambaddho vidyayā sahito bhavet /

brahmatenasatī yāti tata ābhāsate nabhaḥ /72/

When there is a voluntary association of *Pure Brahma* with *avidyā*, then there comes out *Brahmā* (the Creator). From *Brahmā* comes out *ākāśa* (the ether). –72.

तस्मात्प्रकाशते वायुर्वायोरग्निस्ततो जलम् ।

प्रकाशते ततः पृथ्वी कल्पनेयं स्थिता सति ॥७३॥

tasmātprakāśate vāyurvāyoragnistato jalam /

prakaśate tataḥ pṛthvī kalpaneyaṃ sthitā sati /73/

From ether comes air; from air comes fire; from fire comes water; and from water comes the earth. Thus, the creation is originated. –73.

आकाशद्वायुराकाशपवनादग्निसंभवः ।

खवाताग्नेर्जलं व्योमवाताग्निवारितो मही ॥७४॥

ākāśādvāyurākāśapavanādagnisambhavaḥ /

khavātāgnerjalaṃ vyomavātāgnirvārito mahī /74/

From ether came air; from ether and air combined together came fire; from the combination of ether, air and fire came water and from the compound of ether, air, fire and water came the earth. –74.

खं शव्दलक्षणं वायुश्चंचलः स्पर्शलक्षणः ।

स्याद्रुपलक्षणं तेजः सलिलं रसलक्षणम् ॥

गन्धलक्षणिका पृथ्वी नान्यथा भवति ध्रुवम् ॥७५॥

khaṃ śabdalakṣaṇaṃ vāyuścancalaḥ sparśalakṣaṇaḥ /

syādrūpalakṣṇaṃ tejaḥ salilaṃ rasalakṣaṇam /

gandhalakṣaṇikā pṛthvī nānyathā bhavati dhruvam /75/

The quality of ether is sound. Motion and touch are the qualities of air. The quality of fire is *rūpa (*form) and water is taste. Truly, it is never otherwise. –75.

स्यादेकगुणमाकाशं द्विगुणो वायुरुच्यते ।

तथैव त्रिगुणं तेजो भवन्त्यापश्चतुर्गुणाः ॥७६॥

शब्दः स्पर्शश्च रूपं च रसो गन्धस्तथैव च ।

एतत्पंचगुणा पृथ्वी कल्पकैः कल्पतेऽधुना ॥७७॥

syādekaguṇamākāśaṃ dviguṇo vāyurucyate /

tathaiva tiguṇaṃ tejo bhavantyāpaścaturguṇāh /76/

śabdaḥ sparśaśca rūpaṃ ca raso gandhastathaiva ca /

etatpañcaguṇā pṛthvī kalpakaiḥ kalpyate'dhunā /77/

In this way ether has one quality; air two, fire three, water four and earth has five qualities i.e. sound, touch, form, taste and smell. It has been declared so by the wise men. –76-77.

चक्षुषा गृह्यते रूपं गन्धो घ्राणेन गृह्यते ।

रसो रसनया स्पर्शस्त्वचा संगृह्यते परम् ॥

श्रोत्रेण गृह्यते शब्दो नियतं भाति नान्यथा ॥७८॥

cakṣuṣā grihyate rūpaṃ gandho ghrāṇena gṛhyate /

raso rasanayā sparśastvacā saṅgṛhyate param /

śrotreṇa gṛhyate śabdo niyataṃ bhāti nānyathā /78/

Form is perceived by the eyes, smell by the nose, taste by the tongue, touch by the skin and sound by the ear. These sense organs perform their fixed actions and never otherwise. –78.

चैत्न्यात्सर्वमुत्पन्नं जगदेतच्चराचरम् ।

अस्ति चेत्कल्पनेयं स्यान्नास्ति चिन्मयम् ॥७९॥

caitanyātsarvamutpannaṃ jagadetaccarācaram /

asti cetkalpaneyaṃ syānnāsti cedasti cinmayam /79/

This entire universe, movable or unmovable, has come out of Intelligence. Even though the world may seem true through imagination, or may be nonexistent through knowledge, nothing else except the *Pure Intelligence* alone exists. –79.

पृथ्वी शीर्णा जले मग्ना जलं मग्नं च तेजसि ।

लीनं वायौ तथा तेजो व्योम्नि वातो लयं ययौ ।
अविद्यायां महाकाशो लीयते परमे पदे ॥८०॥

pṛthvī śirṇā jale magnā jalaṃ magnaṃ ca tejasi /
līnaṃ vāyau tathā tejo vyomni vāto layaṃ yayau /
avidyāyāṃ mahākāśo līyate parame pade /80/

The earth is dissolved in water; water in fire, fire in air, air is absorbed in ether and ether is dissolved in *avidyā* (the ignorance). Finally, *avidyā* merges into *Paramapada* (literally, the highest position or the Ultimate *Brahman*). –80.

विक्षेपावरणा शक्तिर्दुरन्तासुखरूपिणी ।
जडरूपा महामाया रजः सत्वतमोगुणा ॥८१॥

vikṣepāvaraṇā śaktirdurantāsukharūpinī
jaḍarūpā mahāmāyā rajaḥ satvatamoguṇā /81/

There are two forces with great potentialities and power in the form of happiness *vikṣepa* (the out-going energy) and *āvaraṇa* (the transforming energy). The great *māyā* in material form has three qualities – *sattva* (purity), *rajas* (motion) and *tamas* (inertia). –81.

सा मायावरणाशक्त्यावृताविज्ञानरूपिणी ।
दर्शयेज्जगदाकारं तं विक्षेपस्वभावतः ॥८२॥

sā māyāvaraṇāśaktyāvṛtāvijñānarūpinī /
darśayejjagadākāraṃ taṃ vikṣepasvabhāvataḥ /82/

When that *māyā* is laid on with the veil of *āvaraṇa* force (the transforming energy), then it takes non-intelligent form and manifests itself in the form of universe due to its nature of *vikṣepa* force (the out-going energy). –82.

तमोगुणाधिका विद्या या सा दुर्गा भवेत् स्वयम् ।
ईश्वरस्तदुपहितं चैतन्यं तद्भूद् धवम् ॥८३॥

tamoguṇadhikā vidyā yā sā durgā bhavet svayam

īsvarastadupahitaṃ caitanyaṃ tadbhūd dhruvam /83/

When there is an access of *tamas* in *avidyā*, it manifests itself as *Durgā*, and then the *Intelligence* presiding over her is *Isvara* (*Śiva*). Verily, it is so and not otherwise. –83.

सत्वाधिका च या विद्या लक्ष्मीः स्याद्दिव्यरूपिणी ।

चैतन्यं तदुपहितं विष्णुर्भवति नान्यथा ॥८४॥

sattvādhikā ca yā vidyā laxmiḥ syāddivyarūpinī /

caitanyaṃ tadupahitaṃ viṣṇurbhavati nānyathā /84/

When there is an access of *sattva* in *avidyā,* it manifests itself as *Lakṣmī* in her divine form, and then the *Intelligence* that presides over her becomes *Viṣṇu* and it is not otherwise. –84.

रजोगुणाधिका विद्या ज्ञेया सा वै सरस्वती ।

यश्चित्स्वपो भवति ब्रह्मातदुपधारकः ॥८५॥

rajoguṇādhikā vidyā jñeyā sā vai sarasvatī /

yascitsvarūpo bhavati brahmātadupadhārakaḥ /85/

When the same *avidyā* has an access of *rajas*, it manifests itself as wise *Sarasvatī*; then the form of *Intelligence* that presides over her becomes *Brahmā*. –85.

Absence of Distinction in All Gods

ईशाद्याः सकला देवा दृष्यन्ते परमात्मनि ।

शरीरादिजडं सर्वं सा विद्या तत्तथा तथा ॥८६॥

īśādyāḥ sakalā devā dṛśyante paramātmani /

śarīrādijadaṃ sarvaṃ sā vidyā tattathā tathā /86/

Gods like *Brahmā, Viṣṇu, Śiva*, etc. are all seen in *Paramātmā* (the Universal Self). Bodies and all material objects are the various products of *avidyā*. –86.

एवंरूपेण कल्पन्ते कल्पका विश्वसम्भवम् ।

तत्वातत्वं भवन्तीह कल्पनान्येन चोदिता ॥८७॥

evamrūpeṇa kalpante kalpakā visvasambhavam /

tattvātattvaṃ bhavantīḥ kalpanānyena coditā /87/

In this way, the wise men have spoken of the creation of this universe. likewise, *tattvas* (elements) and *atattvas* (non-elements) are created and never otherwise by any other means. –87.

प्रमेयत्वादिरूपेण सर्वं वस्तु प्रकाश्यते ।

विशेषशब्दोपादाने भेदो भवति नान्यथा ॥८८॥

prameyatvadirūpeṇa sarvaṃ vastu prakāśyate /

viśeṣaśabdopādāne bhedo bhavati nānyathā /88/

All objects are manifested in their finite forms in this universe. Because of the specific names, words, qualities, etc. various distinctions arise; but in reality, there is no difference. –88.

तथैव वस्तुनास्त्येव भासको वर्तकः परः ।

स्वरूपत्वेन रूपेण स्वरूपं वस्तु भाष्यते ॥८९॥

tathaiva vastunāstyeva vāsako vartakaḥ paraḥ /

svarūpatvena rūpeṇa svarūpaṃ vastu bhāṣyate /89/

Therefore, the worldly objects do not exist. *Paramātmā*, the Supreme Father, manifests them and He alone exists. The objects are illusory; as the Supreme Existence reflects them, however, they seem real for the time being. –89.

एकः सत्तापूरितानन्दरूपः पूर्णो व्यापी वर्तत नास्ति किञ्चित् ।

एतज्ज्ञानं यः करोत्येव नित्यं मुक्तः स स्यान्मृत्युसंसारदुःखात् ॥९०॥

ekaḥ sattāpūritānandarūpaḥ purṇo

vyāpī vartate nāsti kiñcit /

etajjñānaṃ yaḥ karotyeva nityam

muktaḥ sa syānmṛtyu samsāraduhkhāt /90/

The One Existence, blissful, whole and omnipresent alone exists and nothing else. One who always practices to realize this knowledge becomes free from the chain of death and miseries in this world. –90.

यस्यारोपापवादाभ्यां यत्र सर्वे लयं गताः ।

स एको वर्तते नान्यत्तच्चित्तेनावधार्यते ॥९१॥

yasyāropāpavādābyāmyatra sarve layaṃ gatāḥ /

sa eko vartate nānyattaccittenāvadhāryate /91/

After the refutation (*apavāda*) of the whole universe as an illusive perception (*āropa*) through the knowledge, it is dissolved into One. Then there exists that One alone and it is firmly held in the mind and nothing else. –91.

Body Bound Self Through Karma

पितुरन्नमयात्कोषाज्जायते पूर्वकर्मणः ।

तच्छरीरं विदुर्दुःखं स्वप्राग्भोगाय सुन्दरम् ॥९२॥

piturannamayātkoṣājjāyate pūrvakarmaṇaḥ /

taccharīraṃ vidurduḥkhaṃ svaprāgbhogāya sundaram /92/

From *annamaya koṣa* (the food-grain body) of the father and according to its past karma, the human body is born. The wise men say that receiving this beautiful body is painful because it is for experiencing both pleasures and pains – the results of one's past karma. –92.

Body – A Temple of Suffering Pain

मांसास्थिस्नायुमज्जादिनिर्मितं भोगमन्दिरम् ।

केवलं दुःखभोगाय नाडीसंतति गुल्फितम् ॥९३॥

māmsāsthisnāyumajjādinirmitaṃ bhogamandiram /

kevalaṃ duḥkhabhogāya nāḍisantati gulphitam /93/

Made of flesh, bones, nerves, marrow, blood, and arteries and veins spread all over, this temple of enjoyment (the human body) is only for experiencing the sorrows and pains. –93.

प्रारमेष्ठ्यमिदं गात्रं पंचभूतविनिर्मितम् ।

ब्रह्माण्डसंज्ञकं दुःखसुखभोगाय कल्पितम् ॥६४॥

pārameṣṭhyamidaṃ gātraṃ pañcabhūtanirmitam /

brahmādasanjñakaṃ duḥkhasukhabhogāya kalpitam /94/

This body, the home of *Parabrahma* (the Universal Self), is composed of five elements and it is known as *brahmāṇḍa* (literally, the egg of *Brahma,* the universe). It has been made for the enjoyment of pleasures and suffering of pains. –94.

Union of Śiva and Śakti – Creation of Beings

बिन्दुः शिवो रजः शक्तिरुभयोर्मिलनात्स्वयम् ।

स्वप्नभूतानि जायन्ते स्वशक्त्या जडरूपया ॥६५॥

vinduḥ śivo rajaḥ śaktirubhayormilanātsvayam /

svapnabhūtāni jāyante svaśaktyā jaḍarūpaya /95/

Through voluntary combination of *vindu* - the seminal fluid (sperm) that is *Śiva* (the Cosmic Self) and *rajah* - the ovarian fluid (ovum) that is *Śakti* (the Cosmic Energy) and through the interaction with their inherent material energy – *māyā*, all living beings are created as in the dream. –95.

तत्पञ्चीकरणात्स्थुलान्यसंख्यानि समासतः ।

ब्रह्माण्डस्थानि वस्तूनि यत्र जीवेऽस्ति कर्मभिः ॥

तद्भूतपञ्चकात्सवं भोगाय जीवसंज्ञिता ॥६६॥

tatpañcīkaraṇātsthulānyasaṅkhyāni samāsataḥ /

brahmāṇḍasthāni vastūni yatra jīvo'sti karmabhiḥ /

tadbhūtapañcakātsarvaṃ bhogāya jīvasaṅjñitā /96/

Through the combination of the five elements, solid innumerable objects are created in this world. In all these objects, the Self remains bound through karma. This entire universe is composed of five elements, and *Jīva* (the embodied Self) is known as the enjoyer of the fruits of its karma. –96.

Cycle of Death and Birth – Result of the Past Karma

पूर्वकर्मानुरोधेन करोमि घटनामहम् ।

अजडः सर्वभूतस्था जडस्थित्या भुनक्ति तान् ॥९७॥

pūrvakarmānurodhena karomi ghaṭanāmaham /

ajaḍaḥ sarvabhūtasthā jaḍasthityā bhunakti tān /97/

I (Lord *Śiva*) control the destiny of *Jīva* according to the effects of its past karma. *Jīva* itself is immaterial; it is the part of the Universal Self that is present in all beings. However, *Jīva* enjoys the fruits of its karma entering into the body. –97.

जडात्स्वकर्मभिर्बद्धो जीवाख्यो विविधो भवेत् ।

भोगायोत्पद्यते कर्म ब्रह्मांडाख्ये पुनः पुनः ॥९८॥

jaḍātsvakarmabhirbaddho jīvākhyo vividho bhavet /

bhogāyotpaddhyate karma brahmāṇḍākhye punaḥ punaḥ /98/

The *Jīva* confined in the material body through its karma is called with various names. It comes in this world repeatedly to go through the results of its past karma. –98.

जीवश्च लीयते भोगावसाने च स्वकर्मणः ॥९९॥

jīvaśca līyate bhogāvasāne ca svakarmaṇaḥ /99/

When experiencing the fruits of its karma is over, the *Jīva* merges into Universal Self. –99.

इति श्रीशिवसंहितायां प्रथमः पटलः समाप्तः ॥१॥

iti śrīśivasamhitāyāṃ

prathamaḥ paṭalaḥ samāptaḥ //1//

Thus, ends the First Chapter of *Śiva Samhitā.*

द्वितीयः पटलः

Dvitīyaḥ Paṭalaḥ

Chapter Two

Discourse on The Reality

Human Body - Replica of Macro Cosmos

देहेऽस्मिन्वर्तते मेरुः सप्तदीपसमन्वितः ।

सरितः सागराः शैलाः क्षेत्रीणि क्षेत्रपालकाः ॥१॥

dehe'sminvartate meruḥ saptadīpasamanvitaḥ /

saritaḥ sāgarāḥ śailāḥ kṣetrāṇi kṣetrapālakāḥ /1/

In this body there is *meru* (the spinal column) connected with seven islands. In addition, there are rivers, oceans, mountains, fields, and the lords of the fields. –1.

ऋषयो मुनयः सर्वे नक्षत्राणि ग्रहास्तथा ।

पुण्यतीर्थानि पीठानि वर्तन्ते पीठदेवताः ॥२॥

ṛṣaya munayaḥ sarve nakṣatrāṇi grahāstathā /

puṇyatīrthāni pīṭhāni vartante pīṭhadevatāḥ /2/

There are (in this body) seers and sages, all the stars and planets, holy places of pilgrimage, main *piṭhas* (the places of worship) and their Gods. –2.

सृष्टिसंहारकर्तारौ भ्रमन्तौ शशिभास्करौ ।

नभो वायुश्च वह्निश्च जलं पृथ्वी तथैव च ॥३॥

sṛṣtisamhārakartārau bhramantau śaśibhāskarau /

nabho vāyuśca vahniśca jalaṃ pṛthvī tathaiva ca /3/

The moon and the sun, the creator and destroyer, travel in this body. There are also ether, air, fire, water and earth in it. –3.

त्रैलोक्ये यानि भूतानि तानि सर्वाणि देहतः ।

मेरुं संवेष्टय सर्वत्र व्यवहारः प्रवर्तत ॥४॥

trailokye yāni bhūtāni tāni sarvāṇi dehataḥ /

meruṃ samveṣṭya sarvatra vyavahāraḥ pravartate /4/

There are in this body all the creatures of the three worlds; encircling the *meru*, they are engaged in their own prescribed duties. –4.

जानाति यः सर्वमिदं स योगी नात्र संशयः ॥५॥

jānāti yaḥ sarvamidaṃ sa yogī nātra samśayaḥ /5/

He who knows all about it is surely a yogi; there is no doubt . – 5.

Psychic Nerve Centers in the Body

ब्रह्माण्डसंज्ञके देहे यथादेशं व्यवस्थितः ।

मेरुश्रृङ्गे सुधारश्मिर्बहिरष्टकलायुतः ॥६॥

brahmāṇḍasañjñake dehe yathādeśaṃ vyavasthitaḥ /

meruśṛṅge sudhāraśmirbahiraṣṭakalāyutaḥ /6/

In this body, which is also called *brahmāṇḍa*, there is the nectar-rayed moon with eight *kalās* (the phases of the moon) properly located in its own place at the top of spinal column. –6.

वर्ततेऽहर्निशं सोऽपि सुधा वर्षत्यधोमुखः ।

ततोऽमृतं द्विधाभूतं याति सुक्ष्मं यथा च वै ॥७॥

vartate'harniśaṃ so'pi sudhā varṣatyadhomukhaḥ /

tato'mṛtaṃ dvidhābhūtaṃ yāti sūkṣmaṃ yathā ca vai /7/

This moon facing downwards constantly pours down its ambrosia day and night (twenty-four hours). The nectar again further divides into two subtle parts. –7.

इडामार्गेण पुष्ट्यर्थं याति मन्दाकिनीजलम् ।
पुष्णाति सकलं देहमिडामार्गेण निश्चितम् ॥८॥

iḍāmārgeṇa puṣṭyarthaṃ yāti mandākinījalam /
pusṇāti sakalaṃ dehamiḍāmārgeṇa niscitam /8/

One of them goes over the body and nourishes it through the psychic channel of *idā* like the waters of *mandākini* (the Heavenly Ganges). This ambrosia certainly nourishes the whole body through the channel of *idā*. –8.

एष पीयूषरश्मिर्हि वामपार्श्वे व्यवस्थितः ।
अपरः शुद्धदुग्धाभो हठात्कर्षति मण्डलात् ॥
मध्यमार्गेण सृष्ट्यर्थं मेरौ संयाति चन्द्रमाः ॥९॥

eṣa pīyūṣaraśmirhi vāmapārśve vyavasthitaḥ /
aparaḥ śuddhadugdhābho haṭhātkarṣati maṇḍalāt /
madyamārgeṇa sṛṣṭyarthaṃ merau samyāti candramāḥ /9/

This ambrosial ray is located on the left side. The other ray, pure, milky and permeated with bliss, enters into the spinal cord through the middle psychic path called *suśumṇā* to which the moon is attached for creation. –9.

मेरुमूले स्थितः सूर्यः कलाद्वादशसंयुतः ।
दक्षिणे पथि रश्मिभिर्वहत्यूर्ध्वं प्रजापतिः ॥१०॥

merumūle sthitaḥ sūryaḥ kalādvādaśasamyutaḥ /
dakṣiṇe pathi raśmibhirvahatyūrdhvaṃ prajāpatiḥ /10/

The sun is located at the base of the spinal column with twelve *kalās*. Through the right psychic path (*piṅgala*), the lord of the creation pushes the nectar upwards with its rays. –10.

पीयूषरश्मिनिर्यासं धातूंश्च ग्रसति ध्रुवम् ।

समीरमण्डले सूर्यो भ्रमते सर्वविग्रहे ॥११॥

pīyūṣaraśminiryāsaṃ dhātūmśca grasati dhruvam /

samīramaṇḍale sūryo bhramate sarvavigrahe /11/

This sun certainly ingests the essence and ray emanated nectar. It travels through the whole body along with the atmosphere. –11.

एषा सूर्यपरामूर्तिः निर्वाणं दक्षिणे पथि ।

वहते लग्नयोगेन सृष्टिसंहारकारकः ॥१२॥

eṣā sūryaparāmūrtiḥ nirvāṇaṃ dakṣiṇe pathi /

vahate lagnayogena sṛṣṭisamhārakārakaḥ /12/

The psychic path on the right side (*piṅgalā*) is another form of the sun, the giver of *nirvāṇa* (liberation). The sun, lord of the creation and destruction, moves in this path through the auspicious zodiacal signs (Aries, Taurus, etc.). –12.

Psychic Nerves in the Body

सार्धलक्षत्रयं नाड्यः सन्ति देहान्तरे नृणाम् ।

प्रधानभूता नाड्यस्तु तासु मुख्याश्चतुर्दशः ॥१३॥

sārdhalakṣatrayaṃ nāṇyaḥ santi dehāntare nṛṇām /

pradhānabhūtā nāḍyastu tāsu mukhyāścaturdaśaḥ /13/

In the human body there are 350,000 *nāḍis* (the psychic channels). Out of them, fourteen are principal. –13.

सुषुम्णेडा पिंगलाच गान्धारी हस्तिजिह्विका ।

कुहूः सरस्वती पूषा शंखिनी च पयस्वनी ॥१४॥

वारुण्यलम्बुसा चैव विश्वोदरी यशस्विनी ।

एतासु तिस्रो मुख्याः स्यूः पिङ्गलेडा सुषुम्णिका ॥१५॥

suṣumṇeḍā piṅgalā ca gāndhāri hastijihvikā /

kuhūḥ sarasvatī pūṣā śaṅkhinī ca payasvinī /14/

vāruṇyalambusā caiva viśvodarī yaśasvinī /

etāsu tisro mukhyāḥ syuḥ piṅgaleḍā suṣumṇikā /15/

These are: *suśumṇā, iḍā, piṅgalā, gāndhārī, hastijihvikā, kuhū, sarasvatī, pūsā, śaṅkhinī, payasvanī, vāruṇī, alambuśā, viśvadarī* and *yaśasvinī*. Of these, *iḍā, piṅgalā* and *suśumṇā* are the major ones. –14-15.

तिसृष्वेका सुषुम्णैव मुख्या सायोगिवल्लभा ।

अन्यास्तदाश्रयं कृत्वा नाड्यः सन्ति हि देहिनाम् ॥१६॥

tisṛṣvekā suṣumṇaiva mukhyā sāyogīvallabhā /

anyāstadāśrayaṃ kṛtvā nāḍyaḥ santi hi dehinām /16/

Among these three, *suśumṇā* is the chief of all and dear to yogis as all the other *nāḍis* take shelter in it. –16.

नाडयस्तु ता अधोवक्त्राः पद्मन्तन्तुनिभाः स्थिताः ।

पृष्ठवंशं समाश्रित्य सोमसूर्याग्निरूपिणी ॥१७॥

nāḍyastu tā adhovaktrāḥ padmatantunibhāḥ sthitāḥ /

pṛṣṭhavamśaṃ samāśritya somasūryāgnirūpiṇī /17/

All these main *nāḍis* have their mouths downwards and are like the fine tissue of the lotus. They are sheltered on the spinal column and are in the form of the moon, the sun and the fire. –17.

तासां मध्ये गता नाडी चित्रा सा मम वल्लभा ।

ब्रह्मरन्ध्रञ्च तत्रैव सूक्ष्मात्सूक्ष्मतरं शुभम ॥१८॥

tāsāṃ madhye gatā nāḍī citrā sā mama vallabhā /

brahmarandhrañca tatraiva sūkṣmātsūkṣmataraṃ śubham /18/

Citrā is the innermost of these three *nāḍis*, and is my beloved one. in there is an auspicious hollow, which is subtlest of the subtle, called *brahmarandhra* (the psychic channel leading to the *Brahma*). –18.

पञ्चवर्णोज्जवला शुद्धा सुषुम्णा मध्यचारिणी ।

देहस्योपाधिरूपा सा सुषुम्णा मध्यरूपिणी ॥१६॥

pañcavarṇojjvalā śuddhā suṣumṇā madhyacāriṇī /

dehasyopādhirūpā sā suṣumṇā madhyarūpiṇī /19/

This *citrā nāḍi* is pure and bright with five colors. it moves in the middle of *suśumṇā*. it is the vital attribute of the human body and the center of the *suśumnā nāḍi* (the middle psychic pathway). –19.

दिव्यमार्गमिदं प्रोक्तममृतानन्दकारकम् ।

ध्यानामात्रेण योगीनद्रो दुरितौघं विनाशयेत् ॥२०॥

divyamārgamidaṃ proktamamṛtānandakārakam /

dhyānamātreṇa yogīndro duritaughaṃ vināśayet /20/

This has been described in the *Śāstras* (the *Vedic* texts) as the Divine Way and the cause of eternal joy and immortality. By meditating on it, the great yogis destroy all their sins. –20.

गुदात्तुद्वयंगुलादूर्ध्वं मेढ्रान्तुद्वयंगुलादधः ।

चतुरंगुलविस्तारमाधारं वर्तते समम् ॥२१॥

gudāttudvayaṅgulādūrdhvaṃ meḍhrāntudvayaṅgulādhaḥ /

caturaṅgulavistāraṃ ādhāraṃ vartate samam /21/

Two finger-width above the anus and two finger-width below the genitals is located the *ādhāra* lotus, which has equal dimensions of four finger-widths. –21.

तस्मिन्नाधारपद्मे च कर्णिकायां सुशोभना ।

त्रिकोणा वर्तते योनिः सर्वतंत्रेषु गोपिता ॥२२॥

tasminnādhārapadme ca karṇikāyām suśovanā /

trikoṇā vartate yoniḥ sarvatantreṣu gopitā /22/

In the core of the *mūlādhāra* lotus, there is a triangular beautiful *yoni* (the womb or the source of creation) that is kept secret in all the *tantras*. –22.

तत्र विद्युल्लताकारा कुण्डली परदेवता ।

सार्द्धत्रिकरा कुटिला सुषुम्णा मार्गसंस्थिता ॥२३॥

tatra viddhullatākārā kuṇḍalī paradevatā /

sārddhatrikara kutilā suṣumṇā margasamsthitā /23/

There abides the Supreme Goddess *Kuṇḍalinī*, in the form of subtle electric fiber and is coiled three and a half times like a serpent in the mouth of *suśumnā*. –23.

जगत्संसृष्टिरूपा सा निर्माणे सततोद्यता ।

वाचामवाच्या वाग्देवी सदा देवैर्नमस्कता ॥२४॥

jagatsamsṛṣṭirūpā sā nirmāṇe satatoddhyatā

vācāmavācyā vāgdevi sadā devairnamaskṛtā /24/

It is the creative force of the universe and constantly engaged in creation. This goddess of speech cannot be expressed by words and all gods always salute her. –24.

इडानाम्नी तु या नाडी वाममार्गे व्यवस्थिता ।

सुषुम्णायां समाश्लिष्य दक्षनाशापुटे गता ॥२५॥

iḍanāmnī tu yā nāḍī vāmamārge vyavasthitā /

suṣumṇāyāṃ samāśliṣyadakṣanāsāpuṭe gatā /25/

The psychic path called *iḍā* is on the left side. Coiling around the middle psychic path, it enters into the right nostril. –25.

पिङ्गला नाम या नाडी दक्षमार्गे व्यवस्थिता ।

मध्यनाडीं समाश्लिष्य वामनासापुटे गता ॥२६॥

piṅgalā nāma yā nāḍī dakṣamārge vyavasthitā

madhyanāḍīṃ samāśliṣya vāmanāsāpuṭe gatā /26/

The psychic channel called *piṅgalā* is on the right side. Coiling around the middle psychic channel, it enters into the left nostrils. –26.

इडापिङ्गलयोर्मध्ये सुषुम्णा या भवेत्खलु ।

षट्स्थानेषु च षट्शक्तिं षट्पद्मं योगिनो विदुः ॥२७॥

iḍāpiṅgalayormadhye suṣumṇā yā bhavetkhalu

ṣaṭsthāneṣu ca ṣaṭśaktiṃ ṣaṭpadmaṃ yogīno viduḥ /27/

The *nāḍi* that lies between *iḍā* and *piṅgalā* is certainly *suśumṇā* (the middle psychic channel). In its six places, there are six energies and six lotuses that are known to yogis. –27.

पञ्चस्थानं सुषुम्णाया नामानि स्युर्बहूनि च ।

प्रयोजनवशात्तानि ज्ञातव्यानीह शास्त्रतः ॥२८॥

pañcasthānaṃ suṣumṇāyā nāmāni syurbahūni ca

prayojanavaśāttāni jñātavyānīha śāstrataḥ /28/

Those five places of *suśumṇā* have various names that are revealed in this *Śāstra* as necessary due to the reason of their application and understanding. –28.

अन्या याऽस्त्यपरा नाडी मूलाधारात्समुत्थिता ।

रसानामेढ्रनयनं पादांगुष्ठे च श्रोत्रकम् ॥२९॥

कुक्षिकक्षांगुष्ठकर्ण सर्वांगं पायुकुक्षिकम् ।

लब्धा तां वै निवर्तन्ते यथादेशसमुद्भवाः ॥३०॥

anyā yā'styaparā nāḍī mūlādhārātsamutthitā

rasanāmeḍhranayanaṃ pādāṅguṣṭhe ca śrotrakam /29/

kukṣikakṣāṅguṣṭhakarṇaṃ sarvāṅgaṃ pāyukukṣikam

labdhvā tāṃ vai nivartante yathādeśasamudbhavāḥ /30/

The other *nāḍis*, which come out of *mūlādhāra*, reach various parts of the body e.g. tongue, sex organ, eyes, feet, toes, ears, the abdomen, the armpit, fingers, the scrotum and the anus. Having come out of their proper place, they reach and stop at their prescribed destinations and return to their place of origination. –29-30.

एताभ्य एव नाडीभ्यः शाखोपशाखतः क्रमात् ।

सार्धलक्षत्रयं जातं यथाभागं व्यवस्थितम् ॥३१॥

etābhya eva nāḍībhyaḥ śākhopaśākhataḥ kramāt /

sārdhalakṣatrayaṃ jātaṃ yathābhāgaṃ vyavasthitam /31/

From these (fourteen) *nāḍis* there gradually arise branches and sub-branches of smaller *nāḍis*, which finally become 350,000 in number and are supplied to their fixed places. –31.

एता भोगवहा नाड्यो वायुसंचारदक्षकाः ।

ओतप्रोताः सुसंव्याप्य तिष्ठन्त्यस्मिन्कलेवरे ॥३२॥

etā bhogavahā nāḍyo vāyusaṇcāradakṣakāḥ /

otaprotāḥ susamvyāpya tiṣṭhantyasminkalevare /32/

These *nāḍis* are well spread all over the human body and they properly regulate the movements of air and carry the sensations throughout. –32.

सूर्यमण्डलमध्यस्थः कलाद्वादशसंयुतः ।

वस्तिदेशे ज्वलद्वह्निर्वर्तते चान्नपाचकः ॥३३॥

एष वैश्वानरोग्निर्वै मम तेजोंशसम्भवः ।

करोति विविधं पाकं प्राणिनां देहमास्थितः ॥३४॥

sūryamaṇḍalamadyasthaḥ kalādvādaśasamyutaḥ /

vastideśe jvaladvahnivartate cānnapācakaḥ /33/

eṣa vaiśvānarognirvai mama tejomśasambhavaḥ /

karoti vividhaṃ pākaṃ praṇināṃ dehamāsthitaḥ /34/

In the central sphere of the sun with twelve *kalās*, there burns the digestive fire located at the middle abdominal area. This is certainly the fire of *vaiśvānara* (the digestive fire in the stomach) that has come out of the part of my energy. Remaining in the bodies of all living beings, it digests various kinds of foods. –33-34.

आयुः प्रदायको वह्निर्बलं पुष्टिं ददाति सः ।
शरीरपाटवञ्चापि ध्वस्तरोगसमुद्भवः ॥३५॥

ayuḥ pradāyako vahnirbalaṃ puṣṭiṃ dadāti saḥ /
śarīrapāṭavañcāpi dhvastarogasamudbhavaḥ /35/

This fire gives longevity, strength and nourishment. It gives the body vitality and destroys all diseases. –35.

तस्माद्वैश्वानराग्निञ्च प्रज्वाल्य विधिवत्सुधीः ।
तस्मिन्नन्नं हुमेद्योगी प्रत्यहं गुरुशिक्षया ॥३६॥

tasmādvaiśvānarāgniñca prajvālya vidhivatsudhī /
tasminnannaṃ humedyogī pratyahaṃ guruśikṣayā /36/

Therefore, the wise yogi should stimulate this fire of *vaisvānara* through proper ritual and rites and offer food to it everyday according to the teachings of his guru. –36.

ब्रह्माण्डसंज्ञके देहे स्थानानि स्युर्बहूनि च ।
मयोक्तानि प्रधानानि ज्ञानव्यानीह शास्त्रके ॥३७॥

brahmāṇḍasaṅjñake dehe sthānāni syurbahūni ca /
mayoktāni pradhānāni jñātavyānīha śāstrake /37/

This body called the replica of *brahmāṇḍa* (the microcosm) has many parts. Here in this *Śāstra* I have explained the major ones. Certainly, the yogi should know them. –37.

नानाप्रकारनामानि विविधानि च ।
वर्तन्ते विग्रहे तानि कथितुं नैव शक्यते ॥३८॥

nānāprakāranāmāni sthānāni vividhāni ca /
vartante vigrahe tāni kathituṃ naiva śakyate /38/

In this human body there are innumerable places and their names are various. Not all of them can be described here fully. –38.

Jīva – Enjoyer of the Fruits of Its Karma

इत्थं प्रकल्पिते देहे जीवो वसति सर्वगः ।
अनादिवासनामालाऽलंकृतः कर्मश्रृखलः ॥३९॥

ittham prakalpite dehe jīvo vasati sarvagaḥ /
anādivāsanāmālā'laṅkṛtaḥ karmaśṛṅkhalaḥ /39/

In the body, composed in this way, lives omnipresent *Jīva*, decorated with the garland of endless desires and confined (to the body) by the chain of its karma. –39.

नानाविधगुणोपेतः सर्वव्यापारकारकः ।
पूर्वार्जितानि कर्मार्णि भुनक्ति विविधानि च ॥४०॥

nānāvidhaguṇopetaḥ sarvavyāpārakārakaḥ /
pūrvārjitāni karmāṇi bhunakti vividhāni ca /40/

The *Jīva* possessing various types of qualities and being the agent of all trades (actions, events, etc.) enjoys the fruits of various karmas gathered in its past life. –40.

यद्यत्संदृश्यते लोके सर्व तत्कर्मसम्भवम् ।
सर्वा कर्मानुसारेण जन्तुर्भोगान्भुनक्ति वै ॥४१॥

yadyatsandṛśyate loke sarvaṃ tatkarmasambhavam /
sarvā karmānusāreṇa janturbhogānbhunakti vai /41/

Whatever trouble or happiness is seen in men in this world, it is all born of karma. All living beings experience pleasure or pain according to results of their karma. –41.

ये ये कामादयो दोषाः सुखदुःखप्रदायकाः ।
ते ते सर्वे प्रवर्तन्ते जीवकर्मानुसारतः ॥४२॥

ye ye kāmādayo doṣāḥ sukhaduḥkhapradāyakāḥ /
te te sarve pravartante jīvakarmānusārataḥ /42/

Whatever offences arise from passions that cause pleasure or pain, they are all activated according to the past karma of *Jīva* – the embodied Self. –42.

पुण्योपरक्तचैतन्ये प्रणान्प्रिणाति केवलम् ।

बाह्ये पुण्यमयं प्राप्य भोज्यवस्तु स्वयम्भवेत् ॥४३॥

puṇyoparakta caitanye prāṇānprīṇāti kevalam /

bāhye puṇyamayaṃ prāpya bhojyavastu svayambhavet /43/

The *Jīva* devoted to virtuous acts receives a best prosperous life. He is full of merit, gets happiness in this world, and enjoys pleasing things without any effort. –43.

ततः कर्मबलात्पुंसः सुखं वा दुःखमेव च ।

पापोपरक्तचैतन्यं नैव तिष्ठति निश्चितम् ॥४४॥

न तद्भिन्नो भवेत्सोऽपि तद्भिन्नो न तु किञ्चन ।

मायोपहित चैतन्यात्सर्वं वस्तु प्रजायते ॥४५॥

tataḥ karmabalātpumsaḥ sukhaṃ vā duḥkhameva ca /

pāpoparaktacaitanyaṃ naiva tiṣṭhati niścitam /44/

na tadbhinno bhavetso'pi tadbhinno na tu kiñcana /

māyopahitaṃ caitanyātsarvaṃ vastu prajāyate /45/

Human beings either enjoy pleasure or suffer pain due to the force of their karma. The *Jīva* attached to sinful acts can never remain happy and it cannot be separate from its karma. There is nothing separate of karma in this world. Everything is created from the *Intelligence* veiled by *māyā*. –44-45.

Knowledge alone Gives Liberation

यथाकालेऽपि भोगाय जन्तूनां विविधोद्भवः ।

यथा दोषवशाच्छुक्तौ रजतारोपणं भवेत् ॥

तथा स्वकर्मदोषाद्वै ब्रह्मण्यारोप्यते जगत् ॥४६॥

yathākāle'pi bhogāya jantūnāṃ vividhodbhavaḥ /

yathā doṣavaśāccuktau rajatāropaṇaṃ bhavet /

tathā svakarmadoṣādvai brahmanyāropyate jagat /46/

As in their fixed time various living beings are born to experience the results of their karma; as by mistake a pearl oyster is seen silver; similarly, through the evil of one's karma, a person superimposes this universe on *Brahman* (the Universal Self). –46.

सवासनाभ्रमोत्पन्नोन्मूलनातिसमर्थनम् ।

उत्पन्नञ्चेदीदृशं स्याज्ज्ञानं मोक्षप्रसाधनम् ॥४७॥

savāsanābhramotpannonmūlanātisamarthanam /

utpannañcedīdṛśaṃ syājjñānaṃ mokṣaprasādhanam /47/

Delusion arises from desire. It is very difficult to eradicate it, as it is very strong. When the liberating knowledge arises, then the desires are eliminated. –47.

साक्षाद्वैशेषदृष्टिस्तु साक्षात्कारिणि विभ्रमे ।

कारणं नान्यथा युक्त्या सत्यं मयोदितम् ॥४८॥

sākṣādvaiśeṣadṛṣṭistu sākṣātkāriṇi vibhrame /

kāraṇaṃ nānyathā yuktyā satyaṃ satyaṃ mayoditam /48/

When a specific vision is immersed into directly visible world, then delusion arises about its *Kartā* (the Main Actor) or the Creator. There is no other reason for this delusion. What I am telling is certainly true, and it is not otherwise. –48.

साक्षात्कारिभमे साक्षात्साक्षात्कारिणि नाशयेत् ।

सो हि नास्तीति संसारे भ्रमो नैव निविर्तते ॥४६॥

sakṣātkāribhrame sakṣātsākṣātkāriṇi nāśayet /

so hi nāstīti sansāre bhramo naiva nivartate /49/

When the Maker of it is realized, the delusion of this world manifested by Him is destroyed. As long as one thinks, "There is not

Brahma", so long his *bhram* (delusion) of the world is not removed at all. –49.

मिथ्याज्ञाननिवृत्तिस्तु बिशेषदर्शनाद्भवेत ।

अन्यथा न निवृत्तिः स्याद्दृश्यते रतजभ्रमः ॥५०॥

mithyājñānanivṛttistu viśeṣadarśanādbhavet /

anyathā na nivṛttih syāddṛśyate rajatabhramaḥ /50/

Through the realization of the Self this false knowledge disappears. One cannot get rid of it otherwise because the delusion of the silver remains. –50.

Human Body a Rare Means of Liberation

यावन्नोत्पद्यते ज्ञानं साक्षात्कारे निरञ्जने ।

तावत्सर्वाणि भूतानि दृश्यन्ते विविधानि च ॥५१॥

yavannotpaddhyate jñānaṃ sākṣātkāre nirañjane /

tāvatsarvāṇibhūtāni dṛśyante vividhāni ca /51/

As long as the knowledge does not arise about the Creator – the *Nirañjana* (the Ultimate Self without any fault or taint), all beings are seen different and various in number. –51.

यदा कर्मार्जितं देहं निर्वाणे साधनं भवेत् ।

तदा शरीरवहनं सफलं स्यान्न चान्यथा ॥५२॥

yadā karmārjitaṃ dehaṃ nirvāṇe sādhanaṃ bhavet /

tadā sarīravahanaṃ saphalaṃ syānna cānyathā /52/

When this body received through past karma is made a means of achieving liberation, then only carrying the load of this body is successful; otherwise, it is worthless and vain. –52.

यादृशी वासना मूला वर्तते जीवसंगिनी ।

तादृशं वहते जन्तुः कृत्याकृत्यविधौ भ्रमम् ॥५३॥

yādṛśī vāśanā mūlā vartate jīvasaṅginī /

tādṛśam vahate jantuḥ kṛtyākṛtyauvidhau bhramam /53/

Whatever (type/nature) be the fundamental desire of the *Jīva*, the same becomes its life companion and travels through life accordingly. It is subjected to delusions of both good and evil or right and wrong. –53.

संसारसागरं तर्तुं यदीच्छेध्योगसाधकः ।

कृत्वा वर्णाश्रमं कर्म फलवर्ज तदाचरेत् ॥५४॥

sansārasāgaraṃ tartuṃ yadīcchedyogasādhakaḥ /

kṛtvā varṇāśramaṃ karma phalavarjaṃ tadācaret /54/

If a yoga practitioner wants to cross the ocean of this world, he should renounce the fruits of all his actions, and perform his duties according to *varṇāśrama* (the four stages of life with one's set duties). –54.

विषयासक्तपुरुषा विषेयषु सुखेप्सवः ।

वाचाभिरुद्धनिर्वाणा वर्तन्ते पापकर्माणि ॥५५॥

viṣayāsaktapuruṣā viṣayeṣu sukhepsavaḥ /

vācābhiruddhanirvāṇā vartante pāpakarmaṇi /55/

People who are attached to worldly objects and sensual pleasures fall into sinful acts, and their words block the path to *nirvāṇa* or liberation (either their use of words are limited to worldly sensual pleasures and attachments only, or they are only talking and intellectualizing about liberation and never going through any particular practice for its realization). –55.

आत्मानमत्मना पश्यन्न किञ्चिदिह पश्यति ।

तदा कर्मपरित्यागे न दोषोऽस्ति मतं मम ॥५६॥

ātmānamātmanā paśyanna kiñcidiha paśyati /

tadā karmaparityāge na doṣo'sti mataṃ mama /56/

Having realized the Universal Self in his own Self, when a person does not see anything else here (except the Universal Self), then he can give up all actions. In doing so, he does not commit any offence; it is my opinion. –56.

कामदयो विलीयन्त ज्ञानादेव न चान्यथा ।

अभावे सर्वतत्वानां स्वयं तत्वं प्रकाशते ॥५७॥

kāmādayo vilīyante jñānādeva na cānyathā /

abhāve sarvatattvānāṃ svayaṃ tattvam prakāśate /57/

All desires disappear through knowledge only and not otherwise. When all elements become nonexistent, then the light or the real essence of Self shines. –57.

इति श्रीशिवसंहितायां द्वितीयः पटलः समाप्त ॥२॥

iti śrīśivasamhitāyāṃ dvitīya paṭalaḥ samāptaḥ //2//

Thus, ends the Second Chapter of *Śiva Samhitā.*

तृतीयः पटलः

Tṛtīya: Paṭalaḥ

Chapter Three

Discourse on Yoga Sādhanā

हृद्यस्ति पङ्कजं दिव्यं दिव्यलिङ्गेन भूषितम् ।

कादिठान्ताक्षरोपेतं द्वादशार्णविभूषितम् ॥१॥

hṛdyasti paṅkajaṃ divyaṃ divyaliṅgena bhūṣitam /

kādiṭhāntākṣaropetaṃ dvādaśārṇavibhūṣitam /1/

There is a brilliant lotus in the heart decorated with twelve petals with brilliant signs. It is ornamented with twelve letters from *ka* to *ṭha*. –1.

Prāṇa Dwells in the Heart

प्राणो वसतितत्रैव वासनाभिरलंकृतः ।

अनादिकर्मसंश्लिष्टः प्राप्याहङ्कारसंयुत ॥२॥

prāṇo vasatitatraiva vāsanābhiralaṅkṛtaḥ /

anādikarmasaṃśliṣṭaḥ prāpyāhaṅkārasaṃyutaḥ /2/

There lives *prāṇa*, decorated with various desires, together with its past karma, which has no beginning, and it is infused with its egoism. –2.

प्राणस्य वृत्तिभेदेन नामानि विविधानि च ।

वर्न्तन्ते तानि सर्वाणि कथितुं नैव शक्यते ॥३॥

prāṇasya vṛttibhedena nāmāni vividhāni ca /

vartante tāni sarvāṇi kathituṃ naiva śakyate /3/

Due to various modifications *prāṇa* has various names. Not all of them can be described here. –3.

प्राणोऽपानः समानश्चोदानो व्यानश्च पञ्चमः ।

नागः कूर्मश्च कृकरो देवदत्तो धनञ्जयः ॥४॥

prāṇo'pānaḥ samānascodāno vyānaśca pañcamaḥ /

nāgaḥ kūrmaśca kṛkaro devadatto dhanañjayaḥ /4/

Prāṇa, apāna, samāna, udāna, vyāna, nāga, kūrma, kṛkara, devadatta and dhanañjaya. –4.

Types of Prāṇa

दश नामानि मुख्यानि मयोक्तानीह शास्त्रके ।

कुर्वन्ति तेऽत्र कार्याणि प्रेरितानि स्वकर्मभिः ॥५॥

daśa nāmāni mukhyāni mayoktānīha śāstrake /

kurvanti te'tra kāryāṇi preritāni svakarmabhiḥ /5/

These are the ten main names of the *prāṇa* told by me in this *Śāstra*. They perform their prescribed duties initiated by their own actions. –5.

अत्रापि वायवः पञ्च मुख्याः स्युर्दशतः पुनः ।

तत्रापि श्रेष्ठकर्तारौं प्रणापानौ मयोदितौ ॥६॥

atrāpi vāyavaḥ pañca mukyāḥ syurdaśatah punaḥ /

tatrapi śreṭhakartārau prāṇāpānau mayoditau /6/

Again, out of these ten *prāṇas* the first five described above are main ones. In my opinion, *prāṇa* and *apāna* are the super most among these five *prāṇas*. –6.

Location of Prāṇa

हृदि प्राणा गुदेऽपानः समानो नाभिमण्डले ।

उदानः कण्ठदेशस्थो व्यानः सर्वशरीरगः ॥७॥

hṛdi praṇo gude'pānaḥ samāno nābhimaṇḍale /

udānaḥ kaṇṭhadeśastho vyānaḥ sarvaśarīragaḥ /7/

Prāṇa remains in the heart and *apāna* in the anus. *samāna* is located in the naval area and *udāna* is on the throat. *vyāna* is pervasive in the whole body. –7.

Functions of Prāṇa

नागादिवायवः पञ्च ते कुर्वन्ति च विग्रहे ।

उद्गारोत्मीलनं क्षुत्तृड्जृम्भा हिक्का च पञ्चमः ॥८॥

nāgādivāyavaḥ pañca te kurvanti ca vigrahe /

udgāronmīlanaṃ kṣuttṛḍjṛmbhā hikkā ca pañcamaḥ /8/

In the body, *nāga* and other five *prāṇas* perform following actions, respectively: belching, opening of the eyes, hunger and thirst, yawning and hiccupping. –8.

अनेन विधिना यो वै ब्रह्माण्डं वेत्ति विग्रहम् ।

सर्वपापविनिर्मुक्तः स याति परमां गतिम् ॥९॥

anena vidhinā yo vai brahmāṇḍaṃ vetti vigraham /

sarvapāpavinirmuktaḥ sa yāti paramāṃ gatim /9/

He, who knows the microcosm of this body in this way, having freed himself from all the sins, comes to the supreme state. –9.

Importance of a Virtuous Guru

अधुना कथयिष्यामि क्षिप्रं योगस्य सिद्धये ।

यज्ज्ञात्वा नावसीदन्ति योगिनो योगसाधने ॥१०॥

adhunā kathayiṣyāmi kṣipraṃ yogasya siddhaye /

yajjñātvā nāvasīdanti yogīno yogasādhane /10/

Now I will tell about receiving perfection quickly in yoga. By knowing it, yogis never fail in their practice of yoga. –10.

भवेद्वीर्यवती विद्या गुरुवक्त्रसमुद्भवा ।
अन्यथा फलहीना स्थान्निर्वीयाप्यतिदुःखदा ॥११॥

bhavedvīryavatī vidyā guruvaktrasamudbhavā /
anyathā phalāhīnā syānnirvīryāpyatiduhkhadā /11/

Only the knowledge imparted through the mouth of the guru becomes powerful; otherwise, it becomes fruitless, feeble and gives a lot of troubles. –11.

गुरुं सन्तोष्य यत्नेन ये वै विद्यामुपासते ।
अवलम्बेन विद्यायास्तस्याः फलमवाप्नुयात् ॥१२॥

guruṃ santoṣya yatnena ye vai vidyāmupāsate /
avalambena vidyāyāstasyāh phalamavāpnuyāt /12/

After satisfying the guru, he who receives *vidyā* (spiritual knowledge) with due care gets the fruits of his learning in no time. – 12.

गुरुः पिता गरुर्माता गुरुर्देवो न संशय ।
कर्मणा मनसा वाचा तस्मात्सर्वैः प्रसेव्यत ॥१३॥

guruḥ pitā gururmātā gururdevo nasamśayaḥ /
karmaṇā manasā vācā tasmātsarvaiḥ prasevyate /13/

There is no doubt that guru is father, he is mother and he is God as well. Therefore, everyone should serve their gurus with all deeds, thoughts and words. –13.

गुरुप्रसादतः सर्वं लभ्यते शुभमात्मनः ।
तस्मात्सेव्यो गुरुर्नित्यमन्यथा न शुभ भवेत् ॥१४॥

guruprasādataḥ sarvaṃ labhyate śubhamātmanaḥ /
tasmātsevyo gururnityamanyathā na śubhaṃ bhavet /14/

All auspicious well-being regarding to one's welfare is received through the grace of the guru. Therefore, a guru should be always served; otherwise, there will be no good. –14.

प्रदिक्षणत्रयं कृत्वा स्पृष्टवा सव्येन पाणिना ।

अष्टांगेन नमस्कुर्याद् गुरुपादसरोरुहम् ॥१५॥

pradakṣiṇatrayaṃ kṛtvā spṛṣṭvā savyena pāṇinā /

aṣṭāṅgena namaskuryād gurupādasaroruham /15/

By going around the guru three times and touching his lotus-feet with the right hand, one should salute him with his eight limbs. –15.

श्रद्धयात्मतां पुंसां सिद्धिर्भवति निश्चिता ।

अन्येषाञ्च न सिद्धिः स्यात्तस्माद्यत्नेन साधयेत् ॥१६॥

śraddhayātmavatāṃ pumsāṃ siddhirbhavati niścitā /

anyeṣāñca na siddhiḥ syāttasmādyatnena sādhayet /16/

The people whose mind and senses are under control certainly receive perfection through faith and respect, and others cannot. Therefore, yoga should be practiced with due respect, faith, and effort. –16.

न भवेत्संगयुक्तानां तथाऽविश्वासिनामपि

गरुपूजाविहीनानां तथा च बहुसंगिनाम् ॥१७॥

मिथ्यावादरतानां च तथा निष्ठुरभाषिणाम् ।

गुरुसन्तोषहीनानां न सिद्धिः स्यात्कदाचन ॥१८॥

na bhavetsaṅgayuktānāṃ tathā'viśvāsināmapi /

gurupūjāvihīnānāṃ tathā ca bahusaṅgināṃ /17/

mithyāvādaratānāṃ ca tathā niṣṭhurabhāṣiṇām /

gurusantoṣahīnānāṃ na siddhiḥ syātkadācana /18/

People who have bad companies, who are disbelievers, who do not respect their guru, who are associated with various companies of people, who are attached to false and vain isms, who are cruel in their words, who do not please and satisfy their guru can never get perfection (success). –17-18.

फलिष्यतीति विश्वासः सिद्धेः प्रथमलक्षणम् ।

द्वितीयं श्रद्धया युक्तं तृतीयं गुरुपूजनम् ॥१६॥
चतुर्थं समताभावं पञ्चमेन्द्रियनिग्रहम् ।
षष्ठं च प्रमिताहारं सप्तमं नैव विद्यते ॥२०॥

phaliṣyatīti viśvāsaḥ siddheḥ prathamalakṣaṇam /
dvitīyaṃ śraddhayā yuktaṃ tṛtīyam gurupūjanam /19/
caturthaṃ samatābhāvaṃ pañcamendriyanigraham /
ṣaṣṭhaṃ ca pramitāhāraṃ saptamaṃ naiva vidyate /20/

The first sign of success is that there should be a strong belief that this *Yogavidyā* (knowledge of yoga) would be fruitful; the second sign is to have faith in it; the third is due respect towards guru; the fourth is equanimous state of mind; the fifth is having control over sense organs. The sixth is moderation in food (neither eating too much, eating too little or not eating at all). There is no seventh sign (for success in yoga). –19-20.

योगोपदेशं संप्राप्य लब्ध्वा योगविदं गुरुम् ।
गरूपदिष्टविधिना धिया निश्चित्य साधयेत् ॥२१॥

yogopadeśaṃ samprāpya labdhvā yogavidaṃ gurum /
gurūpadiṣṭavidhinā dhiyā niścitya sādhayet /21/

Having obtained an experienced guru in yoga and received instructions in (the practice of) yoga from him, a wise yogi should practice yoga without being distracted by anything else, following the method taught by his guru. –21.

Place of Practice

सुशोभने मठे योगी पद्मासनसमन्वितः ।
आसनोपरि संविश्य पवनाभ्यासमाचरेत् ॥२२॥

suśobhane maṭhe yogī padmāsanasamanvitaḥ /
āsanopari samviśya pavanābyāsamācaret /22/

Assuming the *padmāsana* (the lotus pose) and sitting on a seat (deer skin, woolen/straw mattress etc.) in a beautiful place or temple, the yogi should do *pavanābyāsa* (breathing practice i.e. *prāṇāyāma*). –22.

समकायः प्राञ्जलिश्च प्रणम्य च गुरुन् सुधीः ।
दक्षे वामे च विध्नेशं क्षेत्रपालांबिकां पुनः ॥२३॥

samakāyaḥ prañjaliśca prṇamya ca gurūn sudhīḥ /
dakṣe vāme ca vighneśaṃ kṣetrapālāmbikāṃ punaḥ /23/

The wise practitioner should keep his body erect and join his hands together, and salute his guru on the left side and *Gaṇeśa* on the right side. Again, he should salute to Goddess *Ambikā* and *Kṣetrapāla* (the Guardians of the world) on the left side. –23.

Method of Prānāyāma

ततश्च दक्षांगुष्ठेन निरुध्य पिंगलां सुधीः ।
इडया पूरयेद्वायुं यथाश्क्त्या तु कुम्भयेत् ॥
ततस्त्यक्त्वा पिंगलयाशनैरेव न वेगतः ॥२४॥

tataśca dakṣāṅguṣṭhena nirudhya piṅgalāṃ sudhīḥ /
iḍaya pūrayedvāyuṃ yathāśktyā tu kumbhayet /
tatastyaktvā piṅgalayāśanaireva na vegataḥ /24/

Then, the wise practitioner should close the *piṅgalā* (the right nostril) with his right thumb and inhale through *iḍā* (the left nostril) and retain the breath inside as long as possible. Then he should breathe out slowly through the right nostril without forcing the breath. –24.

पुनः पिंगलयाऽऽपूर्य यथाशक्त्या तु कुम्भयेत् ।
इडया रेचयेद्वायुं न वेगेन शनैःशनैः ॥२५॥

punaḥ piṅgalayā''pūrya yathāśaktyā tu kumbhayet /
iḍayā recyedvāyuṃ na vegena śanaiḥ śanaiḥ /25/

Again, he should draw breath through the right nostril, and retain the breath inside as long as possible; then he should expel the air through the left nostril without any force, but slowly and smoothly. –25.

इदं योगविधानेन कुर्याद्विंशतिकुम्भकान् ।

सर्वद्वन्द्वविनिर्मुक्तः प्रत्यहं विगतालसः ॥२६॥

idaṃ yoga vidānena kuryādvimśatikumbhakān

sarvadvandavinirmuktaḥ pratyahaṃ vigatālasaḥ /26/

According to this method of yoga, he should practice twenty *kumbhakas* (retention of the breath). He should practice it daily without neglect, and being free from all dualities. –26.

प्रातःकाले च मध्याह्ने सूर्यास्ते चार्द्धरात्रके ।

कुयदिव चतुर्वारं कालेष्वेतेषु कुम्भकान् ॥२७॥

prātaḥkāle ca madhyāhne sūryāste cārddharātrake /

kuryādevaṃ caturvāraṃ kālaṣveteṣu kumbhakān /27/

He should practice these *kumbhakas* four times a day: - 1) early in the morning, 2) at the middle of the day (noon), 3) at sunset, and 4) at mid-night. –27.

इत्थं मासत्रयं कुर्यादनालस्यो दिने दिने ।

ततो नाडीविशुद्धिः स्यादविलम्बेन निश्चितम् ॥२८॥

itthaṃ māsatrayaṃ kuryādanālasyo dine dine /

tato nāḍīviśuddhiḥ syādavilambena niścitam /28/

While practicing it daily for three months without laziness, the *nāḍis* (the subtle psychic pathways) of the body will certainly be purified immediately. –28.

यदा तु नाडीशुद्धिः स्याद्योगिनस्तत्वदर्शिनः ।

तदा विध्वस्तदोषश्च भवेदारम्भसम्भवः ॥२९॥

yadā tu nāṇīśuddhiḥ syādyogīnastatvadarśinaḥ /

tadā vidhvastadoṣaśca bhavedārambhasambhavaḥ /29/

When the *nāḍis* of the truth-perceiving yogi are purified, his impurities are all destroyed. Then it becomes possible for him to enter into *ārambha avasthā* (the stage or state of beginning). –29.

चिह्नानि योगिनो देहे दृष्यन्ते नाडिसुद्धितः ।

कथ्यन्ते तु समस्तान्यङ्गानि संक्षप्तो मया ॥३०॥

cihnāni yogīno dehe dṛśyante nāṇīśuddhitaḥ /

kathyante tu samastānyaṅgāni saṅkṣepato mayā /30/

When the *nāḍis* are purified, some signs are seen in the body of the yogi. I will describe all about those signs briefly. –30.

समकायः सुगन्धितश्च सुकान्तिः स्वरसाधकः ।

आरम्भघटकश्चैव तथा परिचयस्तदा ॥

निष्पत्तिः सर्वयोगेषु योगावस्था भवन्ति ताः ॥३१॥

samakāyaḥ sugandhiśca sukāntiḥ svarasādhakaḥ /

ārambhaghaṭakaścaiva tathā paricayastadā

niṣpattiḥ sarvayogeṣu yogāvasthā bhavanti tāḥ /31/

The body of the yogi is harmonized, emitting a nice scent and appearing beautiful, and his voice becomes sweet and lovely. There are four stages in all kinds of yoga: 1) *ārambha avasthā* (the state of beginning), 2) *ghaṭa avasthā* (the state of realization of the self), 3) *paricaya avasthā* (the state of knowledge) and 4) *niṣpatti avasthā* (the state of liberation). –31.

आरम्भः कथितोऽस्माभिरधुना वायुसिद्धये ।

अपरः कथ्यते पश्चात्सर्वदुःखौघनाशनः ॥३२॥

ārambhaḥ kathito'smābhiradhunā vāyusiddhaye /

aparaḥ kathyate paścātsarvaduḥkhaughanāśanaḥ /32/

I have already described the *ārambha avasthā* the beginning state of *vāyu siddhi* (perfection in the *prāṇāyama*). Hereafter, the rest will be described. They destroy the multifarious sins. –32.

प्रौढवह्निः सुभोगी च सुखिसर्वाङ्गसुन्दरः ।

संपूर्णहृदयो योगि सर्वोत्साहबलानिवतः ॥

जायते योगिनोऽवश्यमेत्सर्व कलेवरे ॥३३॥

prauḍhavahnih subhogī ca sukhīsarvāṅgasundaraḥ /

sampūrṇa hṛdayo yogī sarvotsāhabalānvitaḥ /

jāyate yogīno'vasyametatsarvaṃ kalevare /33/

Certainly, all these qualities are found in the bodies of the yogi: strong digestive fire, enjoyment of all things, happiness, handsomeness, full satisfaction, great courage, enthusiasm and strength. –33.

अथ वर्ज्य प्रवक्ष्यामि योगविध्नकरं परम् ।

येन संसारदुःखाब्धिं तीर्त्वा यास्यन्ति योगिन ॥३४॥

atha varjyaṃ pravakṣyāmi yogavignakaraṃ param /

yena sansāraduḥkhābdhiṃ tīrtvā yāsyanti yoginaḥ /34/

Now I will describe the great barriers to yoga that should be avoided. By removing these, the yogis cross and go beyond this worldly ocean of miseries and sorrows. –34.

Things to Be Forbidden

आम्लं रूक्षं तथा तीक्ष्णं लवण सार्षपं कटुम् ।

बहुलं भ्रमणं प्रातः स्नानं तैलविदाहकम् ॥३५॥

स्तेयं हिसां जनद्वेषञ्चाहङ्कारमानार्जवम् ।

उपवासमसत्यञ्च मोक्षञ्च प्राणिपीडनम् ॥३६॥

स्त्रीसङ्गमग्निसेवां च बह्वालापं प्रियाप्रियम् ।

अतीव भोजनं योगी त्यजेदेतानि निश्चितम् ॥३७॥

āmlaṃ rūkṣaṃ tathā tīkṣṇaṃ lavaṇaṃ sārṣapaṃ katum /

bahulaṃ bhramaṇaṃ prātaḥ snānaṃ tailavidāhakam /35/

steyaṃ himsāṃ janadveṣañcāhaṅkāramanārjavam /

upavāsamasatyañcā mokṣañca praṇipīḍanam /36/

strīsaṅgamagnisevāṃ ca bahvālāpaṃ priyāpriyām /

atīva bhojanaṃ yogī tyajedetāni niścitam /37/

The yogi should certainly renounce these things: 1) acid, 2) astringent, 3) pungent (hot), 4) salt, 5) mustard, and 6) bitter thing; 7) walking a lot, 8) early bathing and 9) things roasted in oil; 10) theft, 11) killing (of animals), 12) enmity towards any person, 13) pride, 14) deception and 15) wickedness; 16) fasting, 17) telling a lie, 18) desire for liberation, and 19) cruelty towards animals; 20) attachment to men/women, 21) service to (sitting near) fire, 22) too much talking without caring about the pleasing or unpleasing nature of one's speech, and 23) too much eating. –35-37.

Means of Perfection in Yoga

उपायं च प्रवक्ष्यामि क्षिप्रं योगस्य सिद्धये ।

गोपनियं साधकानां येन सिद्धिर्भवेत्खलु ॥३८॥

upāyaṃ ca pravakṣyāmi kṣipraṃ yogasya siddhaye /

gopanīyaṃ sādhakānāṃ yena siddhirbhavetkhalu /38/

Now I will tell you the means of getting success in yoga quickly. The perfection will certainly be achieved in yoga, using this secret method of the practitioners. –38.

घृतं क्षीरं च मिष्टान्नं ताम्बुलं चूर्णवर्जितम् ।

कर्पुरं निष्तुषं मिष्टं सुमठं सूक्ष्मरन्ध्रकम् ॥३९॥

सिद्धान्तश्रवणं नित्यं वैराग्यगृहसेवनम् ।

नामसङ्कीर्तनं विष्णोः सुनादश्रवणं परम् ॥४०॥

धृतिः क्षमा तपः शौचं ह्रीर्मतिर्गुरुसेवनम् ।

सदैतानि परं योगी नियमानि समाचरेत् ।४१॥

ghṛtam kṣīraṃ ca miṣṭhānnaṃ tāmbūlaṃ cūrṇavarjitam /

karpūraṃ niṣtuṣaṃ miṣṭaṃ sumaṭham sūkṣmarandhrakam /39/

siddhānta śravaṇam nityaṃ vairāgyagṛhasevanam /

nāmasaṅkīrtanaṃ viṣṇoḥ sunādaśravanaṃ param /40/

dhṛtiḥ kṣamā tapaḥ śaucaṃ hṝrmatirgurusevanam /

sadaitāni paraṃ yogī niyamāni samācaret /41/

The great yogi should always observe the following rules: He should use 1) butter, 2) milk, 3) sweet foods, 4) betel without lime, 5) camphor; 6) pleasing words, 7) a beautiful cell with a small hole (window); he should: 8) hear discourses on spiritual truth, 9) perform his/her household duties with *vairāgya* (without attachment); 10) chant the name of *Viṣṇu*, and 11) hear the supreme *nāda* (spontaneous inner sound); he should practice: 12) tolerance, 13) forgiveness, 14) austerity, 15) purity, 16) modesty, 17) devotion and 18) service to his guru. – 39-41.

अनिलेऽर्कप्रवेशे च भोक्तव्यं योगिभिः सदा ।

वायौ प्रविष्टे शशिनि शयनं साधकोत्तमैः ॥४२॥

anile'rkapraveśe ca bhoktavyam yogībhiḥ sadā /

vāyau praviṣṭe śaśini śayanaṃ sādhakottamaiḥ /42/

The yogi should always take his food when the air enters into the sun (when the breath flows through *piṅgalā* – the right nostril). When the air enters into the moon (when the breath flows through *iḍā* –the left nostril), it is the best time for the practitioner to go to bed. –42.

सद्यो भुक्तेऽपि क्षुधिते नाभ्यासः क्रियते बुधैः ।

अभ्यासकाले प्रथमं कुर्यात्क्षीराज्यभोजनम् ॥४३॥

sadyo bhukte'pi kṣudhite nābhyāsah kriyate budhaiḥ /

abhyāsakāle prathamaṃ kuryātkṣīrājyabhojanam /43/

The wise yogi should not practice (*prāṇāyāma*) right after eating or when he is hungry. During the practice, first he should take some milk and butter. –43.

ततोऽभ्यासे स्थिरीभूते न तादृङ्नियमग्रहः ।
अभ्यासिना विभोक्तव्यं स्तोकं स्तकमनेकधा ॥
पूर्वोक्तकाले कुर्यात्तु कुम्भकानप्रतिवासरे ॥४४॥

tato 'bhyāse sthirībhūte na tādṛṅniyamagrahaḥ /
abhyāsinā vibhoktavyaṃ stokaṃ stokamanekadhā /
pūrvoktakāle kuryāttu kumbhakānprativāsare /44/

When he is established in his practice, then he need not observe these rules. The practitioner should eat small amounts of food several times a day; and he should practice *kumbhaka* (the retention of the breath) everyday at the specified times. –44.

ततो यथेष्टा शक्तिः स्याद्यागिनो वायुधारणे ।
यथेष्टं धारणाद्वायोः कुम्भकः सिध्यति ध्रवम् ॥
केवले कुम्भके सिद्धे किं न स्यादिह योगिनः ॥४५॥

tato yatheṣṭā śaktiḥ syādyogīno vāyudhāraṇe /
yatheṣṭam dhāraṇādvāyoḥ kumbhakaḥ sidhyati dhruvam /
kevale kumbhake siddhe kiṃ na syādiha yogīnaḥ /45/

From this practice the yogi will achieve enough strength to retain his breath; then being able to hold the breath for certain duration as desired, he will certainly succeed in *kumbhaka*. When he achieves perfection in *kumbhaka* only, then what cannot a yogi do here? –45.

Three Stages of Success in Kumbhaka

स्वेदः संजायते देहे योगिनः प्रथमोद्यमे ।
यदा संजायते स्वेदो मर्दनं कारयेत्सुधीः ॥

अन्यथा विग्रहे धातुर्नष्टो भवति योगिनः ॥४६॥

svedaḥ sañjāyate dehe yogīnaḥ prathamodyame /

yadā sañjāyate svedo mardanaṃ kārayetsudhīḥ /

anyathā vigrahe dhāturnaṣṭo bhavati yogīnaḥ /46/

The body of the yogi perspires during the first effort (in the first stage of *prāṇāyāma*). When there is perspiration from the body, the wise yogi should rub it over his body, otherwise he will lose *dhātu* (the humors) in the body. –46.

द्वितीये हि भवेत्कम्पो दार्दुरी मध्यमे मता ।

ततोऽधिकतराभ्यासाद्गगनेचरसाधकः ॥४७॥

dvitīye hi bhavetkampo dardurī madhyame matā /

tato'dhikatarābhyāsādgaganecarasādhakaḥ /47/

The body of the yogi trembles in the second stage; it starts jumping like a frog in the third; and when greater practice is continued after that, then the practitioner becomes *gaganacara* (the traveler in the air). –47.

Effects of Vāyu Perfection

योगी पदमासनस्थोऽपि भुवमुत्सृज्य वर्तते ।

वायुसिद्धिस्तदा ज्ञेया संसारध्वान्तनाशिनी ॥४८॥

yogī padmāsanastho'pi bhuvamutsṛjya vartate /

vāyusiddhistadā jñeyā samsāradhvāntanāśinī /48/

Seated in *padmāsana*, when the yogi can rise up in the air, leaving the ground, then he should know that he has achieved *vāyusiddhi* (attaining perfection in *prāṇa*), the destroyer of the darkness of the world. –48.

तावत्कालं प्रकुर्वीत योगोक्तनियमग्रहम् ।

अल्पनिद्रा पुरीषं च स्तोकं मूत्रं च जायते ॥४६॥

tāvatkālaṃ prakurvīta yogoktaniyamagraham /

alpanidrā purīṣaṃ ca stokaṃ mūtraṃ ca jāyate /49/

He should continue to follow and observe the set yogic rules specified above until the time of achieving it. The achievement of *vāyusiddhi* results in a yogi needing little sleep, and having small amounts of excrement and urine. –49.

अरोगित्वमदीनत्वं योगिनस्तत्त्वदर्शिनः ।

स्वेदो लाला कृमिश्चैव सर्वथैव न जायते ॥५०॥

arogitvamadīnatvaṃ yogīnastattvadarśinaḥ /

svedo lālā kṛmiścaiva sarvathaiva na jāyate /50/

The truth-perceiving yogi gets into a disease-less and sorrow-less state; he does not ever generate perspiration, saliva and get infested by intestinal worms. –50.

कफपित्तानिलाश्चैव साधकस्य कलेवरे ।

तस्मिनकाले साधकस्य भोज्येष्वनियमग्रहः ॥५१॥

kaphapittānilāścaiva sādhakasya kalevare /

tasminakāle sādhakasya bhojyeṣvaniyamagrahaḥ /51/

When there is no excess of three humors, phlegm, wind and bile, in the body, at that time there may not be any rules regarding the diet of the yogi. –51.

अत्यल्पं बहुधा भुक्त्वा योगी न व्यथत हि सः ।

अथाभ्यावशाद्योगी भूचरीं सिद्धिमाप्नुयात् ॥

यथा दर्दुरजन्तूनां गतिः स्यात्पाणिताडनात् ॥५२॥

atyalpaṃ bahudā bhuktvā yogī na vyathate hi saḥ /

athābhyāsavaśādyogī bhūcarīṃ siddhimāpnuyāt /

yathā dardurajantūnāṃ gatiḥ syātpaṇitāḍanāt /52/

The advanced yogi does not have any pain or trouble if he eats a lot or eats very little or does not eat at all. Due to his regular practice, he achieves *bhucārisiddhi* (attaining perfection in moving in the air); he moves in the air like a frog when the clapping of the hands frightens it. –52.

सन्त्यत्र बहवो विघ्ना दारुण दुर्निवारणाः ।

तथापि साधयेद्योगी प्राणैः कंठगतैरपि ॥५३॥

santyatra bahavo vighnā dāruṇa durnivāraṇāḥ /

tathāpi sādhayedyogī praṇaiḥ kaṇṭhagatairapi /53/

There are many terrible and unpreventable obstacles (in the path of yoga). However, the yogi should continue with his practice even if his *prāṇa* (the vital life force) comes to his throat. –53.

ततो रहस्युपाविष्टः साधकः संयतेन्द्रियः ।

प्रणवं प्रजपेद्दीर्घ विघ्नानां नाशहेतवे ॥५४॥

tato rahasyupāviṣṭaḥ sādhakaḥ samyatendriyaḥ /

praṇavaṃ prajapeddīrghaṃ vignānāṃ nāśahetave /54/

Then the practitioner, living in place of solitude and controlling his senses, should repeat long *praṇava* (the *mantra Om*) in order to destroy all obstacles and barriers. –54.

पूर्वार्जितानि कर्माणि प्राणायामेन निश्चितम् ।

नाशयेत्साधको धीमानिहलोकोद्भवानि च ॥५५॥

pūrvārjitāni karmāṇi prāṇāyāmena niścitam /

nāśayetsādhako dhīmāniha lokodbhavāni ca /55/

By *prāṇāyāma*, the wise practitioner certainly destroys all his karmas, acquired here in this life and in the past. –55.

पूर्वार्जितानि पापानि पुण्यानि विविधानि च ।

नाशयेत्षोडशप्राणायामेन योगि पुंगवः ॥५६॥

pūrvārjitāni pāpāni puṇyāni vividhāni ca

nāśayetṣoḍaśaprāṇāyāmena yogī puṅgava /56/

By the practice of sixteen *prāṇāyāmas*, the great yogi destroys various *pāpas* and *puṇyas* (virtues and vices) that he has collected through his past life. –56.

पापतुलचयानाहो प्रदहेत्प्रलयाग्निना ।

ततः पापाविनिर्मुक्तः पश्चातपुण्यानि नाशयेत् ॥५७॥

pāpatulacayānāho pradahetpralayāgninā /

tataḥ pāpavinirmuktaḥ pascātpuṇyāni nāśayet /57/

As the fire of annihilation burns everything down, this *prāṇāyāma* destroys a multitude of all sins, then it frees the yogi from all sins and after that, it destroys all of his virtuous acts as well. –57.

प्राणायामेन योगीन्द्रो लब्ध्वैश्वर्याण्टकानि वै ।

पापपुण्योदधिं तीर्त्वा त्रैलोक्यचरातामियात् ॥५८॥

prāṇāyāmena yogīndro labdhvaiśvaryāṣṭakāni vai /

pāpapuṇyodadhiṃ tīrtvā trailokyacaratāmiyāt /58/

Having achieved the eight types of perfections (the psychic powers) through *prānāyāma*, and having crossed the worldly ocean of virtue and vices, the great yogi wanders about in all three worlds at will. –58.

ततोऽभ्यासक्रमेणैव घटिकात्रितयं भवेत् ।

येन स्यात्सकलासिद्धिर्योगिनः स्वेप्सिता ध्रुवम् ॥५९॥

tato'bhyāsakrameṇaiva ghatikātritayam bhavet /

yena syātsakalāsiddhiryogīnaḥ svepsitā dhruvam /59/

Then, gradually practicing the *prāṇāyāma*, he should be able to retain the breath for three *ghaṭis* (one hour and twelve minutes). The yogi certainly receives all the desired *siddhis* (the perfections) through this *prāṇāyāma*. –59.

Attainable Perfections by the Yogi

वाक्सिद्धिः कामचारित्वं दूरदृष्टिस्तथैव च ।
दूरश्रुतिः सूक्ष्मदृष्टिः परकायप्रवेशनम् ॥६०॥
विण्मुत्रलेपने स्वर्णमदृष्यकरणं तथा ।
भवन्त्येतानि सर्वाणि खेचरत्वं च योगिनाम् ॥६१॥

vāksiddhiḥ kāmacāritvaṃ dūradṛṣtistathaiva ca /
dūraśrutiḥ sūkṣmadṛṣṭiḥ parakāyapraveśanam /60/
viṇmutralepane svarṇamadṛśyakaraṇam tathā /
bhavantyetāni sarvāṇi khecaratvaṃ ca yogīnām /61/

The yogi acquires these powers: - 1) *vāksiddhi* (what he says comes to be true), 2) *kāmacārī* (traveling anywhere at will), 3) *dūradṛṣṭi* (clairvoyance), 4) *dūraśruti* (clairaudience), 5) *śukṣmadṛṣṭi* (the subtle insight), 6) *parakāyā praveśa* (the power of entering into another's body), 7) changing raw metals into gold by besmearing them with his stool and urine, 8) the power of making oneself invisible, and 9) moving in the air. –60-61.

Ghaṭa Avasthā

यदा भवेदघटावस्था पवनाभ्यासने परा ।
तदा संसारचक्रेऽस्मिन्नास्ति यन्न साधयेत् ॥६२॥

yadā bhavedghaṭāvasthā pavanābhyāsane parā /
tadā samsāracakre'sminnāsti yanna sādhayet /62/

When the yogi reaches *ghaṭa avasthā* (the mastery over the *kumbhaka*) through the practice of *prāṇāyāma*, then there is nothing that he cannot achieve in the wheel of this universe. –62.

प्राणापाननादबिंदुजीवात्मपरमात्मनः ।
मिलित्वा घटते यस्मात्तस्माद्वै घट उच्यते ॥६३॥

prāṇāpānanādabindujīvātmaparamātmanaḥ /
militvā ghaṭate yasmāttasmādvai ghaṭa ucyate /63/

When *prāṇa* and *apāna*, *nāda* and *vindu*, *jīvātma* (the embodied Self) and *Pramātmā* (the Universal Self) combine with each other, then this is called *ghaṭa avasthā*. –63.

यामममात्रं यदा धर्त्तुं समर्थः स्यात्तदादभुतः ।

प्रत्याहारस्तदैव स्यान्नांतरा भवति ध्रुवम् ॥६४॥

yāmamātraṃ yadā dharttuṃ samarthaḥ syāttadādbhutaḥ /

pratyāhārastadaiva syānnāntarā bhavati dhruvam /64/

When he is able to hold his breath for three hours, then he certainly reaches the marvelous state of *pratyāhāra* without any intervals. –64.

यं यं जानाति योगीन्द्रस्तं तमात्मेति भावयेत् ।

यैरिन्द्रियैर्यद्विधानस्तदिन्द्रियजयो भवेत् ॥६५॥

yaṃ yaṃ jānāti yogīndrastaṃ tamātmetibhāvayet /

yairindriyaiyadvidhānastadindriyajayo bhavet /65/

Whatever thing the yogi knows through his senses, he should think it as his own Self. In this way by knowing the working law of the senses, he can have victory over them. –65.

याममात्रं यदा पूर्णं भवेदभ्यासयोगतः ।

एकवारं प्रकुर्वीत तदा योगी च कुम्भकम् ॥६६॥

दण्डाष्टकं यदा वायुर्निश्चलो योगिनो भवेत् ।

स्वसामर्थ्यात्तदांगुष्ठे तिष्ठेद्वातलवत्सुधीः ॥६७॥

yāmamātraṃ yadā pūrṇaṃ bhavedabhyāsayogataḥ /

ekavāraṃ prakurvīta tadā yogī ca kumbhakam /66/

daṇḍāṣṭakaṃ yadā vāyurniścalo yogīno bhavet /

svasāmarthyāttadāṅguṣṭhe tiṣṭhedvātulavatsudhīḥ /67/

When the yogi can perfectly do a single *kumbhaka* for three hours through his practice, when his retention of breath is steady for three hours, then the wise yogi can balance himself on his thumb with his own strength; but he may seem crazy to others. –66-67.

Paricaya Avasthā

ततः परिचयावस्था यागिनोऽभ्यासतो भवेत् ।

यदा वायुश्चंद्रसूर्य त्यक्त्वा तिष्ठति निश्चलम् ॥

वायुः परिचितो वायुः सुषुम्णा व्योम्नि संचरेत् ॥६८॥

tataḥ paricayāvasthā yogīno'bhyāsato bhavet /

yadā vāyuścandrasūryaṃ tyaktvā tiṣṭhati niścalam /

vāyuḥ paricito vāyuḥ suṣumṇā vyomni sañcaret /68/

After that stage, through continuous practice, the yogi arrives at *paricaya avasthā*. When the *prāṇa* moves and remains steady in the ethereal pathway of the *suṣumṇā*, leaving the sun and the moon (the *piṅgalā* and *iḍā*), then it is *paricaya avasthā* (the state of introduction to inner knowledge). –68.

क्रियाशक्तिं गृहीत्वैव चक्रान्भित्वा सुनिश्चितम् ।

यदा परिचयावस्था भवेदभ्यासयोगतः ॥

त्रिकुटं कर्मणां योगि तदा पश्यति निश्चितम् ॥६९॥

kriyāśaktiṃ gṛhītvaiva cakrānbhittvā suniścitam /

yadā paricayāvasthā bhavedabhyāsayogataḥ /

trikutaṃ karmaṇām yogi tadā paśyati niścitam /69/

Having achieved *kriyā śakti* (the perfection over the energy of action) by the practice of yoga, when he penetrates the *cakras* (the psychic energy centers) and aṛves at *paricaya avasthā*; then the yogi certainly perceives *trikūṭa karma - ādyātmika, ādhidaivika* and *ādhibhautika* (the three types of worldly miseries or suffering i.e. spiritual, natural and environmental). –69.

ततश्च कर्मकूटानि प्रणवेन विनाशयेत ।

स योगी कर्मभोगाय कायव्यूहं समाचेरत् ॥७०॥

tataśca karmakūṭāni praṇavena vināśayet /

sa yogī karmabhogāya kāyavyūhaṃ samācaret /70/

Then the yogi should destroy all his amassed karmas through the repetition of *praṇava* (the *mantra Om*). He should perform *kāyavyūha* (the ritual action related to the location and departments of *vāta, pitta, kapha* (the three humors - air, bile, and mucus), skin, blood, flesh, *dhātu* (fluids and juices) and semen of the body) in order to enjoy the fruits of all his karma. –70.

अस्मिन्काले महायोगी पंचधा धारणं चरेत् ।

येन भूरादिसिद्धिः स्यात्ततो भूतभयापहा ॥७१॥

asminakāle mahāyogī pañcadhā dhāraṇaṃ caret /

yena bhūrādisiddhiḥ syāttato bhūtabhayāpahā /71/

During that time, the great yogi should practice five types of *dhāraṇā*; through this practice he achieves *bhūrādisiddhi* (victory over the five elements – the ether, air, fire, water and earth), and fear of harm from any of these elements is eliminated. –71.

आधारे घटिकाः पंच लिंगस्थाने तथैव च ।

तदूर्ध्वं घटिकाः पञ्च नाभिहृन्मध्यके तथा ॥७२॥

भ्रूमध्योर्ध्वं तथा पंच घटिका धारायेत्सुधीः ।

तथा भूरादिना नष्टो योगिन्द्रो न भवेत्खलु ॥७३॥

ādhāre ghatikāḥ pañca liṅgasthāne tathaiva ca /

tadūrdhvaṃ ghatikāḥ pañca nābhihṛnmadhyake tathā /72/

bhrūmadhyordhvaṃ tathā pañca ghatikā dhārayetsudhīḥ /

tathā bhurādinā naṣṭo yogīndro na bhavetkhalu /73/

The wise yogi should practice *dhāraṇā* (concentration) in this way: five *ghaṭis* (two hours) in the *ādhāra* (*mūlādhāra*) lotus; five *ghaṭis* in the area of *liṅga* (*svādhisṭhāna* lotus); five *ghaṭis* in the area above it (*maṇipura* lotus); the same in the heart (*anāhata*) lotus;

five *ghaṭis* in the throat (*viśuddhi* lotus) and at the end he should hold his *dhāraṇā* five *ghaṭis* in *bhrūmadhya* (the space between the two eyebrows). Then certainly, the great yogi cannot be harmed by any of these five elements (through this practice). –72-73.

मेधावी सर्वभूतानां धारणां यः समभ्यसेत् ।
शतब्रह्ममृतेनापि मृत्युस्तस्य न विद्यते ॥७४॥

medhāvi sarvabhūtānāṃ dharaṇāṃ yaḥ samabhyaset /
śatabrahmamṛtenāpi mṛtustasya na vidyate /74/

The wisest yogi among all the creatures, who duly practices this *dhāranā* (concentration) in this way, does not die until the death of one hundred *brahmās*. –74.

Niṣpatti Avasthā

ततोऽभ्यासक्रमेणैव निष्पत्तिर्योगिनो भवेत् ।
अनादिकर्मबीजानि येन तीर्त्वाऽमृतं पिबेत् ॥७५॥

tato'bhyāsakrameṇaiva niṣpattiryogīno bhavet /
anādikarmabījāni yena tīrtvā'mṛtaṃ pibet /75/

Then, through the gradual, having crossed the endless seeds of all his karma, the yogi drinks the nectar of immortality. –75.

यदा निष्पत्तिर्भवति समाधेः स्वन कर्मणा ।
जीवनमुक्तस्य शांतस्य भवेद्धीरस्य योगिनः ॥७६॥
यदा निष्पत्तिसम्पन्नः समाधिः स्वेच्छया भवेत् ।
गृहीत्वा चेतनां वायुः क्रियाशक्तिं च वेगवान् ॥
सर्वाश्चक्रान्विजित्वा च ज्ञानशक्तौ विलीयते ॥७७॥

yadā niṣpattirbhavati samādheḥ svena karmaṇā /
jīvanamuktasya śāntasya bhaveddhīrasya yogīnaḥ /76/
yadā niṣpattisampannaḥ samādhiḥ svecchayā bhevet /
gṛhītvā cetanāṃ vāyuh kṛyāśaktiṃ ca vegavān /

sarvāmścakrānvijitvā ca jñānaśaktau vilīyate /77/

When *jīvan mukta* (the one liberated in the present life), tranquil and persevering yogi reaches *niṣpatti* (the state of final accomplishment) in *samādhi* (the profound state of meditation) through his own practice, and when this state of accomplished *samādhi* is voluntarily induced, then the yogi should grasp his *cetanā* (the conscious intelligence) along with *vāyu* (the vital energy) by the force of his *kriyāśakti* (the power achieved through practice) and should overcome all the *cakras* (the six psychic energy centers) and merge it (the *cetanā*) in *jñāna śakti*. –76-77.

Vāyu Sādhanā (Practice)

इदानीं क्लेशहान्यर्थं वक्तव्य वायुसाधनम् ।

येन संसारचक्रेऽस्मिन् भोगहानिर्भवेद्ध्रुवम् ॥७८॥

idānīṃ kleśahānyarthaṃ vaktavyaṃ vāyusādhanam /

yena samsāracakre'smin bhogahānirbhaveddhruvam /78/

Now I am going to describe about *vāyu sādhanā* (the practice of air or *prāṇa*) in order to remove the obstacles (in the path of yoga practice). Through its knowledge, both the suffering and enjoyment are surely destroyed in the wheel of this world. –78.

रसनां तालुमूले यः स्थापयित्वा विचक्षणः ।

पिबेत्प्राणानिलं तस्य योगानां संक्षयो भवेत् ॥७९॥

rasanāṃ talumūle yaḥ sthāpayitvā vicakṣaṇaḥ /

pivetprāṇānilaṃ tasya rogāṇāṃ sangkṣayobhavet /79/

When the skilled yogi, having placed the tongue at the base of the palate, drinks this *pranic* (vital) air, then his multifarious diseases are destroyed. –79.

काकचंच्वा पिबेद्वायुं शीतलं यो विचक्षणः ।

प्राणापानविधानज्ञः स भवेन्मुक्तिभाजनः ॥८०॥

kākacañcvā pibedvāyuṃ śītalaṃ yo vicakṣaṇaḥ /

prāṇāpānavidhānajñaḥ sa bhavenmuktibhājanaḥ /80/

By knowing the rules of *prāṇa* and *apāna* regarding their functions, the skilled yogi who drinks the cool air through the mouth making it like a beak of a crow, is eligible for liberation. –80.

सरसं यः पिबेद्वायुं पंत्यहं विधिना सुधीः ।

नश्यन्ति योगिनस्तस्य श्रमदाहजरामयाः ॥८१॥

sarasaṃ yaḥ pibedvāyuṃ pratyahaṃ vidhinā sudhīḥ /

naśyanti yogīnastasya śramadāhajarāmayāḥ /81/

The wise yogi who drinks this *sarasam vāyu* (ambrosial air) everyday according to these rules destroys all his fatigue, fever, decay and old age. –81.

रसनामूर्ध्वगां कृत्वा यश्चन्द्रे सलिलं पिबेत् ।

मासमात्रेण योगीन्द्रो मृत्युंजयति निश्चिनम् ॥८२॥

rasanāmūrdhvagāṃ kṛtvā yaścandre salilaṃ pibet /

māsamātreṇa yogīndro mṛtyuñjayati niścitam /82/

Having turned his tongue upward, when the great yogi drinks *salilam* (the ambrosial fluid) flowing down from the moon, surely conquers death within a month. –82.

राजदंतबिलं गाढं संपीडय विधिना पिबेत् ।

ध्यात्वा कुण्डलिनीं देवीं षण्मासेन कविर्भवेत् ॥८३॥

rājadantabilaṃ gāḍham sampīḍya vidhina pibet /

dhyātvā kuṇḍalinīṃ deviṃ ṣaṇmāsena kavirbhavet /83/

After having firmly pressed the front teeth together, the yogi who drinks the vital air with appropriate method through the hole between the teeth, while meditating on the *Goddess Kuṇḍalinī* (the psychic force that lies dormant like a coiled serpent in *mūlādhāra* lotus) turns out to be a poet within six months. –83.

काकचंच्वा पिबेद्वायुं संध्ययोरुभयोरपि ।

कुण्डलिन्या मुखे ध्यात्वा क्षयरोगस्य शान्तये ॥८४॥

kākacañcvā pibdtvāyuṃ sandhyayorubhayorapi /

kuṇḍalinyā mukhe dhyātvā kṣayarogasya śāntaye /84/

The yogi who drinks this air through his mouth like a crow-bill during both dawn and dusk, meditating on the mouth of the *Kuṇḍalinī*, destroys the tuberculosis. –84.

अहर्निशं पिबेद्योगी काकचंच्वा विचिक्षणः ।

पिबेत्प्राणानिलं तस्य रोगाणां सक्षयो भवेत् ॥

दूरश्रुतिर्दूरदृष्टिस्तथा स्याददर्शनं खलु ॥८५॥

aharniśaṃ pibedyogī kākacañcvā vicakṣaṇaḥ /

pibetprāṇānilaṃ tasya rogāṇām saṅkṣayo bhavet /

dūraśrutirdūradṛṣṭistathā syāddarśanaṃ khalu /85/

The yogi who drinks this vital air day and night through a crow-beak shaped mouth, destroys his multifarious diseases; he surely receives the power of *dūraśruti* and *dūradṛṣṭi* (clairaudience, clairvoyance) and subtle vision. –85.

दन्तैर्दन्तान्समापीडय पिबत्वायुं शनैः शनैः ।

ऊर्ध्वजिह्वः सुमेधावी मृत्युं जयति सोचिरात् ॥८६॥

dantairdantānsamāpīḍya pibedvāyuṃ śanaiḥ śanaiḥ /

ūrdhvajihvaḥ sumedhāvī mṛtyuṃ jayati socirāt /86/

The wise yogi, while firmly pressing the upper teeth on the lower with his tongue turned upward, who drinks the air quite slowly, defeats death in no time. –86.

षण्मासमात्रमभ्यासं यः करोति दिने दिने ।

सर्वपापविनिर्मुक्तो रोगान्नाशयते हि सः ॥८७॥

ṣaṇmāsamātramabhyāsaṃ yaḥ karoti dine dine /

arvapāpavinirmukto rogānnāśayate hi saḥ /87/

One who practices this daily for six months frees himself from the multitude of sins and destroys all diseases. –87.

संवत्सरकृताऽभ्यासादभैरवो भवति ध्रुवम् ।

अणिमादिगुणाँल्लब्ध्वा जितभूतगणः स्वयम् ॥८८॥

samvatsarakṛtā'bhyāsādbhairavo bhavati dhruvam /

aṇimādiguṇān labdhvā jitabhūtagṇaḥ svayam /88/

The person who continues this practice for a year surely becomes *bhairava* (one of the form of *Śiva*). Having achieved the power of *aṇimā* etc., he triumphs over the whole class of living beings. –88.

रसनामूर्ध्वगां कृत्वा क्षणार्ध यदि तिष्ठति ।

क्षेणेन मुच्यते योगी व्याधिमृत्युजरादिभिः ॥८६॥

rasanāmūrdhvagāṃ kṛtvā kṣaṇārdhaṃ yadi tiṣṭhati /

kṣaṇena mucyate yogī vyādimṛtyujarādibhiḥ /89/

If the yogi remains for half a second with his tongue turned upward, he immediately liberates himself from disease, death and old age. –89.

रसनां प्राणसंयुक्तां पीड्यमानां विचिंतयेत् ।

न तस्य जायते मृत्युः सत्यं सत्यं मयोदितम् ॥६०॥

rasanāṃ prāṇasamyuktāṃ pīḍyamānāṃ vicintayet /

na tasya jāyate mṛtyuḥ satyaṃ satyaṃ mayoditam /90/

The person who concentrates on *ājñā cakra* (the center of intuition or Third Eye), pressing the tongue (upwards), united with the *prāṇa*, never dies. I am telling you the truth. –90.

एवमभ्यासयोगेन कामदेवा द्वितीयकः ।

न क्षुधा न तृषा निद्रा नैव मूर्च्छा प्रजायते ॥६१॥

evamabhyāsayogena kāmadevo dvitīyakaḥ /

na kṣudhā na tṛṣā nidrā naiva mūrcchā prajāyate /91/

Through yogic practice in this way, he becomes second *kāmadeva* (the God of love). He does not experience hunger and thirst, and does not feel sleepy and faint. –91.

अनेनैव विधानेन योगीन्द्रोऽवनिमण्डले ।

भवेत्स्वच्छन्दचारी च सर्वापत्परिवर्जितः ॥९२॥

anenaiva vidhānena yogīndro'vanimaṇḍale

bhavetsvacchandacārī ca sarvāpatparivarjitaḥ /92/

The great yogi who follows these rules of practice moves and acts independently anywhere in this world, being free from all barriers and obstacles. –92.

न तस्य पुनरावृत्तिर्मोदते ससुरैरपि ।

पुण्यपापैर्न लिप्येत एतदाचरेणेन सः ॥९३॥

na tasya punarāvṛttirmodate sasurairapi /

puṇyapāpairna lipyeta etadācaraṇena saḥ /93/

By following the practice in this way, he is neither reborn in this world, nor can virtue and vice besmear him; he enjoys and lives happily like the gods. –93.

Description of Asanas

चतुरशीत्यासनानि सन्ति नानाविधानि च ।

तेभ्यश्चतुष्कमादाय मयोक्तानि ब्रवीम्यहम् ॥

सिद्धासनं ततः पद्मासनञ्चोग्रं च स्वस्तिकम् ॥९४॥

caturaśītyāsanāni santi nānāvidhāni ca /

tebhyaścatuṣkamādāya mayoktāni bravīmyaham /

siddhāsanaṃ tataḥ padmāsanañcograṃ ca svastikam /94/

There are eighty-four postures and these are of many types. Out of them, four should be taken up, which I am describing: 1) *siddhāsana*, 2) *padmāsana*, 3) *ugrāsana* and 4) *svastikāsana*. –94.

1. Siddhāsana

योनिं संपीड्य यत्नेन पादमूलेन साधकः ।
मढ्रोपरि पादमूलं विन्यसेध्योगवित्सदा ॥९५॥
ऊर्ध्वं निरीक्ष्य भ्रूमध्यं निश्चलः संयतेन्द्रियः ।
विशेषोऽवक्रकायश्च रहस्युद्वेगवर्जितः ॥९६॥

yoniṃ sampīḍya yatnena pādamūlena sādhakaḥ /
meḍhropari pādamūlaṃ vinyasedyogavitsadā /95/
ūrdhvaṃ nirīkṣya bhrūmadhyaṃ niścalaḥ samyatendriyaḥ /
viśeṣo'vakrakāyaśca rahasyudvegavarjitaḥ /96/

The expert yogi with due care should press the *yoni* (the perineum) with the heel and he should place the other heel on the *liṅgam* (the genital organ); fixing his gaze on *bhrūmadhya* (the eyebrow center) he should be steady and senses restrained. Let his body be particularly straight and not tilted in any way. His place of practice should be secluded without any disturbances. –95-96.

एतित्सद्धासनं ज्ञेयं सिद्धानां सिद्धिदायकम् ।
येनाभ्यासवशाच्छीघ्रं योगनिष्पत्तिमाप्नुयात् ॥९७॥
सिद्धासनं सदा सेव्यं पवनाभ्यासिना परम् ।
येन संसारमुत्सृज्य लभते परमां गतिम् ॥९८॥

etatsiddhāsanaṃ jñeyaṃ siddhānāṃ siddhidāyakam /
yenābhyāsavaśātśigraṃ yoganiṣpattimāpnuyāt /97/
siddhāsanaṃ sadā sevyaṃ pavanābhyāsinā param /
yena samsāramutsṛjya labhate paramaṃ gatim /98/

Know that this is *siddhāsana* (the accomplished pose) that gives perfection to ascetics. Through its constant practice, final accomplishment in yoga is quickly achieved. the practitioner of breath (*prāṇāyāma*) should always assume the supreme *siddhāsana* posture. Through the practice of this posture, he attains the highest state while leaving this world. –97-98.

नातः परतरं गुह्यमासनं विद्यते भुवि ।
येनानुध्यानमात्रेण योगी पापाद्विमुच्यते ॥९९॥

nātaḥ parataraṃ guhyamāsanaṃ vidyate bhuvi /
yenānudhyānamātreṇa yogī pāpādvimucyate /99/

In this whole world, there is no *guhya āsana* (secret posture) other than it. By simply contemplating in this posture, the yogi frees himself from sin. –99.

2. Padmāsana

उत्तानौ चरणौ कृत्वा ऊरुसंस्थौ प्रयत्नतः ।
ऊरुमध्ये तथोत्तानौ पाणी कृत्वा तु तादृशौ ॥१००॥
नासाग्रे विन्यसेद्दृष्टिं दन्तमूलञ्च जिह्वया ।
उत्तोल्य चिबुकं वक्ष उत्थाप्य पवनं शनैः ॥१०१॥
यथाशक्त्या समाकृष्य पूरयेदुदरं शनैः ।
यथा शक्त्यैव पश्चात्तु रेचयदविरोधतः ॥१०२॥
इदं पद्मासनं प्रोक्तं सर्वव्याधिविनाशनम् ।
दुर्लभं यन केनापि धीमता लभ्यते परम् ॥१०३॥

uttānau caraṇau kṛtvā ūrusamsthau prayatnataḥ /
ūrumadhye tathottānau pāṇī kṛtvā tu tādṛśau /100/
nāsāgre vinyaset dṛṣṭim dantamūlañca jihvayā /
uttolya cibukaṃ vakṣa utthāpya pavanaṃ śanaiḥ /101/
yathā śaktyā samākṛṣya pūrayedudaraṃ śanaiḥ /
yathā śaktyaiva paścāttu recayedavirodhataḥ /102/
idaṃ padmāsanaṃ proktaṃ sarvavyādhivināsanam /
durlabhaṃ yena kenāpi dhīmatā labhyate param /103/

Having straightened both legs, put each foot on the opposite thigh; similarly, straighten both hands and place them between the thighs; pressing the base of the teeth with the tongue, fix your gaze on the tip of the nose; by expanding the chest with a raised chin, inhale slowly and fill your abdomen as far as your strength allows, and then exhale slowly as far as possible in a smooth harmonious way. This is called *padmāsana* that destroys the multitude of diseases. This is a rare posture and not every one can practice it; only the wise practitioners achieve perfection in this excellent posture. –100-103.

अनुष्ठाने कृते प्राणः समश्चलति तत्क्षणात् ।
भवदभ्यासने सम्यक्साधकस्य न संशय ॥१०४॥

anuṣṭhāne kṛte prāṇaḥ samascalati tatśaṇāt /
bhavedabhyāsane samyaksādhakasya na samśayaḥ /104/

When a practitioner performs this posture, his vital air immediately moves equally, and in the course of practice it runs harmoniously throughout his body. There is no doubt in it. –104.

पद्मासने स्थितो योगी प्राणापानविधानतः ।
पूरयेत्स विमुक्तः स्यात्सत्यं सत्यं वदाम्यहम् ॥१०५॥

padmāsane sthito yogī prāṇāpānavidhānataḥ /
pūrayetsa vimuktaḥ syātsatyaṃ satyaṃ vadāmyaham /105/

The yogi who practices *prāṇāyāma* in *padmāsana* posture, knowing the rule of action of the *prāṇa* and *apāna*, is certainly liberated. Certainly, I tell you the truth. –105.

3. Ugrāsana

प्रसार्य चरणद्वन्द्वं परस्परमसंयुतम् ।
स्वपाणिभ्यां दृढं धृत्वा जानूपरि शिरो न्यसेत् ॥१०६॥
आसनोग्रमिदं प्रोक्तं भवेदनिलदीपनम् ।
देहावसानहरणं पश्चिमोत्तानसंज्ञकम् ॥१०७॥
य एतदासनं श्रेष्ठं प्रत्यहं साधयेत्सुधीः ।
वायुः पश्चिममार्गेण तस्य सञ्चरति ध्रुवम् ॥१०८॥

prasārya caraṇadvandvaṃ parasparasamyutam /

svapāṇibhyām dṛḍham dhṛtvā jānūpari śiro nyaset /106/

āsanogramidaṃ proktaṃ bhavedaniladīpanam /

dehāvasānaharaṇaṃ paścimottānasañjñakam /107/

ya etadāsanam śreṣṭham pratyahaṃ sādhayetsudhīḥ /

vāyuh paścimamārgeṇa tasya sañcarati dhruvam /108/

Stretch out both your legs keeping them apart, firmly grasp the sole of feet with your hands, and place your head on your knees. This is called *ugrāsana* (the Fierce Pose) that stimulates the air and kidnaps death away. This is also called *pascimottānasana* (the back stretching pose). The wise person, who practices this super posture daily, surely moves the air (the vital force) through the posterior path (the middle psychic channel). –106-108.

एतदभ्यासशीलानां सर्वसिद्धः प्रजायते ।

तस्माद्योगी प्रयत्नेन साधयेत्सिद्धमात्मनः ॥१०६॥

etadabhyāsaśīlānāṃ sarvasiddhiḥ prajāyate /

tasmādyogī prayatnena sādhayetsiddhamātmanaḥ /109/

The constant practitioner receives all *siddhis* (the perfections) by its practice. Therefore, the yogi who is desirous of achieving perfection should practice it with due effort. –109.

गोपनीयं प्रयत्नेन न देयं यस्य कस्यचित् ।

येन शीघ्रं मरुत्सिद्धिर्भवेद् दुःखौघनाशिनी ॥११०॥

gopanīyaṃ prayatnena na deyaṃ yasya kasyacit /

yena śīghraṃ marutsiddhirbhaved duḥkhaughanāśinī /110/

This practice should be kept secret with proper effort and should not be imparted to everyone. *vāyusiddhi* (the perfection of vital energy) is quickly attained through its practice, and the multifarious worldly miseries are destroyed. –110.

4. Svastikāsana

जानुर्वोरन्तरे सम्यग्धृत्वा पादतले उभे ।

समकायः सुखासीनः स्वस्तिकं तत्प्रचक्षते ॥१११॥

jānūrvorantare samyagdhṛtvā pādatale ubhe /

samakāyaḥ suskhāsīnaḥ svastikaṃ tatpracakṣate /111/

Lay the sole of each foot under the thigh of the opposite leg. Sit comfortably keeping your back, neck and head straight. This is called *svastikāsana* (the auspicious pose). –111.

अनेन विधिना योगी मारुतं साधयेत्सुधीः ।

देहे न त्क्रमते व्याधिस्तस्य वायुश्च सिध्यति ॥११२॥

anena vidhinā yogī mārutaṃ sādhayetsudhīḥ /

dehe na kramate vyādhistasya vāyuśca siddhyati /112/

The wise yogi should practice *prāṇāyāma* in this way. No diseases cannot attack his body; and he also achieves *vāyusiddhi* (perfection in *prāṇāvāyu*). –112.

सुखासनमिदं प्रोक्तं सर्वदुःखप्राणाशनम् ।

स्वस्तिकं योगिभिर्गोप्यं स्वस्तीकरणमुत्तमम् ॥११३।

sukhāsanamidaṃ proktaṃ sarvaduhkhapraṇāśanam /

svastikaṃ yogibhirgopyaṃ svastīkaraṇamuttamam /113/

This is also called *sukhāsana* (the easy pose) as it is easily performed. It is the destroyer of the multitude of miseries. This excellent auspicious posture, giving welfare and health, is a mystery even to the yogi. –113.

इति श्रीशिवसंहितायां तृतीयः पटलः समाप्तः ॥३॥

iti śrīśivasamhitāyāṃ tṛtīyaḥ paṭalaḥ samāptaḥ //3//

Thus, ends the Third Chapter of *Śiva Samhita.*

चतुर्थपटलः

Caturthapaṭalaḥ

Chapter Four

Discourse on Mudrā

Yoni Mudrā

आदौ पूरक योगेन स्वाधारे पूरयेन्मनः ।
गुदमेढ्रान्तरे योनिस्तामाकुंच्य प्रवर्तते ॥१॥

ādau pūraka yogena svādhāre pūrayenmanaḥ /
gudameḍhrāntare yonistāmākuñcya pravartate /1/

First, inhale deeply and fix your mind in the *ādhāra* lotus; then start to contract the *yoni*, which is located at the perineum. –1.

Union with Cosmic Consciousness and Cosmic Energy

ब्रह्मयोनिगतं ध्यात्वा कामं कन्दुकसन्निभम् ।
सूर्यकोटि प्रतिकाशं चन्द्रकोटिसुशीतलम् ॥२॥
तस्योर्ध्वं तु शिखासूक्ष्मा चिद्रूपा परमाकला ।
तथा सहितमात्मानमेकीभूतं विचिन्तयेत् ॥३॥

brahmayonimgataṃ dhyātvā kāmaṃ kandukasannivam /
sūryakoṭi pratīkāśaṃ chandrakoṭisuśītalam /2/
tasyordhvaṃ tu śikhāsūkṣmā cidrūpā paramākalā /
tayā sahitamātmānamekībhūtaṃ vicintayet /3/

Contemplate that the God of Love resides in that *Brahma Yoni*, and he is beautiful like *bandhuka* (the pentapetes phoenicea) flower, which is as brilliant as tens of millions of suns, and as cool as tens of millions of moons. Above that *yoni* there is a subtle flame in the form of *Intelligence*; imagine that you are united with that *Intelligence* along with its *Śakti*. –2-3.

Drink of Divine Ambrosial Fluid

गच्छति ब्रह्ममार्गेण लिंगत्रयक्रमेण वै ।

अमृतं तद्धि स्वर्गस्थं परमानन्दलक्षणम् ॥४॥

श्वेतरक्तं तेजसाढयं सुधाधाराप्रवर्षिणम् ।

पीत्वा कुलामृतं दिव्यं पुनरेवव विशेत्कुलम् ॥५॥

gacchati brahmamārgeṇa liṅgatrayakrameṇa vai /

amṛtaṃ taddhi svargasthaṃ paramānandalakṣaṇam /4/

svetaraktaṃ tejasāḍhyaṃ sudhādhārāpravarṣiṇam /

pītvā kulāmṛtaṃ divyampunareva viśetkulam /5/

Then you should imagine that the *Jīva* travels up through three bodies (the gross, subtle and causal) in the *suśumṇā* channel. The heavenly nectar is secreted there and its nature is supreme joy. Its color is red-white, full of brilliance that showers down the fountain of the immortal fluid. Drink this divine wine of immortality and then enter the *Kula* (i.e., perineal area) again. –4-5.

पुनरेव कुलं गच्छेन्मात्रायोगेन नान्यथा ।

सा च प्राणसमाख्याता ह्यस्मिंस्तन्त्रे मयोदिता ॥६॥

punareva kulaṃ gachenmātrāyogena nānyathā /

sā ca prāṇāsamākhyātā hyasmintantre mayoditā /6/

Then go to the *kula* again through *mātrāyoga* (the *prāṇāyāma*), and not by any other means. I have described this *yoni* as equal to life in the *tantras*. –6.

पुनः प्रलीयते तस्यां कालाग्न्यादिशिवात्मकम् ।
योनिमुद्रा परा ह्येषा बन्धस्तस्याः प्रकीर्तितः ॥
तस्यास्तु बन्धमात्रेण तन्नस्ति यन्न साधयेत् ॥७॥

punaḥ pralīyate tasyāṃ kālāgnyādiśivātmakam
yonimudrā parā hyeṣā bandhastasyāḥ prakīrtitah
tasyāstu bandhamātreṇa tannāsti yanna sādhayet /7/

Again, the practitioner should absorb in that *yoni*, where the fire of death resides as the form of *Śiva.* In this way, I have described the process of practicing the supreme yoni *mudra* that is called *bandha yoni mudra*. There is nothing that cannot be accomplished by its practice. –7.

Initiated Mantras - Giver of Perfection and Liberation

छिन्नरूपास्तु ये मन्त्राः कीलिताः स्तंभिताश्च ये ।
दग्धामन्त्राः शिखाहीना मलिनास्तु तिरस्कृताः ॥८॥
मन्दा बालास्तथा वृद्धाः प्रौढा यौवनगर्विताः ।
अरिपक्षे स्थिता ये च निर्वीर्याः सत्ववर्जिताः ॥
तथा सत्वेन हीनाश्च खण्डिताः शतधमकृताः ॥६॥
विधानेन च संयुक्ताः प्रभवन्त्यचिरेण तु ॥६॥
सिद्धिमोक्षप्रदाः सर्वे गुरुणा विनियोजिताः ॥१०॥
दीक्षयित्वा विधानेन अभिषिच्य सहस्रधा ।
ततो मन्त्राधिकारार्थमेषा मुद्रा प्रकीर्तिता ॥११॥

chinnarūpāstu ye mantrāḥ kīlitāḥ stambhitāśca ye /
dagdhāmantrāh śikhāhīnā malinastu tiraskṛtāḥ /8/
mandā bālāstathā vṛddhāḥ praudhā yaunagarvitā /
aripakṣe sthitā ye ca nirvīryāḥ sattvavarjitāḥ /
tathā sattvena hīnāśca khaṇḍitāh śatadhākṛtāḥ /9/
vidhānena ca samyuktāḥ prabhavantyachireṇa tu /

siddhimokṣapradāḥ sarve guruṇā viniyojitāḥ /10/

dīkṣayitvā vidhānena abhiṣicya sahasradhā /

tato mantrādhikārārthameṣā mudrā prakīrtitā /11/

Those *mantras* that are impaired, killed, paralyzed, or burnt or which are without their flame or are dull should be given up. Those *mantras* that are slow, young, or old, are proud of their youth, are in the antagonistic position, weak, without vitality and purity, or without essence or which have been broken in a hundred pieces, even then they can be instantly made effective through proper techniques. All the *mantras*, properly initiated by the guru according to rites and rituals, after offering a thousand sprinkles of sacred water (over the disciple) give both perfections and liberation. Therefore, this *mudrā* has been described for the entitlement of *mantra* initiation. –8-11.

ब्रह्महत्यासहस्राणि त्रैलोक्यमपि घातयेत् ।

नासौ लिप्यति पापने योनिमुद्रानिबन्धनात् ॥१२॥

brahmahatyāsahasrāṇi trailokyamapi ghātayet /

nāsau lipyati pāpena yonimudrānibandhanāt /12/

One who masters *bandha yoni mudrā* through practice is not besmeared by the sin even if he killed a thousand *brāhmaṇas* (priests) or all the creatures in the three worlds. –12.

गुरुहा च सुरापी च स्तेयी च चुरुत्ल्पगः ।

एतैः पापैर्न बध्येत योनिमुद्रानिबन्धनात् ॥१३॥

guruhā ca surāpi ca steyī ca gurutalpagaḥ /

etaiḥ pāpairna badhyeta yonirmudrānibandhanāt /13/

Even if he killed his guru, drank alcohol, involved in theft, or violated his teacher's bed, he is not blemished by such sins due to this *yoni mudrā*. –13.

Importance of Practice

तस्मादभ्यासनं नित्यं कर्तव्यं मोक्षकांक्षिभिः ।
अभ्यासाज्जायते सिद्धिरभ्यासान्मोक्षमाप्नुयात् ॥१४॥

tasmādabyāsanaṃ nityaṃ kartavyaṃ mokṣakāṅkṣibhiḥ /
abyāsājjāyate siddhirabhyāsānmokṣamāpnuyāt /14/

Therefore, it is their duty to practice it daily who desire to achieve liberation. It is through practice alone, one achieves perfection (*siddhi*) and again only through practice, he attains liberation. –14.

संविदं लभतेऽभ्यासाद्योगोभ्यासात्प्रवर्तते ।
मुद्राणां सिद्धिरभ्यासादभ्यासाद्वयुसाधनम् ॥१५॥
कालावञ्चनमभ्यासात्तथा मृत्युञ्जयो भवेत् ।
वाक्सिद्धिः कामचारित्वं भवेदभ्यासयोगतः ॥१६॥

samvidaṃ labhate'bhyāsādyogobhyāsātpravartate /
mudrāṇāṃ siddhirabhyāsādabhyāsādvāyusādhanam /15/
kālavañcanamabhyāsāttathā mṛtuñjayo bhavet /
vāksiddhiḥ kāmacaritvaṃ bhavedabyāsayogataḥ /16/

Knowledge is gained through practice. One is established in yoga through practice. Perfections in *mudrās* and *prāṇāyāmas* are attained by practice. A man can deceive death through practice and he can be victorious over it by practice. One gets *vāksiddhi* (the power of whatever one says coming to be true) and the power of going anywhere at will through practice. –15-16.

योनिमुद्रा परं गोप्या न देया यस्य कस्यचित् ।
सर्वथा नैव दात्व्या प्राणैः कण्ठगतैरपि ॥१७॥

yonimudrā paraṃ gopyā na deyā yasya kasyachit /
sarvathā naiva dātavyā prāṇaih kaṇṭhagatairapi /17/

This *yoni mudrā* is a great secret and should not be given to everyone. It should not be given at all even if one's life is threatened. –17.

Awakening of Kuṇḍalinī – Penetration of Cakras

अधुना कथयिष्यामि योगसिद्धिकरं परम् ।
गोपनीयं सुसिद्धानां योगं परमदुर्लभम् ॥१८॥

adhunā kathayiṣyāmi yogasiddhikaraṃ param /
gopaniyaṃ susiddhānāṃ yogaṃ paramadurlabham /18/

Now I am going to tell you the supreme method of attaining perfection in yoga. Practitioners wishing to achieve perfection should keep it secret. It is the most difficult yoga to be found i.e. it is a rare yoga. –18.

सुप्ता गुरुप्रसादेन यदा जागर्ति कुण्डली ।
तदा सर्वाणि पद्मानि भिद्यन्ते ग्रन्थयोऽपि च ॥१९॥

suptā guruprasādena yadā jāgarti kuṇḍalī /
tadā sarvāṇi padmāni bhidyante granthayo'pi ca /19/

When the sleeping *Kunṇḍalinī* is awakened by the grace of the guru, then all the *cakras* (the six psychic centers) and *granthis* (the three psychic knots: *Brahma, Viṣṇu and Rudra*) are penetrated through. –19.

तस्मात्सर्वप्रयत्नेन प्रबोधयितुमीश्वरीम् ।
ब्रह्मरन्ध्रमुखे सुप्तां मुद्राभ्यासं समाचरेत् ॥२०॥

tasmātsarvaprayatnena prabodhayitumīśvarīm /
brahmarandhramukhe suptāṃ mudrābhyāsaṃ samācaret /20/

Therefore, in order to awaken the Goddess that is sleeping in the mouth of *brahmarandhra* (the hollow of the *suṣumṇā channel*) one should practice *mudrās* with all one's effort. –20.

Description of Ten Principal Mudrās

महामुद्रा महाबन्धो महावेधश्च खेचरी ।
जालंधरो मूलबन्धो विपरीतकृतिस्तथा ॥२१॥
उड्डानं चैव वज्रोली दशमे शक्तिचालनम् ।
इदं हि मुद्रादशकं मुद्राणामुत्तमोत्तमम् ॥२२॥

mahāmudrā mahābandho mahāvedhaśca khecarī /
jālandharo mūlabandho viparītakṛtistathā /21/
uḍḍānaṃ caiva vajrolī daśame śakticālanam
idaṃ hi mudrādasakaṃ mudrāṇāmuttamottamam /22/

These ten *mudrās* are the best among the many *mudrās*: 1) *mahāmudrā*, 2) *mahābandha*, 3) *mahā-vedha*, 4) *khecarī*, 5) *jālandhara*, 6) *mūlabandha*, 7) *viparītakaraṇī*, 8) *uḍḍānam* 9) *vajrolī* and 10) *śakti-cālana*. –21-22.

1. Mahāmudrā

अथ महामुद्राकथनम् ।
महामुद्रां प्रवक्ष्यामि तन्त्रेऽस्मिन्मम वल्लभे ।
यां प्राप्य सिद्धाः सिद्धिं च कपिलाद्याः पुरागताः ॥२३॥

atha mahāmudrākathanam /
mahāmudrāṃ pravakṣyāmi tantre'sminmama vallabhe /
yāṃ prāpya siddhāḥ siddhiṃ ca kapilādyāḥ purāgatā /23/

Now *mahāmudrā* is described.

My dear, now I am going to tell you about *mahāmudrā* in this *tantra* from which the ancient sages like *Kapila* and others received perfection in yoga. –23.

अपसव्येन संपीड्य पादमूलेन सादरम् ।
गुरुपदेशतो योनिं गुदमेढ्रान्तरालगाम् ॥२४॥
सव्यं प्रसारितं पादं धृत्वा पाणियुगेन वै ।
नवद्वाराणि संयम्य चिबुकं हृदयोपरि ॥२५॥

चित्तं चित्तपथे दत्वा प्रभवेद्वायुसाधनम् ।
महामुद्रा भवेदेषा सर्वतन्त्रेषु गोपिता ॥२६॥
वामाङ्गेन समभ्यस्य दक्षाङ्गेनाभ्यसेत्पुनः ।
प्रणायामं समं कृत्वा योगी नियतमानसः ॥२७॥

apasavyena sampīḍya pādamūlena sādaram /
gurūpadeśato yoniṃ gudameḍhrāntarālagām /24/
savyaṃ prasāritaṃ pādaṃ dhṛtvā pāṇiyugena vai /
navadvārāṇi samyamya cibukaṃ hṛdayopari /25/
cittaṃ cittapathe dattvā prabhavedvāyusādhanam /
mahāmudrā bhavedeṣā sarvatantreṣu gopitā /26/
vāmāṅgena samabyasya dakṣāṅgenābyasetpunaḥ /
prāṇāyāmaṃ samaṃ kṛtvā yogī niyatamānasaḥ /27/

Press the perineum tenderly with the heel of the left foot according to the instructions of the guru. Outstretch the right foot and grab it with both hands. Having controlled (closed) the nine gateways of the body, lay your chin on the chest. Then focus your mind on the pathway of *Caitanya* (the Intelligence) and involve yourself in the practice of *vāyu* (the *prāṇāyāma*). This *mahāmudrā* is kept secret in all the *tantras*. After practicing it on the left side, the self-controlled yogi should practice it on the right side along with a balanced and steady practice of *praṇāyāma*. –24-27.

अनेन विधिना योगी मन्दभाग्योऽपि सिध्यति ।
सर्वासामेव नाडीनां चालनं बिन्दुमारणम् ॥२८॥
जीवनन्तु कषायस्य पातकानां विनाशनम् ।
सर्वरोगोपशमनं जठराग्नि विविर्धनम् ॥२९॥
वपुषा कान्तिममलां जरामृत्युविनाशनम ।
वांछितार्थफलं सौख्यमिन्द्रियाणाञ्च मारणम् ॥३०॥
एतदुक्तानि सर्वाणि योगारूढस्य योगिनः ।

भवेदभ्यासतोऽवश्यं नात्र कार्या विचारणा ॥३१॥

anena vidhinā yogī mandavāgyo'pi sidhyati /

sarvāsāmeva nāḍīnāṃ cālanaṃ bindumāraṇam /28/

jīvanantu kaṣāyasya pātakānāṃ vināsanam /

sarvarogopaśamanaṃ jaṭharāgni vivardhanam /29/

vapuṣā kāntimamalāṃ jarāmṛtyuvināśanam /

vāñchitārthaphalaṃ saukyamindriyāṇāñca māraṇam /30/

etaduktāni sarvāṇi yogārūḍhasya yoginaḥ /

bhavedabyāsato'vaśyaṃ nātra kāryā vicāraṇā /31/

According to this method, even a yogi with little luck receives success. This activates all the psychic pathways. *vindu* is stabilized; life is prolonged and its decaying is controlled; all the sins are destroyed. All diseases are cured and the digestive fire is stimulated. The body gets a fair and beautiful complexion, and its decay and death are stopped. One receives all happiness, all his desires are fulfilled, and the senses are controlled. A yogi established in yoga certainly attains perfection in all the previously mentioned things through constant practice. It should not be thought otherwise. –28-31

गोपनीयता प्रयत्नेन मुद्रेयं सुरपूजिते ।

यां तु प्राप्य भावाम्भोधेः पारं गच्छन्ति योगिनः ॥३२॥

gopanīyā prayatnena mudreyaṃ surapūjite /

yām tu prāpya bhavāmbhodheḥ pāraṃ gacchanti yoginaḥ /32/

O Goddess, worshipped by gods! This *mudrā* should be kept secret with great care. Having received it, the yogis cross the worldly ocean of deaths and births. –32.

मुद्रा कामदुघा ह्येषा साधकानां मयोदिता ।

गुप्ताचारेण कर्त्तव्या न देया यस्य कस्यचित् ॥३३॥

mudrā kāmadughā hyeṣā sādhakānāṃ mayoditā /

guptācāreṇa karttavyā na deyā yasya kasyacit /33/

This *mudrā* described by me is like *kāmadughā* (a fabulous cow giving all desires) for the yogis. It should be practiced secretly and not be given to everyone. –33.

2. Mahābandha

अथ महाबन्धकथनम् ।

ततः प्रसारितः पादो विन्यस्य तमुरूपरि ।

गुदयोनिं समाकुंच्य कृत्वा चापानमूर्ध्वगम् ॥३४॥

योजयित्वा समानेन कृत्वा प्राणमधोमुखम् ।

बन्धयेदूर्ध्वगत्यर्थं प्राणापानेन यः सुधीः ॥३५॥

कथितोऽयं महाबन्धः सिद्धिमार्गप्रदायकः ।

नाडीजालाद्रसव्यूहो मूर्धानं याति योगिनः ॥

उभाभ्यां साधयेत्पद्भ्यामेकैकं सुप्रयत्नतः ॥३६॥

atha mahābandhakathanam /

tataḥ prasāritaḥ pādo vinyasya tamurūpari /

gudayoniṃ samākuñcya kṛtvā cāpānamūrdhvagam /34/

yojayitvā samānena kṛtvā prāṇamadhomukham /

bandhayedūrdhvagatyarthaṃ prāṇāpānena yaḥ sudhīḥ /35/

kathito'yaṃ mahābandhaḥ siddhimārgapradāyakaḥ /

nāḍījālādrasavyūho mūrdhānaṃ yānti yoginaḥ /

ubhābhyāṃ sādhayetpadbyāmekaikaṃ suprayatnataḥ /36/

Now *Mahābandha* is described.

Then (having practiced the *mahāmudrā*) outstretch the right foot and place it on the left thigh. Contract the perineum and draw the *apāna vāyu* up. Having joined it with the *samāna vāyu*, then force the *prāṇa vāyu* downwards. In this way, the wise yogi should combine the upward forced *apāna* and downward forced *prāṇa* in the navel area to join them with the *samāna.* Now I have told you the *mahābandha*, the giver of the way to liberation. By this practice, all the subtle fluids in the psychic pathways of the yogi's body move up towards the head. The yogi should practice this *mudrā* with both legs alternately with great care. –34-36.

भवेदभ्यासतो वायुः सुषुम्णां मध्यसङ्गतः ।
अनेन वपुषः पुष्टिर्दृढबन्धोऽस्थिपंजरे ॥३७॥
संपूर्णहृदयो योगी भवन्त्येतानि योगिनः ।
बन्धनानेन योगिन्द्रः साधयेत्सर्वमीप्सितम् ॥३८॥

bhavedabyāsato vāyuḥ suṣumṇāṃ madyasaṅgataḥ /
anena vapuṣaḥ puṣṭirdṛḍhabandho'sthipañjare /37/
sampūrṇahṛdayo yogī bhavantyetāni yoginaḥ /
bandhenānena yogīndraḥ sādhayetsarvamīpsitam /38/

The *prāṇa* moves into the middle psychic channel through its practice. It revitalizes the body and firmly binds the skeleton in the body. The heart of the yogi is fully satisfied. The great yogi fulfills all his desires through this *bandha*. –37-38.

3. Mahāveda

अथ महावेधकथनम् ।
अपानप्राणयोरैक्यं कृत्वा त्रिभुवनेश्वरि ।
महावेधस्थितो योगी कुक्षिमापूर्य वायुना ॥
स्फिचौ संताडयेद्धीमान्वेधोऽयं कीर्तितो मया ॥३९॥

atha mahāvedhakathanam /
apānaprāṇayoraikyaṃ kṛtvā tribhuvaneśvari /
mahāvedhasthito yogī kukṣimāpūrya vāyunā /
sphicau santāḍayeddhimānvedo'yaṃ kīrtito mayā /39/

Now *mahāveda* is described.

O Goddess of the three worlds! Having united the *prāṇa* and *apāna vāyus* together in *mahābandha mudrā*, the wise yogi should fill his belly with the air and hit the buttocks. This is the *mahāveda mudrā* described by me. –39.

वेधेनानेन संबिध्य वायुना योगिपुंगवः ।

ग्रन्थि सुषुम्णामार्गेण ब्रह्मग्रन्थिं भिनत्यसौ ॥४०॥

vedhenānena sambidhya vāyunā yogipuñgavaḥ /

granthiṃ suṣumṇāmārgeṇa brahmagranthiṃ bhinattyasau /40/

The greatest yogi after piercing the (psychic) knot with the *vāyu* through this *veda* in the path of *suṣumnā* should penetrate *brahmagranthi* (the psychic knot of *Brahmā*). –40.

यः करोति सदाभ्यासं महावेधं सुगोपितम् ।

वायुसिद्धिर्भवेत्तस्य जरामरणनाशिनी ॥४१॥

yaḥ karoti sadābyāsaṃ mahāvedaṃ sugopitam /

vāyusiddhirbhavettasya jarāmaraṇanāśinī /41/

He who practices this *mudrā,* keeping it highly secret, achieves *vāyusiddhi* (the perfection in the vital energy: *prāṇa*), the destroyer of decay and death. –41.

चक्रमध्ये स्थिता देवाः कम्पन्ति वायुताडनात् ।

कुण्डल्यपि महामाया कैलाशे सा विलियते ॥४२॥

cakramadhye sthitā devāḥ kampanti vāyutāḍanāt /

kuṇḍalyapi mahāmāyā kailāśe sā vilīyate /42/

The gods located in the middle of different *chakras* start trembling due to the beating of the *vāyu* (through the practice of this *mudrā*). The Goddess *Mahā Māyā Kuṇḍalinī* (the Great Cosmic Energy) merges into *Kailāśa*, the abode of Cosmic Consciousness (literally, the peak of the *Himālayas*). –42.

महामुद्रामहाबन्धौ निष्फलौ वेधवर्जितौ ।

तस्माद्योगी प्रयत्नेन करोति त्रितयं क्रमात् ॥४३॥

mahāmudrāmahābandhau niṣphalau vedavarjitau /

tasmādyogī prayatnena karoti tritayam kramāt /43/

The *mahāmudrā* and *mahābandha* bear no fruits without *mahāvedha*. Therefore, the yogi should practice all these three in their due order with great effort. –43.

एतत्त्रयं प्रयत्नेन चतुर्वारं करोति यः ।

षण्मासाभ्यन्तरं मृत्युं जयत्येव न संशयः ॥४४॥

etattrayaṃ prayatnena caturvāram karoti yaḥ /

ṣaṇmāsābhyantaram mṛtyuṃ jayatyeva na samśayaḥ /44/

He who practices these three *mudrā, bandha* and *vedha* four times a day with proper effort, surely conquers death within six months. –44.

एतत्त्रयस्य महात्म्यं सिद्धो जानाति नेतरः ।

यज्ज्ञात्वा साधकाः सर्वे सिद्धिं सम्यग्लभन्ति वै ॥४५॥

etattrayasya mahātmyaṃ siddho jānāti netaraḥ

yajjñātvā sādhakāḥ sarve siddhiṃ samyaglabhanti vai /45/

Only the *siddha* knows the importance of these three and no one else. Having known these, the practitioners achieve all *siddhis* (perfections). –45.

गोपनीया प्रयत्नेन साधकैः सिद्धिमीप्सुभिः ।

अन्यथा च न सिद्धिः स्यान्मुद्राणामेष निश्चयः ॥४६॥

gopanīyā prayatnena sādhakaiḥ siddhimīpsubhiḥ /

anyathā ca na siddhiḥ syānmudrāṇāmeṣa niścayaḥ /46/

The practitioner wishing to achieve perfections should keep his practice secret with due endeavor. Otherwise, no desired perfections can certainly be achieved through the practice of these *mudrās*. –46.

4. Khecarī Mudrā

अथ खेचरीमुद्राकथनम् ।

भ्रूवोरन्तर्गतां दृष्टिं विधाया सुदृढां सुधीः ।

उपविश्यासने वज्रे नानोपद्रववर्जितः ॥४७॥

लम्बिकोर्ध्व स्थिते गर्ते रसनां विपरीतगाम् ।

संयोजयेत्प्रयत्नेन सुधाकूपे विचक्षणः ॥

मुद्रैषां खेचरी प्रोक्ता भक्तानामनुरोधतः ॥४८॥

atha khecarīmudrākathanam /

bhrūvorantargatāṃ dṛṣṭiṃ vidhāya sudṛḍhām sudhīḥ /

upaviśyāsane vajre nānopadravavarjitaḥ /47/

lambikordhvaṃ sthite garte rasanāṃ viparītagām /

samyojayetprayatnena sudhākūpe vicakṣṇaḥ /

mudraiṣāṃ khecarī proktā bhaktānāmanurodhataḥ /48/

Now *mahāveda* is described.

The wise yogi should sit in *vajrāsana* (the thunderbolt pose) in a quite place without any disturbances and steadily fix his eyes on *bhrūmadhya* (the space between the two eyebrows). Taking the tongue up and turning it backwards, he should fix it in the throat pit and join it with the well of nectar with proper effort. This is *khecarī mudrā* described by me upon the request of my devotees. –47-48.

सिद्धीनां जननी ह्येषा मम प्राणधिकप्रिया ।

निरन्तरकृताभ्यासात्पीयूषं प्रत्यहं पिबेत् ॥

तेन विग्रहसिद्धिः स्यान्मृत्युमातङ्गकेशरी ॥४९॥

siddhināṃ jananī hyeṣā mama prāṇadhikapriyā /

nirantarakṛtābyāsātpīyūṣam pratyahaṃ pibet /

tena vigrahasiddhiḥ syānmṛtyumātaṅgakeśarī /49/

O Beloved, dearer than my life! This *mudrā* is mother of all *siddhis* (the perfections). The practitioner should drink the ambrosia daily through its continuous practice. He receives *vigraha siddhi* (the perfection of the body). This *mudrā* is like a lion of immortality over the elephant of death. –49.

अपवित्रः पवित्रो वा सर्वावस्थां गतोऽपिवा ।

खेचरी यस्यं शुद्धा तु स शुद्धो नात्र सशयः ॥५०॥

apavitraḥ pavitro vā sarvāvasthāṃ gato'pivā /

khecarī yasya śuddhā tu sa śuddho nātra samśayaḥ /50/

He who has received perfection in *khecarī mudrā,* whether he is pure, impure or in whatever condition, certainly becomes pure. There is no doubt in it. –50.

क्षणार्ध कुरुते यस्तु तीर्त्वां पापमहार्णवम् ।

दिव्यभोगान्प्रभुक्त्वा च सत्कुले स प्रजायते ॥५१॥

kṣaṇārdham kurute yastu tīrtvām pāpamahārṇavam /

divyabhogānprabhuktvā ca satkule sa prajāyate /51/

He, who practices it even for half a moment, having crossed the great ocean of sins and experienced the divine joy and pleasures (of the heavenly world), is born in a virtuous family. –51.

मुद्रैषा खेचरी यस्तु स्वस्थचित्तो ह्यतन्द्रितः ।

शतब्रह्मगतेनापि क्षणार्ध मन्यते हि सः ॥५२॥

mudraiṣā khecarī yastu svasthacitto hytandritaḥ /

śatabrahmagatenāpi kṣaṇārdhaṃ manyate hi saḥ /52/

He who actively practices this *khecarī mudrā* with a healthy (equanimous) mind, for him even the passing of the life of a hundred *Brahmās* seems half a movement. –52.

गुरूपदेशतो मुद्रा यो वेत्ति खेचरीमिमाम् ।

नानापापरतो धीमान् स याति परमां गतिम् ॥५३॥

gurūpadeśato mudrāṃ yo vetti khecarīmimām /

nānāpāparato dhīmān sa yāti paramāṃ gati /53/

The wise one, who knows this *khecarī mudrā* according to his guru's teaching, attains the supreme state, even while being absorbed in the multifarious sins. –53.

सा प्राणसदृशी मुद्रा यस्मिन्कस्मिन्न दियते ।

प्रच्छाद्यते प्रयत्नेन मुद्रेयं सुरपूजिते ॥५४॥

sā prāṇasadṛśī mudrā yasminkasminna dīyate /

pracchādyate prayatnena mudreyaṃ surapūjite /54/

O Goddess worshiped by Gods! This *mudrā* is equal to *prāṇa* (the life) itself. It should not be given to everyone. It should be kept secret with proper effort. –54.

5. Jālandhara Bandha

अथ जालन्धरबन्धः ।

बद्धागलशिराजालं हृदये चिबुकं न्यसेत् ।

बन्धोजालन्धरः प्रोक्तो देवानापि दुर्लभः ॥५५॥

नाभिस्थवह्निर्जन्तूनां सहस्रकमलच्युतम् ।

पिबेत्पीयूषविस्तारं तदर्थ बन्धयेदिमम् ॥५६॥

atha jālandharabandhakathanam /

baddhāgalaśirājālaṃ hṛdaye cibukaṃ nyaset /

bandhojālandharaḥ prokto devānāmapi durlabhaḥ /55/

nābhisthavahnirjantūnāṃ sahasrakamalacyutam /

pibetpīyūṣavistāraṃ tadarthaṃ bandhayedimam /56/

Now *jālandhara bandha* is described.

Having pressed the net of arteries and veins in the throat, place the chin on the throat. This is called *jālandhara bandha*, rare even to the gods. The digestive fire in the navel area drinks the nectar dripping down from the *sahasrara kamala* (the thousand petalled lotus). Therefore, the practitioner should practice this *bandha* so that the digestive fire does not consume the nectar. –55-56.

बन्धेनानेनपीयूषं पिबति बुद्धिमान् ।

अमरत्वञ्च सम्प्राप्य मोदते भुवनत्रये ॥५७॥

bandhenānena pīyūṣaṃ svayaṃ pibati buddhimān /

amaratvañca samprapya modate bhuvanatraye /57/

The wise practitioner himself drinks the nectar through this *bandha,* and having received immortality, liberally enjoys in all the three worlds. –57.

जालन्धरो बन्ध एष सिद्धिदायकः ।

अभ्यासः क्रियते नित्यं योगिना सिद्धिमिच्छता ॥५८॥

jālandharo bandha eṣa siddhānāṃ siddhidāyakaḥ /

abyāsaḥ kriyate nityaṃ yoginā siddhimicchatā /58/

This *jālandhara bandha* gives perfection to the adepts. The yogi desirous of receiving perfection should practice it constantly. –58.

6. Mūlabandha

अथ मूलबन्धः ।

पादमूलेन संपीड्य गदमार्ग सुयन्त्रितम् ।

बलादपानमाकृष्य क्रमादूर्ध्व सुचारयेत् ॥

कल्पितोऽयं मूलबन्धो जरामरणनाशनः ॥५९॥

atha mūlabandha: /

pādamūlena sampīdya gudamārgaṃ suyantritam /

balādapānamākrisya kramadūrdhvaṃ sucarayet /

kalpito'yaṃ mūlabandho jarāmaraṇanāśanaḥ /59/

Now *mūlabandha* is described.

Pressing the anus properly with the heel, draw up the *apāna vāyu* with force and gradually move it upwards. This *bandha*, destroyer of decay and death, is called *mūla-bandha*. –59.

अपानप्राणयोरैक्यं प्रकरोत्यधिकल्पितम् ।

बन्धेनानेन सुतरां योनिमुद्रा प्रसिद्ध्यति ॥६०॥

apānaprāṇayoraikyaṃ prakarotyadhikalpitam /

bandhenānena sutarām yonimudrā prasiddhyati /60/

It is said that (in the process of practice) when the practitioner unites the *apāna* with the *prāṇa*, then it certainly becomes *yoni mudrā*. –60.

सिद्धिायां योनिमुद्रायां कि न सिध्यति भूतले ।

बन्धस्यास्य प्रसादेन गगने विजितालसः ॥

पद्मासने स्थितो योगी भुवमुत्सृज्य वर्तते ॥६१॥

siddhāyāṃ yonimudrāyāṃ kiṃ na sidhyati bhūtale /

bandhasyāsya prasādena gagane vijitālasaḥ /

padmāsane sthito yogī bhuvamutsṛjya vartate /61/

For he who has perfected *yoni mudrā,* what cannot be achieved in this world? By the grace of this *mudrā,* he travels in space, and conquering idleness, may levitate in the air in *padmāsana*. –61.

सुगुप्ते निर्जने देशे बन्धमेनं समभ्यसेत् ।

संसारसागरं तर्तुं यदीच्छेद्योगि पुंगवः ॥६२॥

sugupte nirjane deśe bandhamenaṃ samabyaset /

samsārasāgaraṃ tartuṃ yadīcchedyogī puṅgavaḥ /62/

If the great yogi is desirous of crossing the worldly ocean, he should practice this *bandha* in a secret and solitary place. –62.

7. Viparītakaraṇī Mudrā

अथ विपरीतकरणी मुद्रा ।

भूतले स्वशिरोदत्वा खे नयेच्चरणद्वयम् ।

विपरीतकृतिश्चैषा सर्वतन्त्रेषु गोपिता ॥६३॥

atha viparītakaraṇīmudrā /

bhūtale svaśirodattvā khe nayeccaraṇadvayam /

viparītakṛtiścaiṣā sarvatantreṣu gopitā /63/

Now *viparītakaraṇī mudrā* is described.

Place the head on the ground and raise both your legs straight up in the air. This *viparītakaraṇī* (inverted) *mudrā* has been kept secret in all the *tantras*. –63.

एतद्यः कुरुते नित्यमभ्यासं याममात्रतः ।

मृत्युं जयति स योगी प्रलये नापि सीदति ॥६४॥

etadhyaḥ kurute nityamabhyāsaṃ yāmamātrataḥ /

mṛtyum jayati sa yogī pralaye nāpi sīdati /64/

In this way the yogi who practices this *mudrā* for three hours everyday conquers death and he is not destroyed even during annihilation. –64.

कुरुतेऽमृतपानं यः सिद्धानां समतामियात् ।

स सेव्यः सर्वलोकानां बन्धमेनं करोति यः ॥६५॥

kurute'mṛtapānam yah siddhānāṃ samatāmiyāt /

sa sevyaḥ sarvalokānāṃ bandhamenaṃ karoti yaḥ /65/

He comes to be equal to the *siddhas* (the perfected sages or seers) who drink the nectar trickling down from the thousand petalled lotus. He who practices this *bandha* is worshiped in all the worlds. –65.

8. Uḍḍāna Bandha

अथ उड्डान बन्धः ।

नाभेरूर्ध्वमधश्चापि तानं पश्चिममाचरेत् ।

उड्डानबंध एष स्यात्सर्वदुःखौघनाशनः ॥६६॥

उदरे पश्चिमं तानं नाभेरुर्ध्व तु कारयेत् ।

उड्डानाख्योऽत्र बन्धोऽयं मृत्युमातङ्गकेशरी ॥६७॥

atha uḍḍyānabandhakathanam /

nābherūrdhvamadhaścāpi tānaṃ paścimamācaret /

uḍḍyānabandha eṣa syātsarvaduhkhaughanāśanaḥ /66/

udare paścimaṃ tānaṃ nābherūrdhvaṃ tu kārayet /

uḍḍānākhyo'tra bandho'yaṃ mṛtyumātaṅgakeśarī /67/

Now *uḍḍyāna bandha* is described.

Pull the area below and above the navel in towards the back. This is *uḍḍāna bandha*, the destroyer of all sins and miseries. While pulling the abdomen towards the back, bring it up above the navel. This is called *uḍḍāna bandha*, a lion of immortality over the elephant of death. –66-67.

नित्यं यः कुरुते योगी चतुर्वारं दिने दिने ।

तस्य नाभेस्तु शुद्धिः स्याद्येन सिद्धो भवेन्मरुत् ॥६८॥

nityaṃ yaḥ kurute yogī caturvāraṃ dine dine /

tasya nāvestu śuddhiḥ syādyena siddho bhavenmarut /68/

When the yogi practices it regularly four times a day, his navel is purified. Through this practice, he receives *vāyusiddhi* (perfection in the vital force). –68.

षण्मासमभ्यसन्योगी मृत्युं जयति निश्चितम् ।

तस्यादराग्निर्ज्वलति रसवृद्धिः प्रजायते ॥६९॥

ṣaṇmāsamabhyasanyogī mṛtyum jayati niścitam /

tasyodarāgnirjvalati rasavṛddhiḥ prajāyate /69/

Through the constant practice of this *bandha* for six months, the yogi certainly wins over death. His digestive fire is stimulated and fluids are increased in the body. –69.

अनेन सुतरां सिद्धिर्विग्रहस्य प्रजायते ।

रोगाणां संक्षयश्चापि योगिनो भवति ध्रुवम् ॥७०॥

anena sutarāṃ siddhirvigrahasya prajāyate /

rogāṇām samkṣayascāpi yogino bhavati dhruvam /70/

Surely, bodily perfection is achieved through it and the multifarious diseases of the yogi are destroyed. –70.

गुरोर्लब्ध्वा प्रयत्नेन साधयेत्तु विचक्षणः ।

निर्जने सुस्थिते देशे बन्धं परम दुर्लभम् ॥७१॥

gurorlabdhvā prayatnena sādhayettu vicakṣaṇaḥ /

nirjane susthite deśe bandhaṃ parama durlabham /71/

Having received the method of practice from the guru, the wise yogi should practice this, the most rare *mudrā*, with due effort in a solitary and pleasant place. –71.

9. Vajrolī Mudrā

अथ वज्रोलीमुद्रा ।

वज्रोली कथयिष्यामि संसारध्वान्तनाशिनीम् ।

स्वभक्तेभ्यः समासेन गुह्यादगुह्यतमामपि ॥७२॥

स्वच्छया वर्तमानोऽपि योगोक्तनियमैर्विना ।

मुक्तो भवति गार्हस्थो वज्रोल्यभ्यासयोगतः ॥७३॥

वज्रोल्यभ्यासयोगोऽयं भोगे युक्तेऽपि मुक्तिदः ।

तस्मादतिप्रयत्नेन कर्तव्यो योगिभिः सदा ॥७४॥

atha vajrolīmudrā /

vajrolī kathayisyāmi samsāradhvāntanāśinīm /

svabhaktebhyaḥ samāsena guhyādguhyatamāmapi /72/

svacchayā vartamāno'pi yogoktaniyamairvinā /

mukto bhavati gārhastho vajrolyabhyāsayogataḥ /73/

vajrolyabhyāsayogo'yaṃ bhoge yukte'pi muktidaḥ /

tasmādatiprayatnena kartavyo yogibhiḥ sadā /74/

Now *vajrolī mudrā* is described.

For the benefit of my devotees, I am going to tell about *vajrolī* in brief; the most secret of all the *mudrās*, it is the dispeller of all worldly illusions and darkness. Even a householder leading his life on his own accord, without following any yogic instructions and rules, can liberate himself through the practice of *vajrolī mudrā*. Liberation is granted through *vajrolī* yoga and its practice even to those people who are fully indulged in sensual pleasures. Therefore, it is the duty of the yogis to always practice it with great effort. –72-74.

आदौ रजः स्त्रियो योन्याः यत्नेन विधिवत्सुधीः ।
आकुंच्य लिंगनालेन स्वशरीर प्रवेशयेत् ॥७५॥
स्वकं स्वकं बिन्दुञ्च सम्बध्य लिंगचालनमाचरेत् ।
दैवाच्चलति चेदूर्ध्व निबद्धो योनिमुद्रया ॥७६॥

ādau rajaḥ striyo yonyāḥ yatnena vidhivatsudhīḥ /
ākuñcya liṅganālena svasarīre praveśayet /75/
svakaṃ svakaṃ vinduñca sambadhya liṅgacālanamācaret /
daivāccalti cedūrdhvam nibaddho yonimudrayā /76/

First, with proper method, the wise practitioner should absorb *raja* (the ovarian fluid) from the vagina of his female partner into his own body by contracting the urethra of his penis. Then he should perform sexual intercourse, controlling the emission of his seminal fluid (without ejaculating his semen). Should his semen tend to emit or fall accidentally, it should be controlled through the practice of *yoni mudrā* (as described above). –75-76.

वाममार्गेऽपि तद्बिन्दुं नीत्वा लिंगं निवारयेत् ।
क्षणमात्रं योनितो यः पुमांश्चालनमाचरेत् ॥७७॥
गुरूपदेशतो योगी हुं हुं कारेण योनितः ।
अपानवायुमाकुंच्य बलदाकृष्य तद्रजः ॥७८॥

vāmamārge'pi tatvindum nītvā liṅgam nivārayet /
kṣaṇamātraṃ yonito yaḥ pumāmścālanamācaret /77/

gurūpadeśato yogī huṃ huṃ kāreṇa yonitaḥ /

apānavāyumākuñcya balādākṛṣya tadrajaḥ /78/

After that, the same seminal fluid should be directed to the left channel (the lunar pathway) and placing it there, the intercourse should be stopped for a while. Then, according to the instructions of his guru, the wise practitioner should again engage in intercourse, uttering the sound '*hum*', '*hum*' and forcing the *praṇa vāyu* upwards while contracting the perineum, he should draw up the ovarian fluid with great effort. –77-78.

अनेन विधिना योगी क्षिप्रं योगस्य सिद्धये ।

भव्यभुक् कुरुते योगी गुरुपादाब्जपूजकः ॥७६॥

anena vidhinā yogī kṣipraṃ yogasya siddhaye /

bhavyabhuk kurute yogī gurupādābjapūjakaḥ /79/

Following this method, the yogi quickly achieves *yoga siddhi* (the perfection in yoga). Being the worshipper of the lotus-feet of his guru, he drinks the divine fluid (the nectar secreted from the thousand petalled lotus). –79.

बिंदुर्विधुमयो ज्ञेयो रजः सूर्यमयस्तथा ।

उभयोर्मेलनं कार्य स्वशरीरे प्रवशयेत् ॥८०॥

vindurvidhumayo jñeyo rajaḥ sūryamayastatha /

ubhayormelanaṃ kāryaṃ svaśarīre praveśayet /80/

Knowing that the seminal fluid is a form of the moon, the ovarian fluid is a form of the sun, and having united both, the practitioner should take them into his body with great effort. –80.

अहं बिन्दू रजः शक्तिरुभयोर्मेलनं यदा ।

योगिनां साधनावस्था भवेद्दिव्यं वपुस्तदा ॥८१॥

मरणं बिन्दुपातेन जीवनं बिन्दुधारणे ।

तस्मादतिप्रयत्नेन कुरुते बिन्दुधारणम् ॥८२॥

ahaṃ vindū rajazh śaktirubhayormelanaṃ yadā /

yogināṃ sādhanāvasthā bhaveddivyaṃ vapustadā /81/

maraṇam vindupātena jīvanaṃ vindudhāraṇe /

tasmādatiprayatnena kurute vindudhāraṇam /82/

I (*Śiva* – the Cosmic Consciousness) am *vindu* (the seminal fluid) and *raja* (the ovarian fluid) is *Śakti* (the Cosmic Energy). When the yogi unites both, then both his body and practice become divine. Death occurs through the discharge of *vindu* and life exists through its preservation. Therefore, it should be preserved with great care and effort. –81-82.

जायते म्रियते लोके बिन्दुना नात्र सशयः ।

एतज्ज्ञात्वा सदा योगी बिन्दुधारणमाचरेत् ॥८३॥

jāyate mṛyate loke vindunā nātra samśayaḥ /

etajjñātvā sadā yogī bindudhāraṇamācaret /83/

There is no doubt that the birth and death of all creatures in this world is certainly due to *vindu*. By knowing this, the yogi should engage himself in the preservation of his *vindu*. –83.

सिद्धे बिन्दौ महायत्ने किं न सिध्यति भूतले ।

यस्य प्रसादान्महिमा ममाप्येतादृशो भवेत् ॥८४॥

siddhe vindau mahāyatne kiṃ na sidhyati bhūtale /

yasya prasādānmahimā mamāpyetādṛśo bhavet /84/

When success is achieved in the preservation of the *vindu* through great effort, what cannot be attained in this world? By its grace, I have received this supreme state and glory. He who attains perfection in preserving his *vindu* becomes equal to me. –84.

बिन्दूः करोति सर्वेषां सुखं दुखं च संस्थितः ।

संसारिणां विमूढानां जरामरणशालिनाम् ॥८५॥

vindūḥ karoti sarveṣāṃ sukhaṃ duḥkhaṃ ca samsthitaḥ

samsāriṇāṃ vimūḍhāṇāṃ jarāmaraṇaśālinām /85/

It is the seminal fluid that establishes all creatures worldly, deluded, and mortals in happiness and miseries. –85.

अयं शांकरो योगो योगिनामुत्तमोत्तमः ।

अभ्यासात्सिद्धिर्माप्नोति भोगयुक्तोऽपि मानवः ॥८६॥

ayaṃ śāṅkaro yogo yogināmuttamuttamaḥ /

abhyāsātsiddhirmāpnoti yogayukto'pi mānavaḥ /86/

This is excellent auspicious yoga (the giver of prosperity and happiness) for all yogis. Every human being attains perfection when he is united with this yoga and its constant practice. –86.

सकलः साधितार्थोऽपि सिद्धो भवति भूतले ।

भुक्त्वा भोगानाशेषान्वै योगनानेन निश्चितम् ॥८७॥

अनेन सकला सिद्धिर्योगिनां भवति ध्रुवम् ।

सुखभोगेन महता तस्मादेनं समभ्यसेत् ॥८८॥

sakalaḥ sādhitartho'pi siddho bhavati bhūtale

bhuktvā bhogānaśeṣānvai yoganānena niścitam /87/

anena sakalā siddhiryogināṃ bhavati dhruvam

sukhabhogena mahatā tasmādenaṃ samabyaset /88/

All the desired things are achieved in this world through its practice. The perfected yogi, through the practice of this yoga, certainly lives happily, experiencing all enjoyments and pleasures. The yogi certainly receives all perfections through the practice of this *mudrā*. –87-88.

सहजोल्यमरोलीं च वज्रोल्या भेदतो भवेत् ।

येन केन प्रकारेण बिन्दुं योगी प्रचारयेत् ॥८९॥

sahajolyamarolīṃ ca vajrolyā bhedato bhavet /

yena kena prakāreṇa vinduṃ yogī pracārayet /89/

Sahajolī and *amarolī* are the two modifications of *vajrolī mudrā*. In any way possible, by any means or methods (through the practice of any one of these *mudrās*), the yogi should preserve his *vindu* (the seminal fluid). –89.

(a) Amarolī Mudrā

देवाच्चलति चेद्वेगे मेलनं चन्द्रसूर्ययोः ।
अमरोलिरियं प्रोक्ता लिंगनालेन शोषयेत् ॥९०॥

daivāccalati cetvege melanaṃ candrasūryayoḥ
amaroliriyaṃ proktā liṅganālena śoṣayet /90/

Should the seminal fluid be inevitably emitted and should there be a union of the sun and the moon (the *vindu* and *raja*), this is called *amarolī*. The yogi should draw them back (in his body) through the urethra of his penis. –90.

(b) Sahajolī Mudrā

गतं बिन्दुं स्वकं योगी बन्धयेद्योनिमुद्रया ।
सहजोलिरियं प्रोक्ता सर्वतन्त्रेषु गोपिता ॥९१॥
संज्ञाभेदात्भवेद्भेदः कार्यं तुल्यगतिर्यदि ।
तस्मात्सर्वप्रयत्नेन साध्यते योगिभिः सदा ॥९२॥

gataṃ vinduṃ svakaṃ yogī bandhayedyonimudrayā /
sahajoliriyaṃ proktā sarvatantreṣu gopitā /91/
saṅjñābhedādbhavedbhedaḥ kāryaṃ tulyagatiryadi /
tasmātsarvaprayatnena sādhyate yogibhiḥ sadā /92/

The yogi should control and retain his seminal fluid that is about to emit from its place through the practice of *yoni mudrā*. It is called *sahajolī* and is kept secret in all *tantras*. *Sahajolī* and *amarolī* are two modified names of *vajrolī*, but their objective and the result are the same. Therefore, the yogi should always engage in achieving perfection in any one of these (*mudrās*) with all his effort. –91-92.

अयं योगो मया प्रोक्तो भक्तानां स्नेहतः प्रिये ।
गोपनीयः प्रयत्नेन न देयो यस्य कस्यचित् ॥९३॥
एतद्गुह्यतमं गुह्यं न भूतं न भविष्यति ।
तस्मादेतत्प्रयत्नेन गोपनीयं सदा बुधैः ॥९४॥

ayaṃ yogo mayā prokto bhaktānāṃ snehataḥ priye /
gopanīyaḥ prayatnena na deyo yasya kasyacit /93/
etadguhyatamaṃ guhyaṃ na bhūtaṃ na bhaviṣyati /
tasmādetatprayatnena gopanīyaṃ sadā budhaiḥ /94/

O Beloved! I have explained this yoga because of my grace and love for my devotees. It should be kept secret with great care and should not be given to anyone. There has never been a more mysterious practice than this one in the past, and never will be one in the future. Therefore, the wise practitioner should always keep it secret with great care. –93-94.

स्वमूत्रोत्सर्गकाले यो बलादाकृष्य वायुना ।
स्तोकं स्तोकं त्यजेन्मूत्रमूर्ध्वमाकृष्य तत्पुनः ॥९५॥
गुरूपदिष्टमार्गेण प्रत्यहं यः समाचरेत् ।
बिन्दुसिद्धिर्भवेत्तस्य महासिद्धिप्रदायिका ॥९६॥

svamūtrotsargakāle yo balādākṛṣya vāyunā /
stokaṃ stokaṃ tyajenmūtramūrdhvamākṛṣya tatpunaḥ /95/
gurūpadiṣṭamārgeṇa pratyahaṃ yaḥ samācaret /
vindusiddhirbhavettasya mahāsiddhipradāyikā /96/

During the time of urination, while forcibly pulling the *apāna vāyu* upwards, the practitioner should urinate little by little, holding it back and drawing it upwards again. He who constantly practices this *mudrā*, according to the methods given by the guru, achieves *vindu siddhi* (the success in controlling and preserving the seminal fluid). This grants him all supreme powers. –95-96.

षण्मासमभ्यसेद्यो वै प्रत्यहं गुरुशिक्षया ।
शताङ्गनानां भोगेऽपि तस्य बिन्दुर्न नश्यति ॥९७॥

ṣaṇmāsamabhyasedyo vai pratyahaṃ guruśikṣayā /
śatāṅganānāṃ bhoge'pi tasya vindurna naśyati /97/

He who practices this *mudrā* for six months according to the instructions of his guru, will not have his *vindu* drained, even if he were to have sexual intercourse with a hundred women. –97.

सिद्धे बिन्दौ महायत्ने किं न सिध्यति पार्वति ।
ईशत्वं यत्प्रसादेन ममापि दुर्लभं भवेत् ॥९८॥

siddhe vindau mahāyatne kiṃ na siddhyati pārvati /
īśatvaṃ yatprasādena mamāpi durlabhaṃ bhavet /98/

O *Pārvati*! when *vindu siddhi* ((the perfection in controlling and preserving the seminal fluid) is achieved with great effort, what cannot be accomplished in this world? I have achieved this divine state of greatness by its grace. Similarly, the practitioner attains great and rare perfection through its practice. –98.

10. Śakticālana Mudrā

अथ शक्तिचालन मुद्रा ।
आधारकमले सुप्तां चालयेत्कुण्डलीं दृढाम् ।
अपानवायुमारुह्य बलादाकृष्य बुद्धिमान् ।
शक्तिचालनमुद्रेयं सर्वशक्तिप्रदायिनी ॥९९॥

atha śakticālanamudrā /
ādhārakamale suptāṃ cālayetkuṇḍalīṃ dṛḍhām /
apānavāyumāruhya balādākṛṣya buddhimān /
śakticālanamudreyaṃ sarvaśaktipradāyinī /99/

Now *śakticālana mudrā* is described.

The wise yogi should firmly move the Goddess *Kuṇḍalinī,* sleeping in the *ādhāra* lotus, up with force, ascending on the *apāna vāyu*. This is *śakticālana mudrā*, giver of all powers. –99.

शक्तिचालनमेवं हि प्रत्यहं यः समाचरेत् ।

आयुर्वृद्धिभेवेत्तस्य रोगाणां च विनाशनम् ॥१००॥

śakticālanamevam hi pratyahaṃ yaḥ samācaret /

āyurvṛddhibhavettasya rogāṇām ca vināśanam /100/

He who practices this *śakticālana mudrā* every day, his life is prolonged and diseases are destroyed. –100.

विहाय निद्रा भुजंगी स्वयमूर्ध्वं भवेत्खलु ।

तस्मादभ्यासनं कार्यं योगिना सिद्धमिच्छता ॥१०१॥

vihāya nidrā bhujaṅgī svayammūrdhvaṃ bhavetkhalu /

tasmādabhyāsanaṃ kāryaṃ yoginā siddhamicchatā /101/

The serpent (*Kuṇḍalinī*), giving up the sleep, surely moves herself up (through this *mudrā*). Therefore, the yogi who is desirous of achieving perfection should duly practice it. –101.

यः करोति सदाभ्यासं शक्तिचालनमुत्तमम् ।

येन विग्रहसिद्धिः स्यादणिमादिगुणप्रदा ॥

गुरूपदेशविधिना तस्य मृत्युभयं कुतः ॥१०२॥

yah karoti sadābhyāsaṃ śakticālanamuttamam /

yena vigrahasiddhiḥ syādaṇimādiguṇapradā /

gurūpadeśavidhinā tasya mṛtyubhayaṃ kutaḥ /102/

He who always practices this excellent *śakticālana mudrā*, according to the instructions of his guru, receives *vigraha siddhi* (the perfection of the body) that gives perfection such as *aṇimā* (one of the perfections – the power of becoming as small as an atom), etc. and for him where is the fear of death? –102.

मुहूर्तद्वयपर्यन्तं विधिना शक्तिचानलम् ।

यः करोति प्रयत्नेन तीय सिद्धिरदूरतः ॥

युक्तासनेन कर्तव्यं योगिभिः शक्तिचालनम् ॥१०३॥

muhūrtadvayaparyantaṃ vidhinā śakticālanam /

yah karoti prayatnena tasya siddhiradūrataḥ /

yuktāsanena kartavyaṃ yogibhiḥ śakticālanam /103/

He who practices *śakticālana mudrā* through proper method for forty-eight minutes, his perfection (success) is not far away. It is the duty of the yogi to practice it in a suitable posture. –103.

एतत्तुमुद्रादशकं न भूतं न भविष्यति ।

एकैकाभ्यासने सिद्धः सिद्धो भवति नान्यथा ॥१०४॥

etattumudrādaśakaṃ na bhūtaṃ na bhaviṣyati /

ekaikāvyāsane siddhaḥ siddho bhavati nānyathā /104/

These ten *mudrās* and their equivalents neither existed in the past nor will exist in the future. The practitioner becomes *siddha* (one who has attained perfection) by achieving *siddhi* (the perfection) through the practice of any one of them. It is surely so, and not otherwise at all. –104.

इति श्रीशिवसंहितायां चतुर्थपटलः समाप्तः ॥४॥

iti śrīśivasamhitāyāṃ caturthapaṭalaḥ samāptaḥ //4//

Thus, ends the Fourth Chapter of *Śiva Samhitā.*

पंचमः पटलः

Pañcamaḥ Paṭalaḥ

Chapter Five

Discourse on Yoga Vidyā

श्री देव्युवाच ॥
ब्रुहि वाक्यमीशान परमार्थधियं प्रति ।
ये विघ्नाः सन्ति लोकानां वद मे प्रिय शंकर ॥१॥

śrī devyuvāca /
brūhi vākyamīśāna paramāthadhiyaṃ prati /
ye vighnāḥ santi lokānāṃ vada me priya śaṅkara /1/

Goddess *Pārvatī* said: – O God, Beloved *Śaṅkara*! Please be graceful and tell me about the obstacles that are faced by those yoga practitioners in this world, on the path of attaining supreme spiritual truth. –1.

Obstacles in Yoga

ईश्वर उवाच ॥
श्रृणु देवी प्रवक्ष्यामि यथा विघ्नाः स्थिताः सदा ।
मुक्तिं प्रति नारायणञ्च भोगः परमबन्धनः ॥२॥

īsvara uvāca /
śṛuṇu devī pravakṣyāmi yathā vighnāḥ sthitāḥ sadā /
muktiṃ prati narāṇāñca bhogaḥ paramabandhanaḥ /2/

Īsvara (Lord *Śiva*) said: – Listen, O Goddess! I am telling you all about the obstacles that always come in the path of yoga. *Bhoga* (enjoyment) is the greatest obstacle to the human beings to the achievement of liberation. –2.

1. Obstacles in Yoga from Enjoyments

अथ भोगरूपयोगविघ्नकथनम् ॥

नारी शय्यासंन वस्त्रं धनमस्य विडम्बनम् ।

ताम्बूलं भक्ष्ययानानि राज्यैश्वर्यविभूतयः ॥३॥

हैमं रौप्यं तथा ताम्रं रत्नञ्चागुरुधेनवः ।

पाण्डित्यं वेदशास्त्राणि नृत्यं गीतं विभूषणम् ॥४॥

वंशी वीणा मृदङ्गाश्च गजेंद्रश्चाववाहनम ।

दारापत्यानि विषयाा विघ्ना ऐते प्रकीर्तिताः ।

भोगरूपा इमे विघ्ना धर्मरूपानिमाञ्छृणु ॥५॥

atha bhogarūpayogabighnakathanam /

nārī śayyāsanaṃ vastraṃ dhanamasya viḍambanam /

tāmbūlaṃ bhakṣyayānāni rājyaiśvaryavibhūtayaḥ /3/

haimaṃ raupyaṃ tathā tāmraṃ ratnañcāgurudhenavaḥ /

pāṇḍityaṃ vedaśāstrāṇi nṛtyaṃ gītaṃ vibhūṣaṇam /4/

vamśī vīṇā mṛdaṅgāśca gajedrāścāśvavāhanam /

dārāpatyāni viṣayā vighnā ete prakīrtitāḥ /

bhogarūpā ime vighnā dharmarūpānimāñchṛuṇu /5/

Now the obstacles that arise from the enjoyments are described.

Women (for men – and vice versa), beds, seats, clothes (uniforms, dresses, etc.), and wealth are deceptive miseries in the path of yoga. Betel, delicious food, vehicles, kingdom, sovereignty, powers; gold, silver and copper, gems, sandal wood, and cattle; profound learning of *Vedas* and *Śāstras* (and its demonstration); dancing, singing and ornaments; *vīṇā* (a large type of lute), flute, drums; elephants and horses; wives and children, and worldly attachments; these are all obstacles that arise from enjoyment. Now listen to the obstacles that arise from religious rituals and rites. –3-5.

2. Obstacles in Yoga from Religious Rituals and Rites

अथ धर्मरूपयोगविघ्नकथनम् ।

स्नानं पूजाविधिर्होमं तथा मोक्षमयी स्थितिः ।
व्रतपवासनियममौनमिन्द्रियनिग्रहः ॥६॥

ध्येयो ध्यानं तथा मन्त्रो दानं ख्यातिर्दिशासु च ।
वापीकूपतडागादिप्रासादारामकल्पना ॥७॥

यज्ञं चान्द्रायणं कृच्छं तीर्थानि विविधानिच ।
दृश्यन्ते च इमे विघ्ना धर्मरूपेण संस्थिताः ॥८॥

atha dharmarūpayogabighnakathanam /

snānaṃ pūjāvidhirhomaṃ tathā mokṣamayī sthitiḥ /
vratopavāsaniyamamaunamindriyanigrahaḥ /6/

dhyeyo dhyānaṃ tathā mantro dānaṃ kyātirdiśāsu ca /
vāpīkūpataḍāgādiprāsādārāmakalpanā /7/

yajñaṃ cāndrāyaṇaṃ kṛcchraṃ tīrthāni vividhāni ca /
dṛśyante ca ime vighnā dharmarūpeṇa samsthitāḥ /8/

Now the obstacles that arise from rituals and rites are described.

These are the obstacles that seem to arise from the religious rituals and rites: – Bathing, worshiping of deities, fire sacrifice, liberating state of mind (indifference to opposites e.g. pleasure and pain), keeping vows, fasting, observation of religious rules and law, silence, sense-control, concentration on the object of contemplation, recitation of *mantras*, giving donation, wide spread fame, construction of water ponds, wells, lakes, luxurious buildings and gardens; sacrifices, *cāndrāyaṇa* and other risky and troublesome vows and fasting and visiting various places of pilgrimage. –6-8.

3. Obstacles in the Form of Knowledge

अथ ज्ञानरूपविघ्नकथनम् ।

यत्तु विघ्नं भवेज्ज्ञानं कथयामि वरानने ।

गोमुखं स्वासनं कृत्वा धौतिप्रक्षालनं च तत् ॥९॥

नाडीसञ्चारविज्ञानं प्रत्याहारनिरोधनम् ।

कुक्षिसंचालनं क्षिप्रं प्रवेश इन्द्रियाध्वना ॥

नाडीकर्माणि भोजनं श्रुयतां मम ॥१०॥

atha jñānarūpayogabighnakathanam /

yattu vighnaṃ bhavejjñānaṃ kathayāmi varānane /

gomukhaṃ svāsanaṃ kṛtva dhautiprakṣālanaṃ ca tat /9/

nāḍīsañcāravijñānaṃ pratyāhāranirodhanam /

kukṣisañcālanaṃ kṣipraṃ praveśa indriyādhvanā /

nāḍīkarmāṇi kalyāṇi bhojanaṃ śrūyatāṃ mama /10/

Now the obstacles that arise in the form of knowledge are described.

O *Pārvati*! Now I am telling you the obstacles that arise from knowledge. Sitting in *gomukhāsana* (the cow-faced pose) and performing *dhauti* (one of the six cleansing practices in *Haṭha Yoga*), knowledge on the science of communication systems of the *nāḍis* (the psychic pathways in the human body) and control of the senses, quick inward and outward movements of the abdomen for awakening the *Kuṇḍalinī Śakti*, entering into the path of the *indriyas* (the senses), and knowledge of the action of the *nāḍis*. O *Kalyāṇī*! Now listen to the wrong concept of food. –9-10.

4. Obstacles from Food and Association

नवधातुरसं छिन्धि शुष्ठिकास्ताडयेत्पुनः ।

एककालं समाधिः स्याल्लिंगभूतमिंद श्रृणु ॥११॥

navadhāturasaṃ chindhi śuṇṭhikāstāḍayetpunaḥ /

ekakālaṃ samādhiḥ syālliṅgabhūtamidaṃ śṛuṇu /11/

It is a mistake to think that *samādhi* (a profound state of meditation) can be attained quickly by drinking nine mineral substances (newly mined) and by eating the beaten dust of *śuṇṭhi* (dried ginger). Now hear (about the association of company). –11.

सङ्गमं गच्छ साधूनां संकोचं भज दुर्जनात् ।
प्रवेशनिर्गमे वायोर्गुरुलक्षं विलोकयेत ॥१२॥

saṅgamaṃ gaccha sādhūnāṃ saṅkocaṃ bhaja durjanāt /
praveśanirgame vāyorgurulakṣaṃ vilokayet /12/

Seeking the association of virtuous people and keeping away from the cruel ones, and observation of the heaviness and lightness of inhaled and exhaled air are both wrong concept. –12.

5. Obstacles from Scriptural Opinions

पिण्डस्थं रूपसंस्थञ्च रूपवर्जितम् ।
ब्रह्मैतस्मिन्मतावस्था हृदयञ्च प्रशाम्यति ॥
इत्येते कथिता विघ्ना ज्ञानरूपे व्यवस्थिताः ॥१३॥

piṇḍasthaṃ rūpasamsthañca rūpasthaṃ rūpavarjitam /
brahmaitasminmatāvasthā hṛdayañca prasāmyati /
ityete kathitā vighnā jñānarūpe vyavasthitāḥ /13/

All the dogmas described here that soothe the heart and mind are obstacles in the form of the knowledge: "The *Brahman* exists in all living beings;" "That (the *Brahman*) is the *Founder* (the Creator) of every thing;" "He has a form;" "He is formless;" and "He is all in all." –13.

Four Types of Yoga

अथ चतुर्विधयोगकथनम् ।
मन्त्रयोगे हठश्चैव लययोगस्तृतीयकः ।
चतुर्थो राजयोगः स्यात्स द्विधाभाववर्जितः ॥१४॥

atha caturvidhayogakathanam /

mantrayogo haṭhaścaiva layayogastritīyakaḥ /

caturtho rājayogaḥ syātsa dvidhābhāvavarjitaḥ /14/

Now the four types of yoga are described.

There are four kinds of yoga: - 1. *Mantra Yoga*, 2. *Haṭha Yoga*, 3. *Laya Yoga* and 4. *Rāja Yoga* which is without duality. –14.

Four Types of Yoga Practitioners

चतुर्धा साधके ज्ञेयो मृदुमध्याधिमात्रकाः ।

अधिमात्रतमः श्रेष्ठो भावाब्धौ लंघनक्षमः ॥१५॥

caturdhā sādhako jñeyo mṛdumadhyādhimātrakāḥ /

adhimātratamaḥ śreṣṭho bhavābdhau laṅghanakṣamaḥ /15/

Know that there are four types of yoga practitioners: – 1) mild, 2) moderate, 3) dedicated, and 4) the most dedicated. Among these four types, the most dedicated practitioner is the most excellent of all, who is capable of crossing the ocean of the world. –15.

1. Characteristics of a Mild Practitioner

अथ मृदुसाधकलक्षणम् ।

मन्दोत्साही सुसंमूढो व्याधिस्थो गुरुदूषकः ।

लोभी पापामतिश्चैव बह्वाशी वनिताश्रयः ॥१६॥

चपलः कातरो रोगी पराधिनोऽतिनिष्ठुरः ।

मन्दाचरो मन्दवीर्यो ज्ञातव्यो मृदुमानवः ॥१७॥

द्वादशाब्दे भवेत्सिद्धिरेतस्य यत्नतः परम् ।

मन्त्रयोगाधिकारी स ज्ञातव्यो गुरुणा ध्रुवम् ॥१८॥

atha mṛdusādhakalakṣaṇam /

mandotsāhī susammūḍho vyādhistho gurudūṣakaḥ /

lobhī pāpamatiścaiva bahvāśī vanitāśrayaḥ /16/

capalaḥ kātaro rogī parādhīno'tiniṣṭhuraḥ /

mandācāro mandaviryo jñātavyo mṛdumānavaḥ /17/

dvādaśābde bhavetsiddhiretasya yatnataḥ param /

mantrayogādhikārī sa jñātavyo guruṇā dhruvam /18/

Now the characteristics of a mild practitioner are described.

Having low enthusiasm, is unmindful and foolish, afflicted with diseases, inimical towards guru, greedy, sinful, gluttonous, attached to beloved one, inconsistent, timid, sick, dependent (on others), cruel, having low character and is weak – know that a man with any of these characteristics is a mild practitioner. He can achieve perfection in his practice with greatest effort in twelve years. The teacher should know that he is certainly entitled to *Mantra Yoga*. – 16-18.

2. Characteristics of a Moderate Practitioner

अथ मध्यम साधकलक्षणम् ।

समबुद्धिः क्षमायुक्तः पुण्याकांक्षी प्रियंवदः ।

मध्यस्थः सर्वकार्येषु सामान्यः स्यान्न संशयः ॥

एत्जज्ञात्वैव गुरुभिर्दीयते मुक्तितो लयः ॥१९॥

atha madhyamasādhakalakṣaṇam /

samabuddhiḥ kṣamāyuktah puṇyākāṅkṣī priyamvadaḥ /

madhyasthaḥ sarvakāryeṣu sāmānyaḥ syānna samśayaḥ /

etajjñātvaiva gurubhirdiyate muktito layaḥ /19/

Now the characteristics of a moderate practitioner are described.

Equanimous and open-minded, compassionate, desirous of virtue, speaking sweet and loving words, indifferent and doubtless in all actions and unaffected by any (favorable or unfavorable) situations – (a person with any of these characteristics) is certainly a moderate practitioner. By knowing it, the guru should initiate him into *Laya Yoga* as the path of liberation. –19.

3. Characteristics of a Dedicated Practitioner

अथ अधिमात्रसाधकलक्षणम् ।

स्थिरबुद्धिर्लये युक्तः स्वाधीनो वीर्यवानपि ।

महाशयो दयायुक्तः क्षमावान् सत्यवानपि ॥२०॥

शूरो वयःस्थः श्रद्धावान् गुरुपादब्जपूजकः ।

योगाभ्यासरतश्चैव ज्ञातव्यश्चाधिमात्रकः ॥२१॥

एतस्यसिद्धिः षड्वर्षे भवेदभ्यासयोगतः ।

एतस्मै दीयते धीरो हठयोगश्च साङ्गतः ॥२२॥

atha adhimātrasādhakalakṣaṇam /

sthirabuddhirlaye yuktaḥ svādhīno vīryavānapi /

mahāśayo dayāyuktaḥ kṣamāvān satyavānapi /20/

śūro vayahsthaḥ śraddhāvān gurupādābjapūjakaḥ /

yogābhyāsarataścaiva jñātavyaścādhimātrakaḥ /21/

etasya siddhiḥ ṣaḍvarṣe bhavedavyāsayogataḥ /

etasmai dīyate dhīro haṭhayogaśca sāṅgataḥ /22/

Now the characteristics of a dedicated practitioner are described.

Steady minded, knower of *Laya Yoga*, independent, full of vitality, noble minded, generous, forgiving, truthful, full of courage, youthful, faithful, worshipper of his guru's lotus feet, involved in the regular practice of yoga- know that a person with any of these characteristics is a dedicated practitioner. Such a practitioner can achieve perfection in six years through the constant practice of yoga. The wise guru should initiate him into *Haṭha Yoga* practice with its all limbs. –20-22.

4. Characteristics of the Most Dedicated Practitioner

महावीर्यान्वितोत्साही मनोज्ञः शौर्यवानपि ।

शास्त्रज्ञोऽभ्यासशीलश्च निर्मोहश्च निराकुलः ॥२३॥

नवयौवनसम्पन्नो मिताहारी जितेन्द्रियः ।

निर्भयश्च शुचिर्दक्षो दाता सर्वजनाश्रयः ॥२४॥

अधिकारी स्थिरो धीमान् यथेच्छावस्थितः क्षमी ।

सुशीलो धर्मचारी च गुप्तचेष्टः प्रियंवदः ॥२५॥

शास्त्रविश्वाससम्पन्नो देवता गरुपूजकः ।

जनसंगविरक्तश्च महाव्याधि विवर्जितः ॥२६॥

अधिमात्रव्रतज्ञश्च सर्वयोगस्य साधकः ।

त्रिभिः संवत्सरैः सिद्धिरेतस्य नात्र सशयः ॥

सर्वयोगाधिकारी स नात्र कार्या विचारणा ॥२७॥

atha adhimātratamasādhakalakṣaṇam /

mahāvīryānvitotsāhī manojñaḥ śauryavānapi /

śāstrajño'bhyāsaśīlaśca nirmohaśca nirākulaḥ /23/

navayauvanasampanno mitāhārī jitendriyaḥ /

nirbhayaśca śucirdakṣo dātā sarvajanāśrayaḥ /24/

adhikārī sthiro dhīmān yathecchāvasthitaḥ kṣamī /

suśīlo dharmacārī ca guptaceṣṭaḥ priyamvadaḥ /25/

śāstraviśvāsasampanno devatā gurupūjakaḥ

janasaṅgaviraktaśca mahavyādi vivarjitaḥ /26/

adhimātravratajñaśca sarvayogasya sādhakaḥ /

tribhiḥ samvatsaraiḥ siddhiretasya nātra samśayaḥ /

sarvayogādhikārī sa nātra kāryā vicāraṇā /27/

Now the characteristics of the most dedicated practitioner are described. Full of great vitality, highly courageous, attractive, full of heroism, knower of the *Śāstras* (the scriptures), engaged in constant practice, unattached to any worldly objects, unconfused, full of youthfulness, moderate eater, self-controlled, fearless, pure (on both mental and physical level), skilled, giver of donations, giver of shelter to everyone, influential, firm, brilliant, remaining according to his will and to the content of his heart, forgiving, humble and gentle, follower of religious codes and conduct, keeping his practice secret, speaking sweet and pleasing words, having faith in the *Śāstras*, worshipper of his god and guru, detached to the company and contacts of people, without any great diseases, knower and keeper of the vows of the *adhimātra* (a highly devoted state of practice) and practitioner of all kinds of yoga. Certainly, a person with any of these characteristics achieves success in three years. There is no doubt that he is entitled to all kinds of yoga. –23-27.

Concentration on Image

अथ प्रतीकोपासनम् ।

प्रतीकोपासना कार्या द्रष्टादृष्टफलप्रदा ।

पुनाती दर्शनादत्र नात्र कार्या विचारणा ॥२८॥

atha pratīkopāsanam /

pratīkopāsanā kāryā dṛṣṭādṛṣṭaphalapradā /

punātī darśanādatra nātra kāryā vicāraṇā /28/

Now the concentration on image is described.

The concentration on one's image gives both seen and unseen fruits to its practitioner. He is purified through its vision alone. There is nothing to think otherwise regarding it. –28.

Method of Concentration on Image

गाढातपे स्वप्रतिविम्बतेश्वरं निरीक्ष्य विस्फारितलोचनद्वयम् ।

यदा नभः पश्यति स्वप्रतीकं नभोङ्गणे तत्क्षणमेव पश्यति ॥२९॥

gāḍhātape svapratibimbateśvaraṃ

nirīkṣya visphāritalocanadvayam /

yadā nabhaḥ paśyati svapratiīkaṃ

nabhoṅgaṇe tatkṣaṇameva paśyati /29/

In a clear sun-lit day, the practitioner should fix his gaze on his divine shadow. When he sees his own image in the sky, he sees the God right in that moment. –29.

प्रत्यहं पश्यते यो वै स्वप्रतीकं नभोङ्गणे ।

आयुवृद्धिर्भवेत्तस्य न मृत्युः स्यात्कदाचन ॥३०॥

pratyahaṃ pasyate yo vai svapratīkaṃ nabhoṅgaṇe /

āyurvṛddhirbhavettasya na mṛtyuḥ syatkadācana /30/

He who sees his image in the sky every day, his life is prolonged and he will never have a sudden death. –30.

यदा पश्यति सम्पूर्ण स्वप्रतीकं नभोङ्गणे ।

तदा जयमवाप्नोति वायुं निर्जित्य सञ्चरेत् ॥३१॥

yadā pasyati sampūrṇaṃ svapratīkaṃ nabhoṅgaṇe /

tadā jayamavāpnoti vāyuṃ nirjitya sañcaret /31/

When he sees his full reflection in the sky, then he gets victory. Having conquered the *vāyu*, he moves everywhere. –31.

Result of the Concentration on Image

यः करोति सदाभ्यासं चात्मानं वन्दते परम् ।

पूर्णानन्दैकपूरुषं स्वप्रतीकप्रसादतः ॥३२॥

yah karoti sadābhyāsaṃ catmānaṃ vandate paraṃ /

pūrṇānandaikapuruṣaṃ svapratikaprasādataḥ /32/

He who always practices it, salutes the *Supreme Personality*, one alone full of bliss and perfect joy athrough the grace of image concentration. –32.

यात्राकाले च विवाहे च शुभे कर्मणि सङ्कटे ।

पापक्षये पुण्यवृद्धौ प्रतीकोपासनञ्चरेत् ॥३३॥

yātrākāle ca vivāhe ca śubhe karmaṇi saṅkaṭe /

pāpakṣaye puṇyavṛddhau pratīkopāsanañcaret /33/

This destroys sins and increases virtue at the beginning of travel, marriage, and auspicious works or at the time of emergency. Therefore, he should practice concentration on his image. –33.

निरन्तरकृताभ्यासादन्तरे पश्यति ध्रुवम् ।

तदा मुक्तिमवाप्नोति योगी नियतमानसः ॥३४॥

nirantarakṛtābhyāsādantare paśyati dhruvam /

tadā muktimavāpnoti yogī niyatamānasaḥ /34/

Through its constant practice, he certainly sees his reflection in his own Self, and then the self-controlled yogi attains *mukti* (liberation). –34.

Practices of Various Dhāraṇā

1. Concentration on the Self as Light

अंगुष्ठाभ्यमुभे श्रोत्रे तर्जनीभ्यां द्विलोचने ।

नासारन्ध्रे च मध्याभ्यामनामाभ्यां मुखं दृढम् ॥३५॥

निरुध्य मारुतं योगी यदैव कुरुते भृशम् ।

तदा लक्षणमात्मानं ज्योतिरूपं स पश्यति ॥३६॥

aṅguṣṭhābhyāmubhe śrotre tarjanībhyāṃ dvilocane /

nāsārandhre ca madhyābhyāṃ

anāmābhyāṃ mukhaṃ dṛḍham /35/

nirudhya mārutaṃ yogī yadaiva kurute bhṛśam /

tadā lakṣaṇamātmānaṃ jyotirūpaṃ sa pasyati /36/

The yogi should close his ears with his thumbs, the eyes with his index fingers, the nostrils with his middle fingers, and then close the mouth firmly with his ring fingers. He who intensely practices (this concentration) retaining the breath in this way, sees the sign of his Self in the form of light. –35-36.

तत्तेजो दृश्यते येन क्षणमात्रं निराकुलम् ।

सर्वपापविनिर्मुक्तः स याति परमां गतिम् ॥३७॥

tattejo dṛśyate yena kṣaṇamātraṃ nirākulam /

sarvapāpavinirmuktaḥ sa yāti paramāṃ gatim /37/

He who clearly sees this light with a calm mind even for a moment is freed from all sins and attains the supreme state. –37.

निरन्तरकृताभ्यासाद्योगी विगतकल्मषः ।

सर्वदेहादि विस्मृत्य तदाभिन्नः स्वयं गतः ॥३८॥

nirantarakṛtābhyāsādyogī vigatakalmaṣaḥ /

sarvadehādi vismṛtya tadbhinnaḥ svayaṃ gataḥ /38/

Through its constant practice, the sin-freed yogi, having forgotten all his bodies (gross, subtle and causal), merges into the Self. –38.

यः करोति सदाभ्यासं गुप्ताचारेण मानवः ।

स वै ब्रह्मसविलीनः स्यात्पापकर्मरतो यदि ॥३९॥

yaḥ karoti sadābyāsaṃ guptācareṇa mānavaḥ /

sa vai brahmavilīnaḥ syātpāpakarmarato yadi /39/

He who regularly practices it in secret is dissolved in the *Brahman* (the Ultimate Self) even though he was involved in sinful acts. –39.

गोपनीयः प्रयत्नेन सद्यः प्रत्ययकारकः ।

निर्वाणदायको लोके योगोऽयं मम वल्लभः ॥

नादः संजायते तस्य क्रमेणाभ्यासतश्च वै ॥४०॥

gopanīyaḥ prayatnena sadyaḥ pratyayakārakaḥ /

nirvāṇadāyako loke yogo'yaṃ mama vallabhaḥ /

nādaḥ sañjāyate tasya krameṇābhyāsataśca vai /40/

This should be kept secret with great care as it instantly produces assurance. It gives liberation to humankind. It is my favorite yoga. Through its gradual practice, the yogi hears *nāda* (subtle sound). –40.

2. Concentration on Anāhata Sound

मत्तभृङ्गवेणुवीणासदृशः प्रथमो ध्वनिः ।
एवमभ्यासतः पश्चात् संसारध्वान्तनाशनम ॥४१॥
घण्टानादसमः पश्चात् ध्वनिर्मेघरवोपमः ।
ध्वनौ तस्मिन्मनो दत्वा यदा तिष्ठति निर्भयः ॥
तदा संजायते तस्य लयस्य मम वल्लभे ॥४२॥

mattabhṛṅgaveṇuvīṇāsadṛśaḥ prathamo dhvaniḥ /
evamabyāsataḥ paścāt samsāradhvāntanāsanam /41/
ghaṇṭānādasamaḥ paścāt dhvanirmegharavopamaḥ /
dhvanau tasminmano dattvā yadā tiṣṭhati nirbhayaḥ /
tadā sañjāyate tasya layasya mama vallabhe /42/

The first sound is like an intoxicated bee, then a flute, next a big lute; and then through its gradual practice, he hears the sounds similar to a bell, the destroyer of all the darkness of the world; after this he hears the sounds of roaring thunder. When he remains fearless, having fixed his mind on this sound, then he is absorbed into deep concentration, O my beloved! –41-42.

तत्र नादे यदा चित्तं रमते योगिनो भृशम् ।
विस्मृत्य सकलं वाह्यं नादेन सह शाम्यति ॥४३॥

tatra nāde yadā cittaṃ ramate yogino bhṛśam /
vismṛtya sakalaṃ bāhyaṃ nādena saha śāmyati /43/

When the mind of the yogi highly rejoices the hearing of this sound, having forgotten all the external objects he is dissolved along with the sound. –43.

एतदभ्यासयोगेन जित्वा सम्यग्गुणान्बहून् ।
सर्वारम्भपरित्यागी चिदाकाशे विलीयते ॥४४॥

etadabhyāsayogena jitvā samyagguṇānbahūn /
sarvārambhaparityāgī cidākāśe vilīyate /44/

Having conquered all the three qualities (*sattva, raja* and *tama*) through the constant practice of this yoga, and giving up all the beginning of passion and abhorrence, he merges into *cidākāśa* (the psychic space of consciousness). –44.

Four Unique Practices

नासनं सिद्धसदृशं न कुम्भसदृशं बलम् ।
न खेचरीसमा मुद्रा न नादसदृशो लय ॥४५॥

nāsanam siddhasadṛsaṃ na kumbhasadṛśam balam /
na khecarīsamā mudra na nādasadṛśo laya /45/

There is no posture similar to *siddhāsana*, no power parallel to *kumbhaka*, no *mudrā* like *khecari*, and no *laya* (dissolution) equal to *nāda* (the mystic psychic sound). –45.

इदानीं कथयिष्यामि मुक्तस्यानुभव प्रिये ।
यज्ज्ञात्वा लभते मुक्तिं पापयुक्तोऽपि साधकः ॥४६॥

idānīṃ kathayiṣyāmi muktasyānubhava priye
yajjñātvā labhate muktiṃ pāpayukto'pi sādhakaḥ /46/

O Dear! Now I am telling you the direct knowledge of liberation. By knowing it, even the sinful practitioner achieves liberation. –46.

3. Concentration on the Pure Self

समभ्यर्च्येश्वरं सम्यक्कृत्वा च योगमुत्तमम् ।
गृह्णीयात्सुस्थितो भूत्वा गुरुं बुद्धिमान ॥४७॥

samabhyarcyeśvaraṃ samyakkṛtvā ca yogamuttamam /
gṛhṇīyātsusthito bhūtvā guruṃ santoṣya buddhimān /47/

Having worshipped the God in a proper way and having completely perfected the most excellent yoga, and by satisfying his guru, the wise yogi should be initiated into this yoga in a stable posture amid a steady mind. –47.

जीवादि सकलं वस्तुं दत्वा योगविदं गुरुम्
सन्तोष्यातिप्रयत्नेन योगोऽयं गृह्यते बुधैः ॥४८॥

jīvādi sakalaṃ vastuṃ dattvā yogavidaṃ gurum /
santoṣyātiprayatnena yogo'yaṃ grzihyate budhaiḥ /48/

Having given all his livestock and wealth to the guru (self-realised spiritual master) who is highly experienced and the knower of the yoga, and satisfied him with great effort, the wise practitioner should be initiated into this yoga. –48.

विप्रान्संतोष्य मेधावी नानामंगलसंयुतः ।
ममालये शुचिर्भूत्वा प्रगृह्णीयाच्छुभात्मकम् ॥४९॥

viprānsantoṣya medhāvī nānāmaṅgalasamyutaḥ /
mamālaye śucirbhūtvā pragṛhṇīyācchubhātmakam /49/

Having satisfied *vipras* (the accomplished sages or yogis), by offering them all kinds of pleasing things, the wise practitioner should receive this auspicious yoga in my abode (in the temple of Lord *Śiva*) with purified body and heart. –49.

संन्यस्यानेन विधिना प्राक्तनं विग्रहादिकम् ।
भूत्वा दिव्यवपुर्योगी गृह्णीयाद्वक्ष्यमाणकम् ॥

sanyasyānena vidhinā prāktanaṃ vigrahādikam /
bhūtvā divyavapuryogī gṛhṇīyādvakṣyamāṇakam /50/

Having renounced all the fruits of his past karmas accumulated by his previous bodies, according to the methods mentioned above, and being in his divine body, the yogi should receive this supreme yoga. –50.

पदमासनस्थितो योगी जनसंगविवर्जितः ।
विज्ञाननाडीद्वितयमङ्गुलीभ्यां निरोधयेत् ॥५१॥

padmāsanasthito yogī janasaṅgavivarjitaḥ /
vijjñānanāḍīdvitayamaṅgulībhyāṃ nirodhayet /51/

Having renounced all social relations and attachments, the yogi seated in *padmāsana* posture should control the two *vijñāna nāḍis* (*iḍā* and *piṅgalā* – ther psychic pathways responsible for worldly knowledge) with his thumb and ring finger. –51.

सिद्धेस्तदाविर्भवति सुखरूपी निरञ्जनः ।

तस्मिनपरिश्रमः कार्यो येन सिद्धो भवेत्खलु ॥५२॥

siddhestadāvirbhavati sukharūpī nirañjanaḥ /

tasminapariśramaḥ kāryo yena siddho bhavetkhalu /52/

When the practitioner achieves perfection through this practice, then there arises all bliss and pure Self in his heart. Therefore, a great effort should be made to surely achieve perfection in it. –52.

यः करोति सदाभ्यासं तस्य सिद्धिर्न दूरतः ।

वायुसिद्धिर्भवेत्तस्य क्रमादेव न सशयः ॥५३॥

yaḥ karoti sadābhyāsaṃ tasya siddhirna dūrataḥ /

vāyusiddhirbhavettasya kramādeva na samśayaḥ /53/

He who regularly practices it comes nearer to success. He undoubtedly also achieves *vāyu Siddhi* through its gradual practice. –53.

सकृद्यः कुरुते योगी पापौघं नाशयेद्ध्रुवम् ।

तस्य स्यान्मध्यमे वायोः प्रवेशो नात्र सशयः ॥५४॥

sakṛdyaḥ kurute yogī pāpaughaṃ nāśayeddhruvam /

tasya syānmadhyame vāyoḥ praveśo nātra samśayaḥ /54/

The yogi who practices it once surely destroys all sins; and undoubtedly, the *vāyu* enters into the middle psychic pathway in his body. –54.

एतदभ्यासशीलो यः स योगी देवपूजितः ।

अणिमादिगुणान् लब्ध्वा विचरेद्भुवनत्रये ॥५५॥

etadabhyāsaśīlo yah sa yogī devapūjitaḥ /

aṇimādiguṇān labdhvā vicaredbhuvanatraye /55/

In this way, even gods worship the yogi who constantly keeps practicing it. Having received the psychic powers like *aṇimā*, etc., he freely travels everywhere in all the three worlds. –55.

यो यथास्यानिलाभ्यासात्तदभवेत्तस्य विग्रहः ।

तिष्ठेदात्मनि मेधावी संयुतः क्रीडते भृशम् ॥५६॥

yo yathāsyānilābhyāsāttadbhavettasya vigrahaḥ /

tiṣṭhedātmani medhāvī samyutaḥ krīḍate bhṛśam /56/

Whichever level the practitioner attains perfection on *vāyu* through the practice; he gets perfection over his body to the same extent. The wise yogi, living together with his Self, highly takes pleasure in his existence. –56.

एतद्योगं परं गोप्यं न देयं यस्य कस्यचित् ।

यः प्रमाणैः समायुक्तस्तमेव कथ्यते ध्रुवम् ॥५७॥

etadyogaṃ paraṃ gopyaṃ na deyaṃ yasya kasyacit /

yaḥ pramāṇaiḥ samāyuktastameva kathyate dhruvam /57/

This is a highly secret yoga. It should not be given to everyone. It should be imparted to one who has certainly proven to have all qualities to be found in a yogi. –57.

4. Concentration on the Throat Pit

योगी पदमासने तिष्ठेत्कण्ठकूपे यदा स्मरन् ।

जिह्वां कृत्वा तालुमूले क्षुत्पिपासा निवर्तते ॥५८॥

yogī padmāsane tiṣṭhetkaṇṭhakūpe yadā smaran /

jihvāṃ kṛtvā tālumūle kṣutpipāsā nivartate /58/

The yogi should sit in *padmāsana* and fix his awareness on the pit of his throat. He should turn his tongue upwards and place it on the base of the palate. His hunger and thirst are satisfied through the practice (of this concentration). –58.

कण्ठकूपादधः स्थाने कूर्मनाडयस्ति शोभना ।

तस्मिन् योगी मनो दत्वा चित्तस्थैर्य लभेद्भृशम् ॥५६॥

kaṇṭhakūpādadhaḥ sthāne kūrmanāḍyasti śobhanā /

tasmin yogī mano dattvā cittasthairyaṃ labhedbhṛśam /59/

A beautiful *nāḍī* called *kūrma* is located below the cavity of the throat. When the yogi concentrates his awareness there, he attains a great steadiness of his mind. –59.

5. Concentration on the Third Eye

शिरः कपाले रुद्राक्षं विवरं चिन्तयेद्यदा ।

तदा ज्योतिः प्रकाशः स्याद्विद्युत्पुञ्जसमप्रभः ॥६०॥

एतच्चिन्तनमात्रेण पापानां संक्षयो भवेत् ।

दुराचारोऽपि पुरुषो लभते परमं पदम् ॥६१॥

śiraḥ kapāle rudrākṣaṃ vivaraṃ cintayedyadā /

tadā jyotiḥ prakāśaḥ syādviddhyutpuñjasamaprabhaḥ /60/

etaccintanamātreṇa pāpānāṃ saṅkṣayo bhavet /

dūrācāro'pi puruṣo labhate paramaṃ padam /61/

When the yogi constantly concentrates on *Rudrākṣa* (literally, the Eye of *Śiva*, Third Eye) in the middle cavity of the forehead, then he perceives brilliant luminous light similar to a multitude of flashes of lightning. Multifarious sins are destroyed by mere concentration on this light; even an immoral person achieves the supreme state (through this practice). –60-61.

अहर्निशं यदा चिन्तां तत्करोति विचक्षणः ।

सिद्धानां दर्शनं तस्य भाषणञ्च भवेद्ध्रुवम् ॥६२॥

aharniśaṃ yadā cintāmtatkaroti vicakṣaṇaḥ /

siddhānāṃ darśanaṃ tasya bhāṣaṇañca bhavetdhruvam /62/

When the wise yogi concentrates on this light day and night, he perceives *siddhas* (the perfected masters/sages) and certainly talks with them. –62.

6. Concentration on the Void

तिष्ठन् गच्छन् स्वपन् भुञ्जन् ध्यायेच्छून्यमहर्निशम् ।
तदाकाशमयो योगी चिदाकाशे विलीयते ॥६३॥

tiṣṭhan gacchan svapan bhuñjan
dhyāyecchūnyaṃ aharniśam /
tadākāśamayo yogī cidākāśe vilīyate /63/

When the yogi concentrates day and night on *śūnya* (the void) while standing or walking, while dreaming or waking, then he becomes fully ethereal and dissolved in *Cidākāśa* (the psychic space of *Intelligence* between the two eyebrows). –63.

एतज्ज्ञानं सदा कार्यं योगिना सिद्धिमिच्छता ।
निरन्तरकृताभ्यासान्मम तुल्यो भवद्ध्रुवम् ॥
एतज्ज्ञानबलाद्योगी सर्वेषां वल्लभो भवेत् ॥६४॥

etajjñānaṃ sadā kāryaṃ yoginā siddhimicchatā /
nirantarakṛtābhyāsānmama tulyo bhavetdruvam /
etajjñānabalādyogi sarveṣāṃ vallabho bhavet /64/

The yogi desirous of success should always receive experiential knowledge of this concentration. He certainly becomes equal to me through constant practice. He becomes dear to everyone by the strength of this knowledge. –64.

Concentration on the Nose Tip

सर्वान् भूतान् जयं कृत्वा निराशीरपरिग्रहः ।
नासाग्रे दृश्यते येन पदमासनगतेन वै ॥
मनसो मरणं तस्य खेचरत्वं प्रसिद्ध्यति ॥६५॥

sarvān bhūtān jayam kṛtvā nirāśīraparigrahaḥ /

nāsāgre dṛśyate yena padmāsanagatena vai /

manaso maraṇam tasya khecaratvam prasiddhyati /65/

Having conquered all the elements and giving up all hopes and worldly possessions, when the yogi seated in *padmāsana* focuses his gaze on the tip of the nose, then his mind dies and attains perfection in *khecarī mudrā*. –65.

ज्योतिः पश्यति योगीन्द्रः शुद्धं शुद्धाचलोपमम् ।

तत्राभ्यासबलेनैव स्वयं तद्रक्षको भवेत् ॥६६॥

jyotiḥ paśyati yogīndraḥ śuddhaṃ śuddhācalopamam /

tatrābhyāsabalenaiva svayaṃ tadrakṣako bhavet /66/

The great yogi sees light as pure as *Śuddhācala* (the Mount *Kailāśa*), and through the power of his practice, he himself becomes the protector of that light. –66.

उत्तानशयने भूमौ सूप्त्वा ध्यायन्निरन्तरम् ।

सद्यः श्रमविनाशाय स्वयं योगी विचक्षणः ॥६७॥

शिरः पश्चात्तु भागस्य ध्याने मृत्युञ्जयो भवेत् ।

भ्रूमध्ये दृष्टिमात्रेण ह्यपरः परिकीर्तितः ॥६८॥

uttānaśayane bhūmau suptvā dhyāyannirantaram /

sadyaḥ śramavināśāya svayaṃ yogī vicakṣaṇaḥ /67/

śiraḥ paścāttu bhāgasya dhyāne mṛtyuñjayo bhavet /

bhrūmadhye dṛṣṭimātreṇa hyaparaḥ parikīrtitaḥ /68/

Laying flat on the floor (in *śavāsana*) the wise yogi should constantly concentrate on this light. This destroys his tiredness right away. By concentrating on the back of his head (the *medulla oblongata*), he conquers death. Focusing concentration between the eyebrows has already been described. –67-68.

Essence of Food and Nourishment of the Body

चतुर्विधस्य चान्नस्य रसस्त्रेधा विभज्यते ।

तत्र सारतमो लिगंदेहस्य परिपोषकः ॥६९॥
सप्तधातुमयं पिण्डमेतिपुष्णाति मध्यगः ।
याति विण्मूत्ररूपेण तृतीयः सप्ततो बहिः ॥७०॥

caturvidhasya cānnasya rasastredhā vibhajyate /
tatra sāratamo liṅgadehasya pariposakaḥ /69/
saptadhātumayaṃ piṇḍameti pusṇāti madhyagaḥ /
yāti viṇmūtrarūpeṇa tṛtīyaḥ saptato bahiḥ /70/

The fluid (chyle) from the digestion of the food that is taken in four different ways: chewing, sucking, licking, and drinking – is divided into three parts. The first part- the finest essence (of the food) is the nourisher of *Liṅga Deha* (the subtle body). The second part - finer middle essence, nourishes the *piṇḍa* (the gross physical body) that is composed of seven *dhātus* (the humors). The third part goes out of the seven-humored body in the form of excrement and urine. –69-70.

आद्यभागद्वयं नाड्यः प्रोक्तास्ताः सकल अपि ।
पोषयन्ति वपुर्वायुमापादतलमस्तकम् ॥७१॥

ādyabhāgadvayaṃ nāḍyaḥ proktāstāḥ sakalā api /
poṣayanti vapurvāyumāpādatalamastakam /71/

The first two essences of the fluid stated above nourish all the *nāḍis* (the psychic pathways), the body and the *vāyus* moving within the body from head to feet. –71.

नाडीभिराभिः सर्वाभिर्वायुः सञ्चरते यदा ।
तदैवान्नरसो देहे साम्येनेह प्रवर्तते ॥७२॥

nāḍībhirābhiḥ sarvābhirvāyuḥ sañcarate yadā /
tadaivānnaraso dehe sāmyeneha pravartate /72/

When the *vāyu* circulates through all the *nāḍis*, then the fluid of the food remains harmonious and even in the whole body. –72.

चतुर्दृशानां तत्रेह व्यापारे मुख्यभागतः ।
ता अनुग्रत्वहीनाश्च प्राणसञ्चारनाडिकाः ॥७३॥

caturdaśānāṃ tatreha vyāpāre mukhyabhāgataḥ /
tā anugratvahīnāśca prāṇasañcāranāḍikāḥ /73/

There are those fourteen main *nāḍis* mentioned earlier that are located in the major parts of the body and they perform their respective functions independently. These *nāḍis* circulate the *prāṇa* in the whole body. –73.

Description of Six Cakras

1. Mūlādhāra Cakra

अथ मूलाधारचक्रविरिणम् ।
गुदाद्व्यंगुलतश्चोर्ध्व मेढ्रैकांगुलतस्त्वधः ।
एवञ्चास्ति समं कन्दं समताच्चतुरंगुलम् ॥७४॥

atha mūlādhāracakravivaraṇam /
gudādvayaṅgulataścordhvaṃ meḍhraikāṅgulatastvadhaḥ /
evañcāsti samaṃ kandaṃ samatāccaturaṅgulam /74/

Now begins the explanation of the *mūlādhāra cakra.*

Two-finger widths above the anus and two-finger widths below *liṅga* (the penis), there is a rectangular space of four-finger widths similar to a bulb. –74.

पश्चिमाभिमुखीः योनिर्गुदमेढ्रान्तरालगा ।
तत्र कन्दं समाख्यातं तत्रास्ति कुण्डली सदा ॥७५॥
संवेष्टय सकला नाडीः सार्द्धत्रिकुटलाकृतीः ।
मुखे निवेश्य सा पुच्छं सुषुम्णाविवरे स्थिता ॥७६॥

paścimābhimukhīḥ yonirgudameḍhrāntarālagā /
tatra kandaṃ samākyātaṃ tatrāsti kuṇḍalī sadā /75/
samveṣṭya sakalā nāḍīḥ sārddhatrikuṭalākṛitīḥ /

mukhe niveśya sā puccham suṣumṇāvivare sthitā /76/

In this space between the anus and the penis there is the *Yoni* facing towards the west (backwards). The space called *kanda* (the bulbous root) is located there, where the *Kuṇḍalinī* always dwells. Encircling all the *nāḍis* and coiled in three and a half rounds, she remains in the hole of the *suṣumṇā* (the middle psychic pathway) with her tail entering into her own mouth. –75-76.

सुप्ता नागोपमा ह्येषा स्फुरन्ती प्रभया स्वया ।
अहिवत्सन्धिसंस्थाना वाग्देवी बीजसंज्ञिका ॥७७॥

suptā nāgopamā hyeṣā sphurantī prabhayā svayā /
ahivatsandhisasthānā vāgdevī bījasajñikā /77/

She remains there sleeping like a serpent and she is luminous by her own light. She dwells between the joints (the *iḍā* and *piṅgalā*) like a serpent. She is the Goddess of speech and she is called *Bīja* (the *Seed* of all existence). –77.

ज्ञेया शक्तिरियं विष्णोर्निर्भरा स्वर्णभास्वरा ।
सत्वं रजस्तमश्चेति गुणत्रयप्रसूतिका ॥७८॥

jñeyā śaktiriyaṃ viṣṇornirvarā svarṇabhāsvarā /
sattvaṃ rajastamaśceti guṇatrayaprasūtikā /78/

"Like glowing gold, know that she is the power of *Viṣṇu*". She is the mother of all three qualities: *sattva*, *rajas* and *tamas*. –78.

तत्र बन्धूकपुष्पाभं कामबीजं प्रकीर्तितम् ।
कलहेमसमं योगे प्रयुक्ताक्षररूपिणम् ॥७९॥

tatra bandhūkapuṣpābhaṃ kāmabījaṃ prakīrtitam /
kalahemasamaṃ yoge prayuktākṣararūpiṇam /79/

It is said that there (in the abode of *Kuṇḍalinī*) is located beautiful *Kāma Bīja* (the seed of love), which is like the *bandhūka* (the pentapetes phoenicea) flower. It is bright like shining gold. In yoga it is regarded as the form of *Akṣara* (the Imperishable or Everlasting One). –79.

सुषुम्णापि च संश्लिष्टा बीजं तत्र वरं स्थितम् ।
शरच्चन्द्रनिभं तेजस्स्वयमेतत्स्फुरीत्स्थितम् ॥८०॥
सूर्यकोटिप्रतीकाशं चनद्रकोटिसुशीतलम् ।
एतत्त्रयं मिलित्वैव देवी त्रिपुरभैरवी ॥
बीजसञ्ज्ञं परंतेजस्तदेव परिकीर्तितम् ॥८१॥

suṣumṇāpi ca samślisṭā bījaṃ tatra varaṃ sthitam /
śaraccandranibhaṃ tejassvayametatsphuratsthitam /80/
sūryakotipratīkāśaṃ candrakotisuśītalam /
etattrayaṃ militvaiva devī tripurabhairavī /
bījasañjñaṃ parantejastadeva parikīrtitam /81/

The beautiful *Bīja* remains there embraced by the *suṣumṇā*. It dwells there shining brightly like the moon in the autumn season, with the radiance of millions of suns and the coolness of millions of moons. *Tripurā Bhairavī* is the combined form of all these three together (the *Kuṇḍalinī*, *Kāma Bīja* and *Suṣumnā* or the fire, sun and moon). She is called the *Bīja* and she is considered an omnipotent Goddess. –80-81.

Svayambhūliṅga

क्रियाविज्ञानशक्तिभ्यां युतं यत्परितो भ्रमत् ।
उत्तिष्ठद्विशतस्त्वम्भः सूक्ष्मं शोणशिखायुतम ॥
योनिस्थं तत्परं तेजः स्वयंभूलिंगसंज्ञितम् ॥८२॥

kriyāvijñānaśaktibhyāṃ yutaṃ yatparito bhramat /
uttiṣṭhadviśatastvambhaḥ sūkṣaṃ śoṇaśikhāyutam /
yonisthaṃ tatparaṃ tejaḥ svayambhūliṅgasañjñitam /82/

That *Bīja* bestowed with the power of *kriyā* (the action) and *vijñāna* (the knowledge) moves throughout the body. Sometimes it rises up and sometimes enters down into the water. It is subtle and bright like the flame of a fire. This supreme radiant *Bīja* dwells in the area of the *yoni* and it is called *Svayambhūliṅga* (the Self-existent Subtle Psychic Body). –82.

आधारपदमेतद्धि योनिर्यस्यास्ति कन्दतः ।

परिस्फुरद्वादिसान्तचतुर्वर्ण चतुर्दलम् ॥८३॥

ādhārapadmetaddhi yoniryasyāsti kandataḥ /

parisphuradvādisāntacaturvarṇaṃ caturdalam /83/

It is (collectively) known as *ādhāra padma* (the foundation lotus). The *yoni* is located at its bulbous root. This brightly budded lotus has four beautiful petals decorated with four letters *va*, *śa*, *ṣa* and *sa*. –83.

कुलाभिधं सुवर्णाभं स्वयंभूलिङ्गसंगतम् ।

द्विरण्डो यत्र सिद्धोऽस्ति डाकिनी यत्र देवता ॥८४॥

तत्पद्ममध्यगा योनिस्तत्र कुण्डलिनी स्थिता ।

तस्या ऊर्ध्वे स्फुरत्तेजः कामबीजं भ्रमन्मतम् ॥८५॥

यः करोति सदा ध्यानं मूलाधारे विचक्षणः ।

तस्य स्याद्दार्दुरी सिद्धिर्भूमित्यागक्रमेण वै ॥८६॥

kulābhidhaṃ suvarṇābhaṃ svayambhūliṅgasaṅgatam /

dviraṇḍo yatra siddho'sti ḍākinī yatra devatā /84/

tatpadmamadhyagā yonistatra kuṇḍalinī sthitā /

tasyā ūrdhve sphurattejaḥ kāmabījaṃ bhramanmatam /85/

yaḥ karoti sadā dhyānaṃ mūlādhāre vicakṣaṇaḥ /

tasya syāddārdurī siddhirbhumityāgakrameṇa vai /86/

There is a golden bright area named *Kula* (the family) united with *Svayambhūliṅga*. There preside the adept named *Dviraṇḍa* and the goddess *Dākinī*. There is the *yoni*, in the center of that lotus, where the *Kuṇḍalinī* dwells. Above it there continuously travels the brilliant *Kāma Bīja.* The wise practitioner who constantly concentrates on *mūlādhāra* receives *dārdurī siddhi* (the power of jumping like a frog) and through gradual practice, he can leave the ground and travel in the air. –84-86.

वपुषः कान्तिरुत्कृष्टा जठराग्निविबर्धनम् ।

आरोग्यञ्च पटुत्वञ्च सर्वज्ञतञ्च जायते ॥८७॥

vapuṣah kāntirutkṛṣṭā jaṭharāgnivibardhanam /

ārogyañca paṭutvañca sarvajñatvañca jāyate /87/

Through concentration on this lotus, the brilliance of the body becomes excellent, the digestive fire is stimulated, and good health, eloquence and omniscient knowledge of everything are all achieved. –87.

भूतं भव्यं भविष्यञ्च वेत्ति सर्व सकारणम् ।

अश्रुतान्यपि शास्त्राणि सरहस्यं भवेद्ध्रुवम् ॥८८॥

bhūtaṃ bhavyaṃ bhaviṣyañca vetti sarvaṃ sakāraṇam /

aśrutānyapi śāstrāṇi sarahasyaṃ bhaveddhruvam /88/

He knows all the happenings with their causes in the past, at present and in the future. Surely, he gains the knowledge of all the unheard *Śāstras* (the scriptures) and unfolds their mysteries. –88.

वक्त्रे सरस्वती देवी सदा नृत्यति निर्भरम् ।

मन्त्रसिद्धिर्भवेत्तस्य जपादेव न सशयः ॥८९॥

vaktre sarasvati devī sadā nṛtyati nirbharam /

mantrasiddhirbhavettasya japādeva na samśayaḥ /89/

Sarasvatī (the goddess of learning) always dances fully on his tongue. He surely gains *mantra siddhi* (the perfection in *mantras*) through mere repetition. –89.

जरामरणदुःखौघान्नाशयति गुरोर्वचः ।

इदं ध्यानं सदा कार्य पवनाभ्यासिना परम् ॥

ध्यानमात्रेण योगीन्द्रमुच्यते सर्वकिल्विषात् ॥९०॥

jarāmaraṇaduhkhaughānnāśayati gurorvacaḥ /

idaṃ dhyānaṃ sadā kāryaṃ pavanābhyāsinā param /

dhyānamātreṇa yogīndromucyate sarvakilviṣāt /90/

There is the saying of the guru: – "It destroys old age, death and the multifarious sins". The practitioner of *prāṇāyāma* should always do this excellent meditation. The great yogi gets rid of all sins by the practice of this meditation only. –90.

मूलपद्मं यदा ध्यायेद्योगी स्वयम्भूलिङ्गकम् ।

तदा तक्षणमात्रेण पापौघं नाशयेद्ध्रुवम् ॥९१॥

mūlapadmaṃ yadā dhyāyedyogī svayambhūliṅgakam /

tadā tatkṣaṇamātreṇa pāpaughaṃ nāśayeddhruvam /91/

When the yogi concentrates on *mūlādhāra* lotus along with the *Svayambhū Liṅga*, then the multitude of his sins are destroyed at once. There is no doubt in it. –91.

यं यं कामयते चिन्ते तं तं फलमवाप्नुयात् ।

निरन्तरकृतभ्यासात्तं पश्यति विमुक्तिदम् ॥९२॥

बहिरभ्यन्तरे श्रेष्ठं पूजनियं प्रयत्नतः ।

ततः श्रेष्ठतमं ह्येतन्नान्यदस्ति मतं मम ॥९३॥

yaṃ yaṃ kāmayate citte taṃ taṃ phalamavāpnuyāt /

nirantarakṛtābhyāsāttaṃ paśyati vimuktidam /92/

bahirabhyantare śresṭhaṃ pūjanīyaṃ prayatnataḥ /

tataḥ śresṭhataṃ hyetannānyadasti mataṃ mama /93/

Whatever the mind of the yogi desires, he obtains them all. Through constant practice, he perceives the One who is the giver of liberation; who is supreme both within and outside, and who is worthy of worshipping with due respect and effort. There does not exist anyone or anything supreme other than Him. This is my (*Śiva's*) opinion. –92-93.

Body: the Real Shrine of God

आत्मसंस्थं शिवं त्यक्त्वा बहिःस्थं यः समर्चयत् ।

हस्तस्थं पिण्डमृत्सृज्य भ्रमते जीविताशया ॥९४॥

ātmasamśthaṃ śivam tyaktvā bahihsthaṃ yaḥ samarcayet /

hastasthaṃ piṇḍamutsṛjya bhramate jīvitāśayā /94/

He who, giving up the *Śiva* (the God) situated within, worships the god that is outside (the external forms of the god e.g. drawing, photograph, statue, idol, icon, etc.) is like a person who throws away the food in his hand and wanders here and there begging for his livelihood. –94.

आत्मलिङ्गार्चनं कुर्यादनालस्यं दिने दिने ।

तस्य स्यात्सकला सिद्धिर्नात्र कार्या विचारणा ॥९५॥

ātmaliṅgārcanaṃ kuryādanālasyaṃ dine dine /

tasya syātsakalā sidhirnātra kāryā vicāraṇā /95/

Hence, one should worship or meditate on his *Ātmaliṅga* (the Subtle Self-body within) everyday without laziness. From this, he attains all the perfections. There is nothing to think otherwise. –95.

निरन्तरकृताभ्यासात्षण्मासैः सिद्धिमाप्नुयात् ।

तस्य वायुप्रवेशोऽपि सषुमग्णायाम्भवेदध्रुवम ॥९६॥

nirantakṛtābhyāsātṣaṇmāsaiḥ siddhimāpnuyāt /

tasya vāyupraveśo'pi suṣumṇāyāmbhaveddhruvam /96/

He achieves perfection in six months through constant practice, and certainly his *vāyu* enters into the middle psychic pathway. –96.

मनोजयञ्च लभते वायुबिन्दुविधारणात् ।

ऐहिकामुष्मिकीसिद्धिर्भवेन्नैवात्र संशयः ॥९७॥

manojayañca labhate vāyubinduvidhāraṇāt /

aihikāmuṣmikīsidhirbhavennaivātra samśayaḥ /97/

He gains mastery over his mind through the control of his *vāyu* and *bindu* (the seminal fluid); there is no doubt he attains perfection in this world and the next beyond it. –97.

2. Svādhiṣṭhāna Cakra

अथ स्याधिष्ठानचक्रविवरणम् ।

द्वितीयन्तु सरोजञ्च लिंगमूले व्यवस्थितम् ।

बादिलान्तं च षड्वर्ण परिभाष्वरषडदलम् ॥९८॥

स्वधिष्ठानाभिधं तत्त् पंकजं शोणरूपकम् ।

बालाख्यो यत्र सिद्धोऽस्ति देवी यत्रास्ति राकिणी ॥९९॥

atha svādhiṣṭhānacakravivaraṇam /

dvitīyantu sarojañca liṅgamūle vyavasthitam /

bādilāntaṃ ca ṣaḍvarṇaṃ paribhāsvaraṣaḍdalam /98/

svādhiṣṭhānābhidhaṃ tattu paṅkajaṃ śoṇarūpakam /

bālākyo yatra siddho'sti devī yatrāsti rākiṇī /99/

Now the explanation of the *Svādhiṣṭhāna Cakra* begins.

The second *cakra* is located at the base of the penis. It has six brilliant petals decorated with the letters *ba*, *bha*, *ma*, *ya*, *ra*, and *la*. The color of this *cakra* called *svādhiṣṭhāna* is red like blood. There preside *Siddha* (the adept) called *Bālā* and the goddess *Rākiṇī*. –98-99.

यो ध्यायति सदा दिव्यं स्वाधिष्ठानारविन्दकम् ।

तस्य कामङ्गनाः सर्वा भजन्ते काममोहिताः ॥१००॥

yo dhyāyati sadā divyaṃ svādhiṣṭhānāravindakam /

tasya kāmāṅganāḥ sarvā bhajante kāmamohitāḥ /100/

He who daily concentrates on *svādhiṣṭhāna* lotus, he is adorned and loved by all the beautiful amorous women infatuated by love. –100.

विविधञ्चाश्रुतं शास्त्रं निःशङ्को वै भवेद्ध्रुवम् ।
सर्वरोगविनिर्मुक्तो लोके चरति निर्भयः ॥१०१॥

vividhañcāśrutaṃ śāstraṃ nihśaṅko vai bhaveddhruvam /
sarvarogavinirmukto loke carati nirbhayaḥ /101/

He certainly explains the various *Śāstras* unheard to him before without any doubt. He fearlessly moves throughout this world being free from all diseases. –101.

मरणं खाद्यते तेन स केनापि न खाद्यते ।
तस्य स्यात्परमा सिद्धिरणिमादिगुणप्रदा ॥१०२॥
वायु सञ्चरते देहे रसवृद्धिर्भवेद्ध्रुवम् ।
आकाशपङ्कजगलत्पीयूषमपि वर्द्धते ॥१०३॥

maraṇam khādyate tena sa kenāpi na khādyate /
tasya syātparamā siddhiraṇimādiguṇapradā /102/
vāyu sañcarate dehe rasavṛddhirbhaveddhruvam /
ākāśapaṅkajagalatpīyūṣamapi varddhate /103/

He eats death; he is not eaten by anything. He receives the supreme powers like *aṇimā*, etc.; the *vāyu* moves harmoniously throughout his body. Surely, the fluids are increased in his body. The nectar secreting from the *ākāśa paṅkaja* (the thousand petalled lotus) is also increased in his body. –102-103.

3. Maṇipura Cakra

अथ मणिपुरचक्रविवरणम् ।
तृतीयं पङ्कजं नाभौ मणिपुरसंज्ञकम् ।
दशारण्डादिफान्तार्णं शोभितं हेमवर्णकम् ॥१०४॥

atha maṇipuracakravivaraṇam /
tṛtīyaṃ paṅkajaṃ nābhau maṇipurasañjñakam /
daśāraṇḍādiphāntārṇaṃ śobhitaṃ hemavarṇakam /104/

Now *maṇipura cakra* is described.

The third *cakra* called *maṇipura* is located on the navel. It has a golden colour. The ten petals of this *cakra* are decorated with the letters from *ḍa* to *pha* (they are: *ḍa*, *ḍha*, *ṇa*, *ta*, *tha*, *da*, *dha*, *na*, *pa* and *pha*). –104.

रुद्राख्यो यत्र सिद्धोऽस्त सर्वमङ्गलदायकः ।

तत्रस्था लाकिनी नाम्नी देवी परमधार्मिका ॥१०५॥

rudrākyo yatra siddho'ti sarvamaṅgaladāyakaḥ /

tatrasthā lākinī nāmnī devī paramadhārmikā /105/

The adept called *Rudra*, the giver of all auspicious objects, and the most virtuous Goddess, named *Lākinī*, preside there. –105.

तस्मिन् ध्यानं सदा योगी करोति मणिपूरके ।

तस्य पातालसिद्धिः स्यान्निरन्तरसुखावहा ॥१०६॥

ईप्सितञ्च भवेल्लोके दुःखरोगविनाशनम् ।

कालस्य वञ्चनञ्चापि परदेहप्रवेशनम् ॥१०७॥

tasmin dhyānaṃ sadā yogī karoti maṇipūrake /

tasya pātālasiddhiḥ syānnirantarasukhāvahā /106/

īpsitañca bhavelloke duḥkharogavināśanam /

kālasya vañcanañcāpi paradehapraveśanam /107/

The yogi who always concentrates on *maṇipura cakra* achieves *pātāla siddhi* (the perfection that constant happiness flows to the yogi). All his desires are fulfilled in this world; his miseries and diseases are destroyed. He deceives death and also can enter into the body of another. –106-107.

जाम्बूनदादिकरणं सिद्धानां दर्शनं भवेत् ।

औषधिदर्शनञ्चापि निधीनां दर्शनं भवेत् ॥१०८॥

jāmbūnadādikaraṇaṃ siddhānāṃ darśanaṃ bhavet /

auṣadhidarśanañcāpi nidhīnāṃ darśanaṃ bhavet /108/

He can create gold; can have the vision of the adepts, recognize the medicines and see the wealth underground. –108.

4. Anāhata Cakra

अथ अनाहतचक्रविवरणम् ।

हृदयेऽनाहतं नाम चतुर्थ पङ्कजं भवेत् ।

कादिठान्तार्णसंस्थानं द्वादशारसमन्वितम ॥

अतिशोणं वायुबीजं प्रसादस्थानमीरितम् ॥१०६॥

atha anāhatacakravivaraṇam

hṛdaye'nāhataṃ nāma caturthaṃ paṅkajaṃ bhavet /

kādiṭhāntārṇasamsthānaṃ dvādasārasamanvitam /

atiśoṇaṃ vāyubījaṃ prasādasthānamīritam /109/

Now here is the description of *Anāhata Cakra.*

The fourth *cakra* called *anāhata* is located in the heart. The twelve petals of this lotus are followed by the letters *ka*, *kha*, *ga*, *gha*, *ṅa*, *ca*, *cha*, *ja*, *jha*, *ña*, *ṭa* and *ṭha*. Its color is bright red. Its *bīja* (the seed) is of *vāyu*. It is a pleasing place. –109.

पद्मस्थ तत्परं तेजो बाणलिङ्गं प्रकीर्तितम् ।

यस्य स्मरणमात्रेण दृष्टादृष्टफलं लभेत् ॥११०॥

padmasthaṃ tatparaṃ tejo bāṇaliṅgaṃ prakīrtitam /

yasya smaraṇamātreṇa dṛṣṭādṛṣṭaphalaṃ labhet /110/

There is a highly brilliant energy called *bāṇaliṅga* in this *cakra*. One can receive both seen and unseen things through mere concentration on this. –110.

सिद्धः पिनाकी यत्रास्ते काकिनी यत्र देवता ।

एतस्मिन्सततं धयानं हृत्पाथोजे करोति यः ॥

क्षुभ्यन्ते तस्य कान्ता वै कामार्ता दिव्ययोषितः ॥१११॥

siddhaḥ pinākī yatrāste kākinī yatra devatā /

etasminsatataṃ dhyānaṃ hṛtpāthoje karoti yaḥ /

kṣubhyante tasya kāntā vai kāmārtā divyayoṣitaḥ /111/

The adept *Pinākī* and the goddess *Kākinī* preside there. He who constantly concentrates on this heart lotus is fascinated by beautiful women and amorous divine maidens. –111.

ज्ञानञ्चाप्रतिमं तस्य त्रिकालविषयम्भवेत् ।

दूरश्रुतिर्दूरदृष्टिः स्वेच्छया खगतां व्रजेत् ॥११२॥

jñānañcāpratimaṃ tasya trikālaviṣayambhavet /

dūraśrutirduradṛṣṭiḥ svecchayā khagatāṃ vrajet /112/

He gets incomparable knowledge, knows the subject matter of all time (past, present and future); attains the power of clairaudience, clairvoyance and moves in space at his own will. –112.

सिद्धानां दर्शनञ्चापि योगिनी दर्शनं तथा ।

भवेत्खेचरसिद्धिश्च खेचराणां जयन्तथा ॥११३॥

siddhānāṃ darśanañcāpi yoginī darśanaṃ tathā /

bhavetkhecarasiddhiśca khecarāṇāṃ jayantathā /113/

He visualizes adepts and *Yoginis* (the female attendants of *Śiva* or *Durgā*); he receives *khecarī siddhi* (the perfection of flying in space), and gains mastery over all the creatures moving in the air. – 113.

Bāṇaliṅga

यो ध्यायति परं नित्यं बाणलिंगं द्वितीयकम् ।

खेचरी भूचरी सिद्धिर्भवेत्तस्य न सशयः ॥११४॥

yo dhyāyati paraṃ nityaṃ bāṇaliṅgaṃ dvitiyakam /

khecarī bhūcarī siddhirbhavettasya na samśayaḥ /114/

He who regularly concentrates on the second *Vāṇaliṅga* (the *Śiva Liṅga* located in the middle of the *anāhata cakra*), certainly achieves *khecarī siddhi* (the perfection moving in space) and *bhūcārī siddhi* (the perfection of traveling the universe at one's will). –114.

एतदुध्यानस्य महात्म्य कथितुं नव शक्यते ।

ब्रह्माद्याः सकला देवा गोपयन्ति परन्त्विदम् ॥११५॥

etaddhyānasya māhātmyaṃ kathituṃ naiva śakyate /

brahmādyāḥ sakalā devā gopayanti parantvidam /115/

The glory of the meditation on *anāhata cakra* cannot be described fully; even the gods like *Brahmā* etc., keep it secret. –115.

5. Viśuddhi Cakra

अथ विशुद्धचक्रविरिणम् ।

कण्ठस्थानस्थितं पद्मं विशुद्धं नामपञ्चमम् ।

सुहेमाभं स्वरोपेतं षोडशस्वरसंयुतम् ॥११६॥

atha viśuddhicakravivaraṇam

kanṭhasthānasthitaṃ padmaṃ viśuddhaṃ nāmapañcamam /

suhemābhaṃ svaropetaṃ ṣoḍaśasvarasamyutam /116/

Now *viśuddhi cakra* is described.

The fifth *cakra* located in the throat is called *viśuddhi.* Its color is bright gold. Its sixteen petals are decorated with sixteen vowel letters (*a, ā, i, ī, u, ū, ṛ, ṝ, lṛ, lṝ, e, ai, o, au, aṃ, aḥ*). –116.

छगलाण्डोऽस्ति सिद्धोऽत्र शाकिनी चाधिदेवता ।

ध्यानं करोति यो नित्यं स योगीश्वरपण्डितः ॥११७॥

chagalāṇḍo'sti siddho'tra śākinī cādhidevatā

dhyānaṃ karoti yo nityaṃ sa yogīśvarapaṇḍitaḥ /117/

The adept called *Chagalāṇḍa* and the goddess *Śākinī* preside there. He who regularly meditates on this *cakra* becomes lord of the yogis and the wise. –117.

किन्त्वस्य योगिनोऽन्यत्र विशुद्धाख्या सरोरुहे ॥

चतुर्वेदा विभासन्ते सरहस्या निधेरिव ॥११८॥

kintvasya yogino'nyatra viśudākhye saroruhe /

caturvedā vibhāsante sarahasyā nidheriva /118/

Why would a yogi who has a mastery over *viśuddhi cakra* need to pursue knowledge elsewhere? The four *Vedas* are revealed to him with their mysteries, just like someone finds a treasury by chance. – 118.

इह स्थाने स्थितो योगी यदा क्रोधवशो भवेत् ।

तदा समस्तं त्रलोक्यं कम्पते नात्र संशय ॥११९॥

iha sthāne sthito yogī yadā krodhavaśo bhavet /

tadā samastaṃ trailokyaṃ kampate nātra saṃśayaḥ /119/

When the yogi situated (having his mind fixed) on this place becomes angry, then all the three worlds tremble without a doubt. – 119.

इह स्थाने मनो यस्य दैवाद्यातिलयं यदा ।

तदा बाह्यं परित्यज्य स्वान्तरे रमते ध्रुवम् ॥१२०॥

iha sthāne mano yasya daivādyātilayaṃ yadā /

tadā bāhyaṃ parityajya svāntare ramate dhruvam /120/

If luckily, the mind of the yogi is absorbed in this place, then he, giving up the external world, certainly enjoys the inner world. –120.

तस्य न क्षतिमायाति स्वशरीरस्य शक्तितः ।

संवत्सरसहस्रेऽपि वज्रातिकठिनस्य वै ॥१२१॥

tasya na kṣatimāyāti svaśarīrasya śaktitaḥ /

samvatsarasahasre'pi vajrātikaṭhinasya vai /121/

His body does not decay, he lives for a thousand years through the energy of his own body; it becomes harder than a thunderbolt. – 121.

यदा त्यजति तदध्यानं योगींन्द्रोऽवनिमण्डले ।

तदा वर्षसहस्राणि मन्यते तत्क्षणं कृति ॥१२२॥

yadā tyajati taddhyānaṃ yogīndro 'vanimaṇḍale /

tadā varṣasahasrāṇi manyate tatkṣaṇaṃ kṛtī /122/

When the great yogi draws his mind out of this meditation in this world, then a thousand years seems to him a few moments only. –122.

6. Ājñācakra

अथ आज्ञाचक्रविवरणम् ।

आज्ञापद्मं भ्रुवोमध्ये हक्षोपेतं द्विपत्रकम् ।

शुक्लाभं तन्महाकालः सिद्धो देव्यत्र हाकिनी ॥१२३॥

atha ājñācakravivaraṇam /

ājñāpadmaṃ bhrūvormadhye hakṣopetaṃ dvipatrakam /

śuklābhaṃ tanmahākālaḥ siddho devyatra hākinī /123/

Now here follows the description of *ājñācakra.*

The lotus with two petals called *ājñā* is endowed with two letters *ham* and *kṣam* and is located between the two eyebrows. Its color is bright white. There preside the adept *Mahākāla* and the goddess *Hākinī*. –123.

शरच्चन्द्रनिभं तत्राक्षरबीजं विजृंभितम् ।

पुमान् परमहंसोऽयं यज्ज्ञात्वा नावसीदति ॥१२४॥

śaraccandranibhaṃ tatrākṣarabījaṃ vijṛmbhitam /

pumān paramahamso 'yaṃ yajjñātvā nāvasīdati /124/

Brilliant as the moon in autumn, there is the manifestation of the *Eternal Bīja*. Having known it, the wise *Paramahaṃsa* (the ascetic in the highest order) does not fall down. –124.

एतदेव परन्तेजः सर्वतन्त्रेषु मन्त्रिणः ।

चिन्तयित्वा परां सिद्धिं लभते नात्र संशयः ॥१२५॥

etadeva parantejaḥ sarvatantreṣu mantriṇaḥ /

cintayitvā parāṃ siddhiṃ labhate nātra samśayaḥ /125/

This supreme light is kept secret in all the *tantras*. There is no doubt that the highest perfection is achieved by pondering over it. – 125.

Turīya Liṅga

तुरीयं त्रितयं लिङ्गं तदाहं मुक्तिदायकः ।

ध्यानमात्रेण योगीन्द्रो मत्समो भवति ध्रुवम् ॥१२६॥

turīyaṃ tritayaṃ liṅgaṃ tadāhaṃ muktidāyakaḥ /

dhyānamātreṇa yogīndro matsamo bhavati dhruvam /126/

I am the *Turīya* (the fourth and final state of the Self in which it becomes one with the Universal Self), the *Third Liṅga* located in the *ājñācakra* and the giver of liberation. The yogi certainly becomes equal to me by merely meditating on it. –126.

Iḍā and Piṅgalā – Varaṇā and Asī

इडा हि पिंगला ख्याता वरणासीति होच्यते ।

वाराणसी तयार्मध्ये विश्वनाथोऽत्र भाषितः ॥१२७॥

iḍā hi piṅgalā khyātā varaṇāsīti hocyate /

vārāṇasī tayormadye viśvanātho'tra bhāṣitaḥ /127/

The two psychic pathways known as *iḍā* and *piṅgalā* are called *Varaṇā* And *Asi*. Situated between them is *Vārāṇasi* (the holy shrine of Lord *Śiva*). It is said that *Viśvanātha* (the Lord of the whole universe –*Śiva*) presides there. –127.

एतत्क्षेत्रस्य महात्म्यमृषिभिस्तत्वदर्शिभिः ।

शास्त्रेषु बहुधा पोक्तं परं तत्वं सुभाषितम् ॥१२८॥

etatkṣetrasya māhātmyamṛṣibhistattvadarśibhiḥ /

śāstreṣu bahudhā proktaṃ paraṃ tattvaṃ subhāṣitam /128/

The sages and truth-seers have beautifully described in many ways the glory of this sacred shrine and *Parama Tattva* (the Ultimate Reality) in the various scriptures. –128.

सुषुम्णा मेरुणा याता ब्रह्मरन्ध्रं यतोऽस्ति वै ।
ततश्चैषा परावृत्य तदाज्ञापद्मदक्षिणे ॥
वामनासापुटं याति गंगेति परिगीयते ॥१२६॥

suṣumṇā meruṇā yātā brahmarandhraṃ yato'sti vai /
tataścaiṣā parāvṛtya tadājñāpadmadakṣiṇe /
vāmanāsāputaṃ yāti gaṅgeti parigīyate /129/

Suṣumṇā passes through *meru* (the spinal column) up to the area where *brahmrandhra* is located. From there, *iḍā* turns back on the right side of *ājñācakra* and goes to the left nostril. It is called the *Gaṅgā*. –129.

ब्रह्मरन्ध्रे हि यत्पद्मं सहस्रारं व्यवस्थितम् ।
तत्र कन्देहि या योनिस्तस्यां चन्द्रो व्यवस्थितः ॥१३०॥
त्रिकोणाकारतस्तस्याः सुधा क्षरति सन्ततम् ।
इडायामामृतं तत्र समं स्रवति चन्द्रमाः ॥१३१॥
अमृतं वहति धारा धारारूपं निरन्तरम् ।
वामनासापुटं याति गंगेत्युक्ता हि योगिभिः ॥१३२॥

brahmarandhre hi yatpadmaṃ sahasrāraṃ vyavasthitam /
tatra kandehi yā yonistasyāṃ candro vyavasthitaḥ /130/
trikoṇākāratastasyāḥ sudhā kṣarati santatam /
iḍāyāmamṛtaṃ tatra samaṃ sravati candramāḥ /131/
amṛtaṃ vahati dhārā dhārārūpaṃ nirantaram /
vāmanāsāputaṃ yāti gaṅgetyuktvā hi yogibhiḥ /132/

It is in the *brahmarandra* where *sahasrāra cakra* (the thousand petalled lotus) is located. At the base of it there is the *yoni* in which the moon presides. The nectar is constantly secreted through that triangular shaped *yoni*. This immortal fluid of the moon continuously trickles down through the *iḍā*. The fountain of the nectar flows constantly in a stream and reaches the left nostril. Thus it is called the *Gaṅgā* by the yogis. –130-132.

आज्ञापङ्कजदक्षांसाद्वामनासापुटंगता ।

उदग्वहेति तत्रेडा वरणा समुदाहृता ॥१३३॥

ājñāpaṅkajadakṣāmsādvāmanāsāpuṭam gatā /

udagvaheti tatreḍā varaṇā samudāhṛtā /133/

From the right side of the *ājñācakra* the *iḍā* goes to the left nostril. Here this end point of the *iḍā* is called *Varaṇā* (the northward flowing *Gaṅgā*). –133.

ततो द्वयोर्हिमध्ये तु वाराणसीति चिन्तयेत् ।

तदाकारा पिंगलापी तदाज्ञाकमलाल्तरे ॥

दक्षनासापुट याति प्रोक्तास्माभिरसीति वै ॥१३४॥

tato dvayorhi madhye tu vārāṇasīti cintayet /

tadākārā piṅgalāpi tadājñākamalāntare /

dakṣanāsāpuṭe yāti proktāsmābhirasīti vai /134/

The yogi should concentrate on the space between the two (the *iḍā* and *piṅgalā*) regarding it as *Vārāṇasī*. Similar to the *iḍā*, the *piṅgalā* goes from the left side of the *ājñācakra* to right nostril. Here we have called it *Asi*. –134.

मूलाधारे हि यत्पदेमं चतुष्पत्र व्यवस्थितम् ।

तत्र मध्येहि या योनिस्तस्यां सूर्यो व्यवस्थितः ॥१३५॥

mūlādhāre hi yatpadmaṃ catuṣpatraṃ vyavasthitam /

tatra madhye hi yā yonistasyāṃ sūryo vyavasthitaḥ /135/

The *cakra* located in the *mūlādhāra* has four petals. There is the *yoni* in its center where the sun dwells. –135.

तत्सूर्यमण्डलद्वाराद्विषं क्षरति सन्ततम् ।

पिंगलायां विषं तत्र समर्पयति तापनः ॥१३६॥

tatsūryamaṇḍaladvārādviṣaṃ kṣarati santatam /

piṅgalāyāṃ viṣaṃ tatra samarpayati tāpanaḥ /136/

There a poison continuously oozes through the orb of the sun. The sun passes that poison over to the *piṅgalā* pathway. –136.

विषं तत्र वहन्ती या धारारूपं निरन्तरम् ।

दक्षनासपुटे याति कल्पितेयन्तु पूर्ववत् ॥१३७॥

viṣaṃ tatra vahantī yā dhārārūpaṃ nirantaram /

dakṣanāsāpuṭe yāti kalpiteyantu pūrvavat /137/

The poison (from the sun) continuously flows there in a stream and it goes to the right nostril, as the previously mentioned nectar of the moon goes to the left nostril. –137.

आज्ञापङ्कजवामास्याद्दक्षनासापुटं गता ।

उदग्वहा पिंगलापि पुरासीति प्रकीर्तिता ॥१३८॥

ājñāpaṅkajavāmāsyāddakṣanāsāpuṭam gatā /

udagvahā piṅgalāpi purāsīti prakīrtitā /138/

The pathway that passes through *ajñācakra* on the left and goes to the right nostril is the northward flowing *piṅgalā.* It has also been known as *Purā* (former or of yore) *Asi.* –138.

Ājñācakrā – the Supreme Temple of Śiva

आज्ञापद्ममिदं प्रोक्तं यत्र देवो महेश्वरः ।

पीठत्रयं ततश्चोर्ध्व निरुक्तं योगचिन्तकैः ॥

तद्बिन्दुनादशक्त्याख्यं भालपद्मे व्यवस्थितम् ॥१३९॥

ājñāpadmamidaṃ proktaṃ yatra devo maheśvaraḥ /

pīṭhatrayaṃ tataścordhvaṃ niruktaṃ yogacintakaiḥ /

tadbindunādaśaktyākhyaṃ bhālapadme vyavasthitam /139/

In the *ajñācakra* described here, presides the god *Maheśvara* (the Great Lord). *yogacintakas* (literally, the thinkers of yoga, yogis) give certain details of three shrines above this *cakra*. They are called *Vindu*, *Nāda* and *Śakti*, and they are properly placed in *bhālapadma* (the lotus in the forehead i.e. the *ajñācakra*). –139.

यः करोति सदाध्यानमाज्ञापद्‌मस्य गोपितम् ।

पूर्वजन्मकृतं कर्म विनश्येदविरोधतः ॥१४०॥

yah karoti sadādhyānamājñāpadmasya gopitam /

pūrvajanmakṛtaṃ karma vinaśyedavirodhataḥ /140/

He, who always meditates on this *ajñācakra* in secrecy, destroys all the karmas done in his past life in a congenial (cordial) way. –140.

Meditation on Ājñācakra

इह स्थिते यदा योगी ध्यानं कुर्यान्निरन्तरम् ।

तदा करोति प्रतिमां पूजाजपमनर्थवत् ॥१४१॥

iha sthite yadā yogī dhyānaṃ kuryānnirantaram /

tadā karoti pratimāṃ pūjājapamanarthavat /141/

When the yogi constantly meditates focusing in this place, then for him the worship of idols or statues (the external forms of gods/deities) and repetition of *mantras* seem to be worthless. –141.

यक्षराक्षसगन्धर्वा अप्सरो गणकिन्नराः ।

सेवन्ते चरणौ तस्य सर्वे तस्य वशानुगाः ॥१४२॥

yakṣarākṣasagandharvā apsarogaṇakinnarāḥ

sevante caraṇau tasya sarve tasya vaśānugāḥ /142/

The *Yakṣas* (the attendants and the guards of *Kubera*, the God of wealth), *Rākṣasas* (the demons), *Gandharvas* (the celestial singers or musicians of gods) *Apsarā Gaṇa* (the class of celestial dancing girls at the court of *Indra*, the king of heaven), and *Kinnaras* (the mythical beings with human bodies and horses' heads reckoned among the *Gandharvas*) serve at his feet. –142.

करोति रसनां योगी प्रविष्टां विपरितगाम् ।

लम्बिकोर्ध्वेषु गर्तेषु धृत्वा ध्यानं भयापहम् ॥१४३॥

अस्मिन् स्थाने मनो यस्य क्षणार्ध वर्ततेऽचलम् ।

तस्य सर्वाणि पापानि संक्षयं यान्ति तत्क्षणात् ॥१४४॥

karoti rasanāṃ yogī praviṣṭāṃ viparītagām /

lambikordhveṣu garteṣu dhṛtvā dhyānaṃ bhayāpaham /143/

asmin sthāne mano yasya kṣaṇārdhaṃ vartate'calam /

tasya sarvāṇi pāpāni saṅkṣayaṃ yānti tatkṣaṇāt /144/

Turning the tongue upward, inserting it into the pit of the palate and holding it there, the yogi should meditate, which will destroy all fear. He whose mind stays steady here even for a moment, his multifarious sins are destroyed right away. –143-144.

Results of All Cakras from Ājñācakra Meditation

यानि यानि हि प्रोक्तानि पंचपद्मे फलानि वै ।

तानि सर्वाणि सुतरामेतज्ज्ञानाद्भवन्ति हि ॥१४५॥

yāni yāni hi proktāni pañcapadme phalāni vai /

tāni sarvāṇi sutarāmetajjñānādbhavanti hi /145/

All types of perfections that have been described earlier resulting from the meditation on each of the other five *cakras*, are certainly received through the knowledge (the experienced meditative skillfulness) of *ajñācakra* alone. –145.

यः करोति सदाभ्यासमाज्ञा पद्मे विचक्षणः ।

वासनाया महाबन्ध तिरस्कृत्य प्रमोदते ॥१४६॥

yaḥ karoti sadābhyāsamājñāpadme vicakṣaṇaḥ /

vāsanāyā mahābandhaṃ tiraskṛtya pramodate /146/

The wise man who constantly practices meditation on the *ajñācakra*, having disregarded the great bondage of passion, lives happily. –146.

प्राणप्रायाणसमये तत्पदमं यः स्मरन्सुधीः ।

त्यजेत्प्राण स धर्मात्मा परमात्मनि लीयते ॥१४७॥

prāṇaprayāṇasamaye tatpadaṃ yaḥ smaransudhīḥ /

tyajetprāṇaṃ sa dharmātmā paramātmani līyate /147/

When the yogi meditates on this *cakra* at the time of his death, after leaving the body, the virtuous one is merged in the *Paramātmā* (the Ultimate Self). –147.

तिष्ठन् गच्छन् जाग्रत् यो ध्यानं कुरुते नरः ।

पापकर्मविकुर्वाणो नहि मज्जति किल्विषे ॥१४८॥

tiṣṭhan gacchan svapan jāgratyo dhyānaṃ kurute naraḥ /

pāpakarmavikurvāṇo nahi majjati kilviṣe /148/

He who meditates on this *cakra* while sitting, walking, sleeping and waking, is not smeared by the sins even if he were to involve in sinful acts. –148.

योगी बन्धाद्विनिर्मुक्तः स्वीयया प्रभया स्वयम् ।

द्विदलध्यानमाहात्म्यं कथितुं नैव शक्यते ॥

ब्रह्मादिदेवताश्चैव किञ्चिन्मतो विदन्ति ते ॥१४९॥

yogī bandhādvinirmuktaḥ svīyayā prabhayā svayam /

dvidaladhyānamāhātmyaṃ kathituṃ naiva śakyate /

brahmādidevatāścaiva kiñcinmatto vidanti te /149/

The yogi himself is freed from the shackle of bondage through his own endeavor. The significance of the meditation of the two-petalled *cakra* cannot be described completely. Even the gods like *Brahma*, etc., know a little bit about it from me. –149.

7. Sahasrāra Cakra

अतः ऊर्ध्वं तालुमूले सहस्रारं सरोरुहम् ।

अस्ति यत्र सुषम्णाया मूलं सविवरं स्थितम् ॥१५०॥

ata ūrdhvaṃ tālumūle sahasrāraṃ saroruham /

asti yatra suṣumṇāyā mūlaṃ savivaraṃ sthitam /150/

Sahasrāra cakra (the thousand petalled lotus) is at the base of the palate above *ajñācakra* where the root of *suṣumnā*, with its hollow, is located. –150.

तालुमूले सुषुम्णा सा अधोवक्त्रा प्रवर्तते ।

मूला धारेणयोन्यस्ताः सर्वनाड्यः समाश्रिताः ॥

ता बीजभूतास्तत्त्वस्य ब्रह्ममार्गप्रदायिकाः ॥१५१॥

tālumūle suṣumṇā sā adhovaktrā pravartate /

mūlādhāreṇayonyastāḥ sarvanāḍyaḥ samāśritāḥ /

tā bījabhūtāstattvasya brahmamārgapradāyikāḥ /151/

The *suṣumṇā* located at the base of the palate has its face turned downward. All the *nāḍis* from the base of the palate down to *mūlādhāra* and *yoni* are entirely under its shelter. These *nāḍis* are the seeds of elements and guide one to the path of *Brahma* (the Ultimate Self). –151.

तालुस्थाने च यत्पद्मं सहस्रारं पुराहितम् ।

तत्कन्दे योनिरेकास्ति पश्चिमाभिमुखी मता ॥१५२॥

tālusthāne ca yatpadmaṃ sahasrāraṃ puroditam /

tatkande yonirekāsti paścimābhimukhī matā /152/

The *cakra* located at the base of the palate is called *sahasrāra.* In its bulbous root there is a *Yoni* with its face downwards. –152.

तस्या मध्ये सुषुम्णाया मूलं सविवरं स्थितम् ।

ब्रह्मरन्ध्रं तदेवोक्तमामूलाधारपङ्कजम् ॥१५३॥

tasyā madhye suṣumṇāyā mūlaṃ savivaraṃ sthitam /

brahmarandhraṃ tadevoktamāmūlādhārapaṅkajam /153/

In the middle of it (the *yoni*), there is the root of *suṣumṇā*, with its hollow, called *brahmarandhra* (the hole that leads to *Brahma*) that expands down to *mūlādhāra*. –153.

ततस्तद्रन्ध्रे तच्छक्तिः सुषुम्णा कुण्डली सदा ।

सुषुम्णायां सदा शक्तिश् चित्रा स्यान्मम वल्लभे ॥

तस्यां मम मते कार्या ब्रह्मरन्ध्रादिकल्पना ॥१५४॥

tatastadrandhre tacchaktiḥ suṣumṇā kuṇḍalī sadā /

suṣumṇāyāṃ sadā śaktiścitrā syānmama vallabhe /

tasyāṃ mama mate kāryā brahmarandhrādikalpanā /154/

In that hollow of the *suṣumṇā*, its energy the *Kuṇḍalinī* always dwells. There is also a dynamic energy in the *suṣumṇā* that is called *citrā*, which is dear to me. In my opinion it is known or understood as *brahmarandhra* according to its actions. –154.

यस्याः स्मरमात्रेण ब्रह्मज्ञत्वं प्रजायते ।

पापक्षयश्च भवति न भूयः पुरुषो भवेत् ॥१५५॥

yasyāḥ smaraṇamātreṇa brahmajñatvaṃ prajāyate /

pāpakṣayaśca bhavati na bhūyaḥ puruṣo bhavet /155/

One gains the knowledge of *Brahma* by merely remembering it; his sins are destroyed, and he is not born again. –155.

प्रवेशितं चलाङ्गुष्ठं मुखे स्वस्य निवेशयेत् ।

तेनात्र न वहत्येव देहचारी समीरणः ॥१५६॥

praveśitaṃ calāṅguṣṭhaṃ mukhe svasya niveśayet /

tenātra na vahatyeva dehacārī samīraṇaḥ /156/

The *sādhaka* (the practitioner) should insert his right hand thumb into his mouth and close it. By this the *prāṇa* that flows in the body is stopped. –156.

Only Kuṇḍalinī Able to Pierce Through the Knots

तेन संसारचक्रेऽस्मिन् भ्रमतीत्येव सर्वदा ।
तदर्थं ये प्रवर्तन्ते योगीनः प्राणधारणे ॥१५७॥
तत एवाखिला नाडी विरुद्धा चाष्टवेष्टनम् ।
इयं कुण्डलिनी शक्ति रन्ध्रं त्यजति नान्यथा ॥१५८॥

tena samsāracakre'smin bhramatītyeva sarvadā /
tadarthaṃ ye pravartante yogīnaḥ prāṇadhāraṇe /157/
tata evākhilā nāḍī niruddhā cāṣṭaveṣṭanam /
iyaṃ kuṇḍalinī śakti randhraṃ tyajati nānyathā /158/

It is due to (the flow of) this *prāṇa* that all beings always wander in the cycle of death and birth in this world. Therefore, the yogis make an effort to hold the *prāṇa* suspended. All the *nāḍis* are bound by the eight knots (bondages) i.e. passion, anger etc., only this *Kuṇḍalinī* force is capable of piercing through the hollow of *suṣumṇā* and there is no other way out. –157-158.

यदा पूर्णासु नाडीषु सन्निरुद्धानिलास्तदा ।
बन्धत्यागेन कुण्डल्या मुखं रन्ध्रात् बहिर्भवेत् ॥
सुषुम्णायं सदैवायं वहेत्प्राणसमीरणः ॥१५९॥

yadā pūrṇāsu nāḍiṣu sanniruddhānilāstadā /
bandhatyāgena kuṇḍalyā mukhamrandhrāt bahirbhavet /
suṣumṇāyāṃ sadaivāyaṃ vahetprāṇasamīraṇaḥ /159/

When the *prāṇa* is fully suspended in all the *nāḍis*, then the *Kuṇḍalinī* leaving those knots penetrates and passes out through the hollow of *brahmarandhra*. After that the *prāṇa* constantly flows through the *suṣumṇā*. –159.

मूलपद्मस्थिता योनिर्वामदक्षिणकोणतः ।
इडापिंगलयोर्मध्ये सुषुम्णा योनिमध्यगा ॥१६०॥

mūlapadmasthitā yonirvāmadakṣiṇakoṇataḥ /
iṇāpiṅgalayormadhye suṣumṇā yonimadhyagā /160/

Iḍā and *piṅgalā* are on the right and the left side of the *yoni* situated in the *mūlādhāra cakra. Suṣumṇā* (the middle psychic channel) passes through in the middle of the *yoni* between the *iḍā* and *piṅgalā*. –160.

ब्रह्मरन्ध्रं तु तत्रैव सुषुम्णाधारमण्डले ।

यो जानति स मुक्तः स्यात्कर्मबन्धाद्विचक्षणः ॥१६१॥

brahmarandhraṃ tu tatraiva suṣumṇādhāramaṇḍale /

yo jānāti sa muktaḥ syātkarmabandhādvicakṣaṇaḥ /161/

There is also *brahmarandhrā* (literally, the hole or way to *Brahma*) in the orb of the *ādhāra cakra*. The wise yogi who knows it is liberated from the bondage of karma. –161.

The Holy Bath at Triveṇi/Prayāga

ब्रह्मरन्ध्रमुखे तासां संगमः स्यादसंशयः ।

तस्मिन्स्नाने स्नातकानां मुक्तिः स्यादविरोधतः ॥१६२॥

brahmarandhramukhe tāsāṃ saṅgama syādasaṃśayaḥ /

tasminsnāne snātakānāṃ muktiḥ syādavirodhataḥ /162/

The meeting point of all three psychic channels is certainly in the mouth of *brahma- randhra*. He who takes a holy bath there achieves unfailing liberation. –162.

Iḍā, Piṅgala and Suṣumṇā – Gaṅgā, Jamunā and Sarasvatī

गंगायमुनयोर्मध्ये बहत्येषा सरस्वती ।

तासां तु संगमे स्नात्वा धन्यो याति परां गतिम् ॥१६३॥

gaṅgāyamunayormadhye vahatyeṣā sarasvatī /

tāsām tu saṅgame snātvā dhanyo yāti parāṃ gatim /163/

This *Sarasvatī* flows in between the *Gaṅgā* and *Jamunā*. By taking a holy bath at their confluence, the practitioner becomes fortunate enough and attains *Parama Gati* (the highest state – liberation). –163.

इडा गंगा पुरा प्रोक्ता पिंगला चार्कपुत्रिका ।
मध्या सरस्वती प्रोक्ता तासां संगोऽतिदुर्लभः ॥१६४॥

iḍā gaṅgā purā proktā piṅgalā cārkaputrikā /
madhyā sarasvatī proktā tāsāṃ saṅgo'tidurlabhaḥ /164/

It has already been said that *iḍā* is the *Gaṅgā*, *piṅgalā* is the *Jamunā* the daughter of the sun and *suṣumṇā* in the middle is the *Sarasvatī*; the confluence of all these three is the most rare. –164.

सितासिते संगमे यो मनसा स्नानमाचरेत् ।
सर्वपापविनिर्मुक्तो याति ब्रह्म सनातनम् ॥१६५॥

sitāsite saṅgame yo manasā snānamācaret /
sarvapāpavinirmukto yāti brahma sanātanam /165/

He who takes a mental bath at the confluence of the *White Gaṅgā* (the *iḍā*) and the *Black Jamunā* (the *piṅgalā*), being freed from all sins, reaches the eternal *Brahma*. –165.

Triveṇī – the Best Shrine for Obsequial Rites

त्रिवेण्यां संगमे यो वै पितृकर्म समाचरेत् ।
तारयित्वा पितन्सर्वान्स याति परामां गतिम् ॥१६६॥

triveṇyāṃ saṅgame yo vai pitṛkarma samācaret /
tārayitvā pitṝnsarvānsa yāti paramāṃ gātim /166/

He who performs the obsequial rites (oblation or sacrifice offered to one's ancestors) at the confluence of this *Triveṇī* (the meeting point of three rivers) delivers liberation to his ancestors and also attains the highest state. –166.

नित्यं नैमित्तिकं काम्यं प्रत्यहं यः समाचरेत् ।
मनसा चिन्तयित्वा त सोऽक्षयं फलमाप्नुयात् ॥१६७॥

nityaṃ naimittikaṃ kāmyaṃ yaḥ samācaret
manasā cintayitvā tu so'kṣayaṃ phalamāpnuyāt /167/

He who mentally performs *nitya* (regular), *naimittika* (periodical) and *kāmya* (optional) karmas every day here receives imperishable fruit. –167.

सकृद्यः कुरुते स्नानं स्वर्गे सौख्यं भुनक्ति सः ।

दग्धवा पापानशेषान्वै योगी शुद्धमतिः स्वयम् ॥१६८॥

sakṛdhyaḥ kurute snānam svarge saukhyaṃ bhunakti saḥ /

dagdhvā pāpanaśeṣānvai yogī śuddhamatiḥ svayam /168/

He who takes a bath here once enjoys heavenly happiness, his multifarious sins are totally burnt down, and he himself becomes a pure-minded yogi. –168.

अपवित्रः पवित्रो वा सर्वावस्थां गतोऽपि वा ।

स्नानाचरणमात्रेण पूतो भवति नान्यथा ॥१६९॥

apavitraḥ pavitro vā sarvāvasthāṃ gato'pi vā /

snānācaraṇamātreṇa pūto bhavati nānyathā /169/

Whether the practitioner is pure or impure, or in whatever condition he may be, by merely taking a bath here, he is certainly purified. –169.

मृत्युकाले प्लुतं देहं त्रिवेण्याः सलिले यदा ।

विचिन्त्य यस्त्यजेत्पाणान्स तदा मोक्षमाप्नुयात् ॥१७०॥

mṛtyukāle plutaṃ dehaṃ triveṇyāḥ salile yadā /

vicintya yastyajetprāṇānsa tadā mokṣamāpnuyāt /170/

At the time of death, he who dies thinking that his body is floating in the holy water of *Triveṇī*, attains *mokṣa* (liberation) right then. –170.

The Holy Shrine of All Three Worlds

नातः परतरं गुह्यं त्रिषु लोकेषु विद्यते ।

गोप्तव्यं तत्प्रयत्नेन न व्याख्येयं कदाचन ॥१७१॥

nātaḥ parataraṃ guhyaṃ triṣu lokeṣu vidyate /

goptavyaṃ tatprayatnena na vyākhyeyaṃ kadācana /171/

There is no greater secret than this one in all the three worlds. It should be kept secret and it should never be explained. –171.

ब्रह्मरन्ध्रे मनो दत्वा क्षणाध यदि तिष्ठति ।

सर्वपापविनिर्मुक्तः स याति परमां गतिम् ॥१७२॥

brahmarandre mano dattvā kṣaṇārdhaṃ yadi tiṣṭhati /

sarvapāpavinirmuktaḥ sa yāti paramāṃ gatim /172/

If the mind remains concentrated even for half a moment after fixing it on the *brahma- randhra*, one is freed from all his sins and attains the highest state. –172.

अस्मिन लीन मनो यस्य स योगी मयि लीयते ।

अणिमादिगुणान्भुक्त्वा स्वेच्छया पुरुषोत्तमः ॥१७३॥

asmin līnaṃ mano yasya sa yogī mayi līyate /

aṇimādiguṇānbhuktvā svecchayā puruṣottamaḥ /173/

The excellent yogi, whose mind is dissolved in it, merges in me after enjoying the perfection of *aṇimā*, etc. and the three qualities of nature, at his will. –173.

एतद्रन्ध्रध्यानमात्रेण मर्त्यः संसारेऽस्मिन्वल्लभो मे भवेत्सः ।

पापाञ्जित्वा मुक्तिमार्गाधिकारी ज्ञानं दत्वा तारयत्यद्भुतं वै ॥१७४॥

etadrandhradhyānamātreṇa martyaḥ

samsāre'sminvallabho me bhavetsaḥ /

pāpāñjitvā muktimārgādhikarī

jñānaṃ dattvā tārayatyadbhutaṃ vai /174/

Through the meditation of the *brahmarandhra* alone the practitioner becomes dear to me in this world. After conquering his sins, he is entitled to liberation, and by giving the spiritual knowledge, he delivers liberation to other people as well. –174.

चतुर्मुखादित्रिदशैरगम्यं योगिवल्लभम् ।

प्रयत्नेन सगोप्य तदब्रह्मरन्ध्रं मयोदितम् ॥१७५॥

caturmukhāditridaśairagamyaṃ yogivallabham /

prayatnena sugopyaṃ tadbrahmarandhraṃ mayoditam /175/

This knowledge, beloved to yogis, is not accessible even to four-faced *Brahmā* and the other thirty-three gods. This knowledge of *brahmarandhra* (literally, the hole of *Brahma*) given by me should be kept secret with great care. –175.

Meditation of the Divine Sphere of the Moon

पुरा मयोक्ता या योनिः सहस्रारे सरोरुहे ।

तस्याऽधो वर्तते चन्द्रस्तदध्यानं क्रियते बुधैः ॥१७६॥

purā mayoktā yā yoniḥ sahasrāre saroruhe /

tasyā'dho vartate candrastaddhyānaṃ kriyate budhaiḥ /176/

I have explained earlier that there is a *yoni* in the *sahasrāra cakra*. The moon is located below it. The wise yogi should meditate on this moon. –176.

यस्य स्मरमात्रेण योगीन्द्रोऽवनिमण्डले ।

पूज्यो भवति देवानां सिद्धानां सम्मतो भवेत् ॥१७७॥

yasya smaraṇamātreṇa yogīndro'vanimaṇḍale /

pūjyo bhavati devānāṃ siddhānāṃ sammato bhavet /177/

By remembering it alone, the great yogi is honored in this world and he becomes similar and equal to gods and adepts. –177.

शिरःकपालविवरे ध्यायदुदुग्धमहोदधिम ॥

तत्र स्थित्वा सहस्रारे पदमे चन्द्रं विचिन्तयेत् ॥१७८॥

śirahkapālavivare dhyāyaddugdhamahodadhim /

tatra sthitvā sahasrāre padme candraṃ vicintayet /178/

The yogi should meditate on the great ocean of milk in the cavity of the forehead; remaining there he should meditate on the moon located in the *sahasrāra* lotus. –178.

Meditation of Haṃsa

शिरःकपालविवरे द्विरष्टकलायुतः ।

पीयुषभानुहंसाख्यं भावयेत्तं निरंजनम ॥१७९॥

निरन्तरकृताभ्यासात्त्रिदिने पश्यति ध्रुवम् ।

दृष्टिमात्रण पापौघं दहत्वेव स साधकः ॥१८०॥

śirahkapālavivare dvirașṭakalāyutaḥ /

pīyūṣabhānuhamsākhyaṃ bhāvayettaṃ nirañjanam /179/

nirantarakṛtābhyāsāttridine paśyati dhruvam /

dṛṣṭimātreṇa pāpaughaṃ dahatveva sa sādhakaḥ /180/

In the cavity of the forehead there is the brilliant nectar-shedding moon called *Haṃsa*, with its sixteen *kalās* (the digits of the moon). The yogi should meditate on this *Nirañjana* (the *Stainless Pure Being*). He certainly sees it within three days through constant practice. The practitioner burns down all his sins merely by seeing it. –179-180.

अनागतञ्च स्फुरति चित्तशुद्धिर्भवेत्खलु ।

सद्यः कृत्वापि दहति महापातकपञ्चकम् ॥१८१॥

anāgatañca sphurati cittaśuddhirbhavetkhalu /

sadyaḥ kṛtvāpi dahati mahāpātakapañcakam /181/

He knows the future and his mind becomes pure. Through a moment of concentration on this, he at once burns down the five great sins (killing a *Brahman*, taking any types intoxicants, thievery, violating the guru's bed, and the associating with those who have committed these four great sins) even if he were to commit them. – 181.

आनुकूल्यं ग्रहा यान्ति सर्वे नश्यन्त्युपद्रवाः ।

उपसर्गाः शमं यान्ति युद्धे जयमवाप्नुयात् ॥१८२॥

खेचरीभूचरीसिद्धिर्भवेत्क्षीरेन्दुदर्शनात् ।

ध्यानादेवभवेत्सर्वे नात्र कार्या विचारणा ॥१८३॥
सतताभ्यासयोगेन सिद्धो भवति नान्यथा ।
सत्यं सत्यं पुनः सत्यं मम तुल्यो भवेद्ध्रुवम् ॥
योगशास्त्रेऽप्यभिरतं योगिनां सिद्धिदायकम् ॥१८४॥

ānukūlyaṃ grahā yānti sarve naśyantyupadravāḥ /
upasargāḥ śamaṃ yānti yuddhe jayamavāpnuyāt /182/
khecarībhūcarīsiddhirbhavetkṣīrendudarśanāt /
dhyānādevabhavetsarvaṃ nātra kāryā vicāraṇā /183/
satatābhyāsayogena siddho bhavati nānyathā /
satyaṃ satyaṃ punaḥ satyaṃ mama tulyo bhaveddhruvam /
yogaśāstre'pyabhirataṃ yogināṃ siddhidāyakam /184/

All the planets become favorable; all calamities are destroyed; all diseases come to an end; victory is gained in war; the *khecarī* and *bhūcarī* perfections are achieved through the visualization of the moon in the ocean of milk. There is no doubt that all these are results of the meditation on the moon. Through the constant practice of this yoga, the practitioner certainly becomes an adept. It is a reality and the truth again that he becomes equal to me. The constant devotion to the discipline of yoga is the giver of perfection to the yogis. –182-184.

Description of Rāja Yoga

अथ राजयोगकथनम् ।
अतः ऊर्ध्वं दिव्यरूपं सहस्रारं सरोरुहम् ।
ब्रह्माण्डाख्यस्य दहस्य बाह्ये तिष्ठति मुक्तिदम् ॥१८५॥

atha rājayogakathanam /
ataḥ ūrdhvaṃ divyarūpaṃ sahasrāraṃ saroruham /
brahmāṇḍākhyasya dehasya bāhye tiṣṭhati muktidam /185/

Now the *Rāja Yoga* is described.

There is the brilliant *sahasrāra* lotus above the orb of the moon. It is out of this body called *brahmāṇḍa* (the egg of *Brahma* or miniature form of the macro cosmos). It is the giver of liberation. – 185.

Divine Mount Kailāśa

कैलासो नाम तस्यैव महेशो यत्र तिष्ठति ।

नकुलाख्योऽविनाशी च क्षयवृद्धिविवर्जितः ॥१८६॥

kailāso nāma tasyaiva maheśo yatra tiṣṭhati /

nakulākhyo'vināśī ca kṣayavṛddhivivarjitaḥ /186/

It is called Mount *Kailāśa.* There resides *Maheśa* (the great God). He is called *Nakula* (another name of *Śiva*) and is non-decaying, and without reduction or growth. –186.

स्थानस्यास्य ज्ञानमात्रेण नृणां संसारेऽस्मिन्सम्भवो नैव भूयः ।

भूतग्राम सन्तताभ्यासयोगात् कर्तुं हर्तुं स्याच्च शक्तिः समग्रा ॥१८७॥

sthānasyāsya jñānamātreṇa nṝṇāṃ

samsāre'sminsambhavo naiva bhūyaḥ /

bhūtagrāmaṃ santatābhyāsayogāt

kartuṃ hartuṃ syācca śaktiḥ samagrāḥ /187/

When men get the knowledge of this place, it is not possible for them to be born again in this world. The yogi, through the constant practice of yoga, achieves the total power of creating and destroying anything – the collective creation of five elements. –187.

स्थाने परे हंसनिवासभूते कैलासनाम्नीह निविष्टचेताः ।

योगी हृतव्याधिरधः कृताधिर्मायुश्चिरं जीवति मृत्युमुक्तः ॥१८८॥

sthāne pare haṃsanivāsabhūte

kailāsanāmnīha niviṣṭacetāḥ /

yogī hṛtavyādiradhaḥ kṛtādhir-

māyuściraṃ jīvati mṛtyumuktaḥ /188/

When the yogi steadily fixes his mind on the place named *Kailāśa*, the abode of *Parama Haṃsa*, then he destroys all his *vyādhi* (physical diseases, miseries, accidents, etc.) and prolongs his life indefinitely. He lives liberated from death. –188.

चित्तवृत्तिर्यदा लीना कुलाख्ये परमेश्वरे ।

तदा समाधिसाम्येन योगी निश्चलतां व्रजेत् ॥१८६॥

cittavṛttiryadā līnā kulākhye parameśvare /

tadā samādhisāmyena yogī niścalatāṃ vrajet /189/

When the mind of the yogi is dissolved in the *Parameśvara* (the Supreme God) called *kula*, then by the evenness of the *samādhi* (profound state of meditation) he remains in a stable state. –189.

निरन्तरकृते ध्याने जगद्विस्मरणं भवेत् ।

तदा विचित्रसामथ्य योगीनो भवति ध्रुवम् ॥१६०॥

nirantarakṛte dhyāne jagadvismaraṇaṃ bhavet /

tadā vicitrasāmarthyaṃ yogino bhavati dhruvam /190/

Through this constant meditation he forgets the world, and then he certainly achieves miraculous powers. –190.

तस्माद्गलितपीयूषं पिबेद्योगी निरन्तरम् ।

मृत्योर्मृत्युं विधायाशु कुलं जित्वा सरोरुहे ॥६१॥

अत्र कुण्डलिनी शक्तिर्लयं याति कुलाभिधा ।

तदा चतुर्विधा सृष्टिर्लीयते परमात्मनि ॥१६२॥

tasmādgalitapīyūṣaṃ pibedyogī nirantaram /

mṛtyormṛtyuṃ vidhāyāśu kulaṃ jitvā saroruhe /191/

atra kuṇḍalinī śaktirlayaṃ yāti kulābhidhā /

tadā caturvidhā sṛṣṭirlīyate paramātmani /192/

The yogi should constantly drink the nectar that drops down from it (the *sahasrara*); he rules over death, and wins over the *kula* in the lotus. When the *Kuṇḍalinī* force called *kulā* comes to be dissolved here, then the fourfold creation (*jarāyujaḥ*– men or animals born from the womb or viviparous, *aṇḍajaḥ*– birds or fish born from the egg or oviparous, *svedajaḥ*– insects generated by warm vapor or sweat and *udbhijjaḥ*– plants germinated from the earth) is also dissolved in the *Paramātman* (the Ultimate Self). –191-192.

यज्ज्ञात्वा प्राप्य विषयं चित्तवृत्तिर्विलीयते ।

तस्मिन्परिश्रमं योगी करोति निरपेक्षकः ॥१९३॥

yajjñātvā prāpya viṣayaṃ cittavṛttirvilīyate /

tasminpariśramaṃ yogī karoti nirapekṣakaḥ /193/

Upon gaining the knowledge of this *cakra*, all the mental modifications from the sense-objects are dissolved. Therefore, being free from worldly attachments, the yogi should make an effort to gain the experiential knowledge of it. –193.

चित्तवृत्तिर्यदालीना तस्मिन् योगी भवेद् ध्रुवम् ।

तदा विज्ञायतेऽखण्डज्ञानरूपी निरञ्जनः ॥१९४॥

cittavṛttiryadālīnā tasmin yogī bhaved dhruvam /

tadā vijñāyate'khaṇḍajñānarūpī nirañjanaḥ /194/

When the mental modifications of the yogi are dissolved, then he certainly becomes a true yogi; only then does he know Indivisible Pure Self in the form of knowledge. –194.

Meditation of the Great Void

ब्रह्माण्डबाह्ये संचिंत्य स्वप्रतीकं यथोदितम् ।

तमावेश्य महच्छून्यं चिन्तयेदविरोधतः ॥१९५॥

brahmāḍabāhye sañcintya svapratikaṃ yathoditam /

tamāveśya mahacchūnyaṃ cintayedavirodhataḥ /195/

Beyond this microcosm (the body), the practitioner should concentrate on his image as mentioned earlier. Entering into it, he should ponder over *Mahāśūnnya* (the Great Void) constantly. –195.

आद्यान्तमध्यशून्यं तत्कोटीसूर्यसमप्रभम् ।

चन्द्रकोटिप्रतिकाशमभ्यस्य सिद्धिमाप्नुयात् ॥१९६॥

ādyantamadhyaśūnyaṃ tatkotisūryasamaprabham /

candrakotipratīkāśamabhyasya siddhimāpnuyāt /196/

It is void in the beginning, void in the middle and void at the end. It is as brilliant as tens of millions of suns and is as cool as tens of millions of moons. The practitioner should ponder over this *Mahāśūnnya* constantly. –196.

एतदुध्यानं सदा कुर्यादनालस्यं दिने दिने ।

तस्य स्यात्सकला सिद्धिर्वत्सरान्नात्र संशयः ॥१९७॥

etaddhyānaṃ sadā kuryādanālasyaṃ dine dine /

tasya syātsakalā siddhirvatsarānnātra samśayaḥ /197/

He should always practice this meditation without laziness, and he surely receives all perfections within a year. –197.

क्षणार्ध निश्चलं तत्र मनो यस्य भवेद् ध्रुवम् ।

स एव योगी सद्भक्तः सर्वलोकेषु पूजितः ॥

तस्य कल्मषसंघातस्तत्क्षणादेव नश्यति ॥१९८॥

kṣaṇārdhaṃ niścalaṃ tatra mano yasya bhaved dhruvam /

sa eva yogī sadbhaktaḥ sarvalokeṣu pūjitaḥ /

tasya kalmaṣasaṅghātastatkṣaṇādeva naśyati /198/

He whose mind is stable there (in meditation on the Great Void) even for half a moment is certainly a yogi and a virtuous devotee. He is worshipped in all the worlds. His multitudes of sins are destroyed immediately. –198.

यं दृष्ट्वा न प्रवर्तन्ते मृत्युसंसारवर्त्मनि ।

अभ्यसेत्तं प्रयत्नेन स्वाधिष्ठानेन वर्त्मना ॥१९९॥

yaṃ dṛṣṭvā na pravartante mṛtyusamsāravartmani /

abhyasettaṃ prayatnena svādhiṣṭhānena vartmanā /199/

After seeing this Great Void, he does not return to the path of this mortal world; hence, the yogi should practice it with great effort through the path of *svādhiṣṭhāna*. –199.

एतद्ध्यानस्य महात्म्यं मया वक्तुं न शाक्यते ।

यः साधर्यात जानाति सोऽस्माकमपि सम्मतः ॥२००॥

etaddhyānasya māhātmyaṃ mayā vaktuṃ na śakyate /

yaḥ sādhayati jānāti so'smākamapi sammataḥ /200/

I cannot fully describe the glory of this meditation. He who practices it, knows it. I honor the knower of it. –200.

ध्यानादेव विजानाति विचित्रेफलसम्भवम् ।

अणिमादिगुणोपेतो भवत्येव न संशयः ॥२०१॥

dhyānādeva vijānāti vicitrephalasaṃbhavam /

aṇimādiguṇopeto bhavatyeva na saṃśayaḥ /201/

The practitioner knows the various miraculous results that are possible right away through the meditation of it (the Great Void). It is certain that he is endowed with supernatural perfections like *aṇimā*, etc. –201.

Rājādhirāja Yoga

राजयोगो मयाख्यातः सर्वतन्त्रेषु गोपितः ।

राजाधिराजयोगोऽयं कथयामि समासतः ॥२०२॥

rājayogo mayākhyātaḥ sarvatantreṣu gopitaḥ /

rājādhirājayogo'yaṃ kathayāmi samāsataḥ /202/

The *Raja Yoga* that I have described has been kept secret in all the *tantras*. Now I am going to describe the *Rājādhirāja Yoga* (literally, yoga of the king of the kings i.e. the highest yoga) in brief. –202.

स्वस्तिकञ्चासनं कृत्वा सुमठे जन्तुवर्जिते ।

गुरुं संपूज्य यत्नेन ध्यानमेतत्समाचरेत् ॥२०३॥

svastikañcāsanaṃ kṛtvā sumaṭhe jantuvarjite /

guruṃ sampūjya yatnena dhyānametatsamācaret /203/

In a beautiful temple or place without any animals (men, also cattle), the yogi should sit in *svastikāsana* (the auspicious pose). Having properly worshipped his guru, he should practice this meditation with proper effort. –203.

Meditation of the Self Alone

निरालम्बं भवेज्जीवं ज्ञात्वा वेदान्तयुक्तितः ।

निरालम्बं मनः कृत्वा न किञ्चिच्चिन्तयेत्सुधीः ॥२०४॥

nirālambaṃ bhavejjīvaṃ jñātvā vedāntayuktitaḥ /

nirālambaṃ manaḥ kṛtvā na kiñcit cintayetsudhīḥ /204/

By knowing through the arguments of *Vedānta* (one of the six systems of *Hindu* philosophy) that the *Jīva* is self-supported, the wise practitioner should also make his mind independent, and think of nothing else. –204.

एतदुध्यानान्महासिद्धिर्भवत्येव न संशयः ।

वृत्तिहीनं मनः कृत्वा पूर्णरूपं स्वयं भवेत् ॥२०५॥

etaddhyānānmahāsiddhirbhavatyeva na samśayaḥ /

vṛttihīnaṃ manaḥ kṛtvā pūrṇarūpaṃ svayaṃ bhavet /205/

He achieves *mahā siddhi* (the highest perfection) through this meditation. Having made the mind free of its modifications, he becomes *pūrṇa* (completely perfect) in himself. –205.

The Supreme Experience of "I am That"

साधयेत्सततं यो वै स योगी विगतस्पृहः ।

अहंनाम न कोऽप्यस्ति सर्वदात्मैव विद्यते ॥२०६॥

sādhayetsatataṃ yo vai sa yogī vigataspṛhaḥ /

ahamnāma na ko'pyasti sarvadātmaiva vidhyate /206/

In this way, he who constantly practices it becomes a yogi free of passion and desire. He does not utter the word, " I "; for him *Ātmā* (the Self) exists in the whole universe. –206.

को बन्धः कस्य वा मोक्ष एकं पश्येत्सदा हि सः ।

एतत्करोति या नित्यं स मुक्तो नात्र संशयः ॥२०७॥

ko bandhaḥ kasya vā mokṣa ekaṃ paśyetsadā hi saḥ /

etatkaroti yo nityaṃ sa mukto nātra samsayaḥ /207/

What is bondage, what is liberation? He always sees the *One* (the Universal Self) in all. Without a doubt, he who always practices it is truly liberated. –207.

स एव योगी सद्भक्तः सर्वलोकेषु पूजितः ।

अहमस्मीति यन्मत्वा जीवात्मपरमात्मनोः ।

अहं त्वमेतदुभयं त्यक्त्वाऽखण्डं विचिन्तयेत् ॥२०८॥

अध्यारोपापवादाभ्यां यत्र सव विलीयते ।

तदवीजमाश्रयेद्योगी सर्वसंगविवर्जितः ॥२०९॥

sa eva yogī sadbhaktaḥ sarvalokeṣu pūjitaḥ /

ahamasmīti yanmatvā jīvātmaparamātmanoḥ /

ahaṃ tvametadubhayaṃ tyaktvā'khaṇḍaṃ vicintayet /208/

adhyāropāpavādābhyāṃ yatra sarvaṃ vilīyate /

tadbījamāśrayedyogī sarvasaṅgavivarjitaḥ /209/

He is the yogi, he is the virtuous devotee, and he is worshipped in all the worlds who regards that *Jīvātmā* and *Paramātmā* are the same and one as *"I"* and *"Am"* and who gives up both *"I"* and *"Thou"* and thinks over the *Indivisible One* alone. The yogi, being free from all the worldly attachments, should take shelter in that *Bīja* (the *Seed* of the universe) in which this entire illusive world is dissolved by the knowledge of superimposition and refutation. –208-209.

अपरोक्षं चिदानन्दं पूर्णं त्यक्त्वा भ्रमाकुलाः ।

परोक्षं चापरोक्षं च कृत्वा मूढा भ्रमन्ति वै ॥२१०॥

aparokṣaṃ cidānandaṃ pūrṇaṃ tyaktvā bhramākulāḥ /

parokṣaṃ cāparokṣaṃ ca kṛtvā mūḍhā bhramanti vai /210/

The deluded ones, giving up the Supreme who is manifest and who is *Intelligence*, *Bliss* and *Complete*, roam about debating the manifest and the unmanifest. –210.

चराचरमिदं विश्वं परोक्षं यः करोति च ।

अपरोक्षं परं ब्रह्म त्यक्तं तस्मिन् प्रलीयते ॥२११॥

carācaramidaṃ viśvaṃ parokṣaṃ yaḥ karoti ca /

aparokṣaṃ paraṃ brahma tyaktaṃ tasminpralīyate /211/

He who thinks that this movable and immovable universe is unmanifest; he renounces the Supreme *Brahman* – the manifest. Thus, he is dissolved in this universe. –211.

ज्ञानकारणमज्ञानं यथा नोत्पद्यते भृशम् ।

अभ्यासं कुरुत योगी सदा सङ्गविवर्जितम् ॥२१२॥

jñānakāraṇamajñānaṃ yathā notpadyate bhṛśam /

abhyāsaṃ kurute yogī sadā saṅgavivarjitaḥ /212/

The yogi, being free from the worldly attachments, endeavors constantly for the practice of yoga that give rise to knowledge, so that ignorance may not rise up its head excessively. –212.

सर्वेन्द्रियाणि संयम्य विषयेभ्यो विचक्षणः ।

विषयेभ्यः सुषुप्त्यैव तिष्ठेत्संगविवर्जितः ॥२१३॥

sarvendriyāṇi saṃyamya viṣayebhyo vicakṣaṇaḥ /

viṣayebhyaḥ suṣuptyaiva tiṣṭhetsaṅgavivarjitaḥ /213/

Having controlled all his senses from their respective objects, the wise yogi, being free from all types of worldly attachments, stays in the middle of them as he were in a deep sleep. –213.

एवमभ्यासतो नित्यं स्वप्रकाशते ।
श्रोतुं बुद्धिसमर्थाथ निवर्तन्ते गुरोर्गिरः ।
तदभ्यासवशादेकं स्वता ज्ञानं प्रवर्तते ॥२१४॥

evamabhyāsato nityaṃ svaprakāśaṃ prakāśate /
śrotuṃ buddhisamarthārthaṃ nivartante gurorgiraḥ /
tadabhyāsavaśādekaṃ svato jñānaṃ pravartate /214/

In this way, through constant practice the Self-luminous becomes visible. Here comes to an end of all the teachings of the guru that were meant to empower the knowledge of the practitioner. From now on, through his own practice he gains the knowledge spontaneously without any external help. –214.

यतो वाचो निवर्तन्ते अप्राप्य मनसा सह ।
साधनादमलं ज्ञानं स्वयं स्फुरति तद्ध्रुवम् ॥२१५॥

yato vāco nivartante aprāpya manasā saha /
sādhanādamalaṃ jñānaṃ svayaṃ
sphurati taddhruvam /215/

Both the mind and speech are unable to reach that *Ultimate Knowledge* and they return altogether. Certainly, that *Pure Knowledge* (which cannot be described by words and cannot be grasped by the mind) itself shines forth through the constant practice. –215.

Haṭha Yoga and Rāja Yoga – Complementary to One Another

हठं विना राजयोगो राजयोगं विना हठः ।
तस्मात्प्रवर्तते योगी हठे सद्गुरुमार्गतः ॥२१६॥

haṭhaṃ vinā rājayogo rājayogaṃ vinā haṭhaḥ /

tasmātpravartate yogī haṭhe sadgurumārgataḥ /216/

Haṭha Yoga (the physical discipline of yoga) cannot be gained without *Raja Yoga* (the mental discipline yoga) and *Raja Yoga* cannot be attained without *Haṭha Yoga*. Therefore, the yogi should first learn *Haṭha Yoga* through the guidelines of a virtuous guru. – 216.

Life is Meaningless without Spiritual Practice

स्थिते देहे जीवति च यागं न श्रियते भृशम् ।

इन्द्रियार्थोपभोगेषु च जीवति न संशयः ॥२१७॥

sthite dehe jīvati ca yogaṃ na śriyate bhṛśam /

indriyārthopabhogeṣu ca jīvati na samśayaḥ /217/

He who does not devote himself to the practice of yoga while he is still living in this physical body, undoubtedly, he is only living for the enjoyment of sensual pleasures. –217.

अभ्यासपाकपर्यन्तं मितान्नं स्मरणं भवेत् ।

अन्यथा साधनं धीमान् कर्तुं पारयतीहन ॥२१८॥

abhyāsapākaparyantaṃ mitānnaṃ smaraṇaṃ bhavet /

anyathā sādhanaṃ dhīmān kartuṃ pārayatīhana /218/

The wise yogi should always remember that he should be eating little (i.e. be moderate in his diet) until the time he achieves perfection in his practice. Otherwise, he cannot be successful in his practice. –218.

Total Renunciation of Association

अतीवसाधुसंलापोवदेत् संसदिबुद्धिमान् ।

करोति पिण्डरक्षार्थं बह्वालापविवर्जितः ॥२१९॥

त्यज्यते त्यज्यते सङ्गं सर्वथा त्यज्यते भृशम् ।

अन्यथा न लभेन्मुक्तिं सत्यं सत्यं मयोदितम् ॥२२०॥

atīvasādhusamlāpovadet samsadibuddhimān /

karoti piṇḍarakṣyārthaṃ bahvālāpavivarjitaḥ /219/

tyajyate tyajyate saṅgaṃ sarvathā tyajyate bhṛśam /

anyathā na labhenmuktiṃ satyaṃ satyaṃ mayoditam /220/

The wise yogi should speak a few highly auspicious words in a gathering (of people), but not too much. He should eat very little just to sustain his physical body. He should renounce all types of attachments to people and associations; he should definitely renounce them altogether. Otherwise, he cannot achieve liberation. Surely, I am telling you the truth and the truth alone. –219-220.

Execution of Duties as a Detached Actor

गुप्त्यैव क्रियतेऽभ्यासः संगं त्यक्त्वा तदन्तरे ।

व्यवहाराय कर्तव्यो बाह्येसंगानुरागतः ॥२२१॥

स्वे स्वे कर्माणि वर्तन्ते सर्वे ते कर्मसम्भवाः ।

निमित्तमात्रं करणे न दोषोऽस्ति कदाचन ॥२२२॥

guptyaiva kriyate'bhyāsaḥ saṅgaṃ tyktvā tadantare /

vyavahārāya kartavyo bāhyesaṅgānurāgataḥ /221/

sve sve karmaṇi vartante sarve te karmasambhavāḥ /

nimittamātraṃ karaṇe na doṣo'sti kadācana /222/

Giving up all types of attachments to people and associations, he should practice yoga in privacy in an isolated place. He should fulfill all his prescribed duties of his profession according to his social status (caste, rank and stage of life, etc.), while remaining detached from relations outside. He should perform all these simply as a nominal doer. There is no fault in doing so. –221-222.

Householder Unified with Yoga –

Entitled to Liberation

एवं निश्चित्य सुधिया गृहस्थोऽपि यदाचरेत् ।

तदा सिद्धिमवाप्नोति नात्र कार्या विचारणा ॥२२३॥

evam niścitya sudhiyā gṛhastho'pi yadā caret /

tadā siddhimavāpnoti nātra kāryā vicāraṇā /223/

Being mentally certain in this way, even the householder who performs the practice (of yoga) in a wise manner achieves perfection. There is nothing to think otherwise. –223.

पापपुण्यविनिर्मुक्तः परित्यक्ताङ्गसाधकः ।

यो भवेत्स विमुक्तः स्याद्गृहे तिष्ठन्सदा गृही ॥२२४॥

न पापपण्यैर्लिप्येत योगयुक्तो सदा गृही ।

कुर्वन्नपि तदा पापान्स्वकार्ये लोकसंग्रहे ॥२२५॥

pāpapuṇyavinirmuktaḥ parityaktāṅgasādhakaḥ /

yo bhavetsa vimuktaḥ syādgṛhe tiṣṭhansadā gṛhī /224/

na pāpapuṇyairlipyeta yogayukto sadā gṛhī /

kurvannapi tadā pāpānsvakārye lokasaṅgrahe /225/

The yogi who is free from merits and demerits, has controlled his senses, and lives with his family always fulfilling his duties as householder, attains liberation. The householder always unified with yoga (engaged in the practice of yoga) is not besmeared by either merits or sins. Even if he commits sins acting for the welfare of humanity, they do not contaminate him. –224-225.

Mantra Sādhanā (Practice)

अधुना संप्रवक्ष्यामि मन्त्रसाधनमुत्तमम् ।

ऐहिकामष्मिकसुखं येन स्यादविरोधतः ॥२२६॥

adhunā sampravakṣyāmi mantrasādhanamuttamam /

aihikāmuṣmikasukhaṃ yena syādavirodhataḥ /226/

Now I am going to tell you the excellent practice of *mantra* (subtle sound vibration or a formula of prayer sacred to any god or deity). The practitioner attains uninterrupted happiness in this world and beyond it through this practice. –226.

यस्मिन्मन्त्रे वरे ज्ञाते योगसिद्धिर्भवेत्खलु ।
योगेन साधकेन्द्रस्य सर्वैस्वर्यसुखप्रदा ॥२२७॥

yasminmantre vare jñāte yogasiddhirbhavetkhalu /
yogena sādhakendrasya sarvaisvaryasukhapradā /227/

The yogi certainly achieves perfection through the knowledge of this excellent *mantra.* This yoga gives all perfections and happiness to the virtuous yogi focused within. –227.

1. Bīja Mantras

मूलाधारेऽस्ति यत्पद्मं चतुर्दलसमन्वितम् ।
तन्मध्ये वाग्भवं बीजं विस्फुरन्तं तडित्प्रभम् ॥२२८॥

mūlādhāre'sti yatpadmaṃ caturdalasamanvitam /
tanmadhye vāgbhavaṃ bījaṃ
visphurantaṃ taḍitprabham /228/

The lotus located in the *mūlādhāra* is endowed with four petals. There is the vibrating *bīja* (the mystical syllable or letter of a *mantra*) of speech, brilliant as lightning. –228.

हृदये कामबीजन्तु बन्धूककुसुमप्रभम् ।
आज्ञारविन्दे शक्त्याख्यं चन्द्रकोटिसमप्रभम् ॥२२९॥
बीजत्रयंमिदं गोप्यं भुक्तिमुक्तिफलप्रदम् ।
एतन्मन्त्रत्रयं योगी साधयेत्सिद्धिसाधकः ॥२३०॥

hṛdaye kāmabījantu bandhūkakusumaprabham /
ājñāravinde śaktyākhyaṃ candrakoṭisamapravam /229/
bījatrayamidaṃ gopyaṃ bhuktimuktiphalapradam /
etanmantratrayaṃ yogī sādhayetsiddhisādhakaḥ /230/

The *bīja* of *kāma* (love), bright as the *bandhūka* (the pentapetes phoenicea) flower, is located in the heart (the *anāhata cakra*). In the *ajñācakra* there is the *bīja* of *Śakti*, brilliant as tens of millions of moons. These three *bījas* are to be kept secret as they give both *bhukti* (enjoyment) and *mukti* (liberation). Therefore, the *siddhi sādhaka* (one who practices for achieving perfection) yogi should practice the repetition of these three *bīja mantras*. –229-230.

2. Method of Mantra Practice

एतन्मन्त्रं गुरुर्लब्ध्वा न द्रुतं न विलम्बितम् ।

अक्षराक्षरसन्धानं निःसन्दिग्धमना जपेत् ॥२३१॥

etanmantraṃ gurorlabdhvā na drutaṃ na vilambitam /

akṣarākṣarasandhānaṃ nihsandigdhamanā japet /231/

After receiving this *mantra* from his guru, he should repeat it neither fast nor slow, without any doubts in his mind, knowing the integral relationship between the mystic syllables of the *mantra*. – 231.

तद्गतश्चैकचित्तश्च शास्त्रोक्तविधिना सुधीः ।

देव्यास्तु पुरतो लक्षं हुत्वा लक्षत्रयं जपेत् ॥२३२॥

tadgataścaikacittaśca śāstroktavidhinā sudhīḥ /

devyāstu purato lakṣaṃ hutvā lakhsatrayaṃ japet /232/

Having firmly fixed his mind on this *mantra*, the wise yogi according to the ordinance of the scripture, should perform a fire sacrifice, offer one hundred thousand oblations and repeat the *mantra* three hundred thousand times in front of the goddess *Devī*. – 232.

करवीरप्रसूनन्तु गुडक्षीराज्यसंयुतम् ।

कुण्डे योन्याकृत धीमाञ्जपान्ते जुहुयात्सुधीः ॥२३३॥

karavīraprasūnantu guḍakṣīrājyasamyutam /

kuṇḍe yonyākṛte dhīmāñjapānte juhuyātsudhīḥ /233/

The wise yogi, at the end of *japa* (the repetition of the *mantra*), should perform the fire sacrifice in a *kuṇḍa* (the hole in the ground made for fire sacrifice) having the shape of the *Yoni* (the womb or source), and offer oblation mixing sugar, milk, butter and the flower of *Karavīra* (the nerium odorum) together. –233.

अनुष्ठाने कृते धीमान्पूर्वसेवा कृता भवेत् ।
ततो ददाति कामान्वै देवी त्रिपरभैरवी ॥२३४॥

anuṣṭhāne kṛte dhīmānpūrvasevā kṛtā bhavet /
tato dadāti kāmānvai devī tripurabhairavī /234/

By the observance of the fire sacrifice, *japa*, and worship in the described way, the goddess *Tripurā Bhairavī* is satisfied, and she fulfills all the desires of the yogi. –234.

गुरुं सन्तोष्य विधिवल्लब्ध्वा मन्त्रवरोत्तमम् ।
अनेन विधिना युक्तो मन्दभाग्योऽपि सिध्यति ॥२३५॥

guruṃ santoṣya vidhivallabdhvā mantravarottamam /
anena vidhinā yukto mandabhāgyo'pi sidhyati /235/

Having satisfied the guru and received this excellent *mantra* properly and by following the prescribed methods of practice in this way, even the yogi destined with little luck attains perfection. –235.

3. Fruit of the Mantra Japa

लक्षमेकं जपेद्यस्तु साधको विजितेन्द्रियः ।
दर्शनात्तस्य क्षुभ्यन्ते योषितो मदनातुराः ॥
पतन्ति साधकस्याग्रे निर्लज्जा भयवर्जिताः ॥२३६॥

lakṣamekaṃ japedyastu sādhako vijitendriyaḥ /
darśanāttasya kṣubhyante yoṣito madanāturāḥ /
patanti sādhakasyāgre nirlajjā bhayavarjitāḥ /236/

The amorous women become infatuated by the sight of the yogi who has controlled his senses, and who repeats the *mantra* one hundred thousand times; they fall down in front of him, regardless of their status, without shame or fear. –236.

जप्तेन चेदद्विलक्षेण य यस्मिन्विषये स्थिताः ।

आगच्छन्ति यथातीर्थं विमुक्तकुलविग्रहाः ॥
ददति तस्य सर्वस्वं तस्यैव च वशे स्थिताः ॥२३७॥

japtena ceddvilakṣena ye yasminviṣaye sthitāḥ /
āgacchanti yathā tīrthaṃ vimuktakulavigrahāḥ /
dadati tasya sarvasvaṃ tasyaiva ca vaśe sthitāḥ /237/

If the yogi repeats it two hundred thousand times, then people of all lifestyles come to him easily, as the women of high-class families travel to places of pilgrimage freely. They offer him all their possessions and remain under his control –237.

त्रिभिर्लक्षेस्तथजप्तैर्मण्डलीकाः समण्डलाः ।
वशमायान्ति ते सर्वे नात्र कार्या विचारणा ॥२३८॥

tribhirlakṣaistathā japtairmaṇḍalīkāḥ samaṇḍalāḥ /
vaśamāyānti te sarve nātra kāryā vicāraṇā /238/

By repeating this *mantra* three hundred thousand times, he comes to control all the *Maṇḍalīkās* (the deities that preside in the mystical orbs) along with their *maṇḍalās* (the spheres). There is no doubt in it. –238.

षड्भिलक्षैर्महीपालं सभृत्यबलवाहनम् ॥२३९॥

By repeating it (the *mantra*) six hundred thousand times, he becomes the protector of the world and is accompanied by servants, armies and transports. –239.

लक्षैर्द्वादशभिर्जप्तैर्यक्षरक्षोरगेश्वराः ।
वशमायान्ति ते सर्वे आज्ञां कुर्वन्ति नित्यशः ॥२४०॥

lakṣairdvādaśabhirjaptairyakṣarakṣorageśvarāḥ /
vaśamāyānti te sarve ājñāṃ kurvanti nityaśaḥ /240/

By repeating it twelve hundred thousand times, he comes to command the lords of the *Yakṣas*, *Rākṣas* and *Nāgas* (the kings of the serpents) and they all constantly follow his orders. –240.

त्रिपञ्चलक्षजप्तैस्तु साधकेन्द्रय धीमतः ।

सिद्धिविद्याधराश्चैव गन्धर्वाप्सरसांगणाः ॥२४१॥

वशमायान्ति ते सर्वे नात्र कार्य विचारणा ।

हठाच्छ्वणविज्ञानं सर्वज्ञत्वं प्रजायते ॥२४२॥

tripañcalakṣajaptaistu sādhakendrasya dhīmataḥ /

siddhavidhyādharāścaiva gandharvāpsarasāṅgaṇāḥ /241/

vaśamāyānti te sarve nātra kāryā vicāraṇā /

haṭhācchravaṇavijñānaṃ sarvajñatvaṃ prajāyate /242/

Through repetition of it fifteen hundred thousand times, the *Siddhas* (the adepts), *Vidyādharas* (a class of demi-gods), *Gandharvas* and *Apsarās* come under the control of the wise yogi focused within. There is no doubt in it. He at once achieves the power of clairaudience and knowledge of everything. –241-242.

तथाष्टादशभिर्लक्षैर्देहेनानेन साधकः ।

उत्तिष्ठेन्मेदिनीं त्वक्त्वा दिव्यदेहस्तु जायते ॥

भ्रमते स्वच्छया लोके छिद्रां पश्यति मेदिनोम् ॥२४३॥

tathāṣṭādaśabhirlakṣairdehenānena sādhakaḥ /

uttiṣṭhenmedinīṃ tyaktvā divyadehastu jāyate /

bhramate svecchayā loke chidrāṃ paśyati medinīm /243/

By repeating it eighteen hundred thousand times, the yogi rises up in his body and leaves the earth. His body becomes divine and he freely travels everywhere in the universe at his will. He sees the tiny pores of the earth. –243.

अष्टाविंशतिभिर्लक्षैर्विद्याधरपतिर्भवेत् ।

साधकस्तु भवेद्धीमात्कामरूपो महाबलः ॥२४४॥

त्रिंशल्लक्षैस्तथाजप्तैर्ब्रह्मविष्णुसमो भवेत _ ।

रुद्रत्वं षष्टिभिर्लक्षैरमरत्वमशीतिभिः ॥२४५॥

कोट्यैकया महायोगी लीयते परमे पदे ।

साधकस्तु भवेद्योगी त्रैलोक्ये सोऽतिदुर्लभः ॥२४६॥

aṣṭāviṃśatibhirlakṣairvidhyādharapatirbhavet /

sādhakastu bhaveddhīmānkāmarūpo mahābalaḥ /244/

triṃśallakṣaistathājaptairbrahmaviṣṇusamo bhavet /

rudratvaṃ ṣaṣṭibhirlakṣairamaratvamaśītibhiḥ /245/

koṭyaikayā mahāyogī līyate parame pade /

sādhakastu bhavedyogī trailokye so'tidurlabhaḥ /246/

By repeating this *mantra* twenty-eight hundred thousand times, he becomes the lord of the *Vidyādharas*; the wise yogi becomes *kāmarūpī* (identical to *Kāmadeva*) and all-powerful. By repeating three million times, he becomes equal to *Brhamā* (the Creator) and *Viṣṇu* (the Protector). He becomes *Rudra* (*Śiva*) through the repetition of it six million times. He gains immortality by performing eight million repetitions. By repeating it ten million times, he is dissolved in the *Parama Brahma* (the Ultimate Reality). Such a yogi is a rare practitioner to be found in all the three worlds. –244-246.

Achievement of Liberation –

The Final Aim of the Yogi

त्रिपुरे त्रिपुरन्त्वेकं शिवं परमकारणम् ।

अक्षयं तत्पदं शान्तमप्रमेयमनामयम् ॥

लभतेऽसौ न सन्देहो धीमान्सर्वमभीप्सितम् ॥२४७॥

tripure tripurantvekaṃ śivaṃ paramakāraṇam /

akṣayaṃ tatpadaṃ śāntamaprameyamanāmayam /

labhate'sau na sandeho dhīmānsarvamabhīpsitam /247/

O Goddess! *Śiva*, the destroyer of the *Tripura*, is the One alone (without duality) and the Supreme Cause. His supreme state is non-decaying, full of peace, infinite and pure. Undoubtedly, the yogi attains Him the ultimate desired objective of his life. –247.

Śivavidyā is Mahāvidyā

शिवविद्या महाविद्या गुप्ता चाग्रे महेश्वरी ।

मद्‌भाषितमिदं शास्त्रं गोपनियमतो बुधैः ॥२४८॥

śivaviddhyā mahāvidyā guptā cāgre maheśvarī /

madbhāṣitamidaṃ śāstraṃ gopanīyamato budhaiḥ /248/

O *Maheśvarī* (the Great Goddess)! *Śivavidyā* (the spiritual science of *Śiva*) is *mahāvidyā* (the greatest science or learning) and it is preeminent. It has been kept secret. The wise should keep secret this science spoken by me. –248.

हठविद्या परगोप्या योगिना सिद्धिमिच्छता ।

भवेद्वीर्यवती गुप्ता निर्वीया च प्रकाशिता ॥२४९॥

haṭhavidyā paraṃgopyā yoginā siddhimicchatā /

bhavedvīryavatī guptā nirvīryā ca prakāśitā /249/

The yogi who is desirous of perfection should keep *Haṭha Yoga* highly secret. It becomes fruitful if kept secret, and becomes powerless if disclosed. –249.

य इदं पठते नित्यमाद्योपान्तं विचक्षणः ।

योगसिद्धिर्भवेत्तस्य क्रमेणैव न संशयः ।

समोक्षं लभते धीमान्य इदं नित्यमर्चयेत् ॥२५०॥

ya idam paṭhate nityamādyopāntam vicakṣaṇaḥ /

yogasiddhirbhavettasya krameṇaiva na samśayaḥ /

sa mokṣaṃ labhate dhīmānya idaṃ nityamarcayet /250/

The wise man who always reads it, from beginning to end, receives gradual success in yoga without doubt. He who worships it daily achieves liberation. –250.

Achievement of Perfection Through Practice Alone

मोक्षार्थिभ्यश्च सर्वेभ्यः साधुभ्यः श्रावयेदपि ।

क्रियायुक्तस्य सिद्धिः स्यादक्रियस्य कथम्भवेत् ॥२५१॥

mokṣārthibhyaśca sarvebhyaḥ sādhubhyaḥ śrāvayedapi /

kriyāyuktasya siddhiḥ syādakriyasya kathambhavet /251/

This knowledge should be spoken to all those who are desirous of liberation, and to all virtuous ones. Uniting oneself with steady practice, one attains perfection. How can one achieve success without practice? –251.

तस्मात्क्रियाविधानेन कर्तव्या योगिपुंगवैः ।

यदृच्छालाभासन्तुष्टः सन्त्यक्त्वान्तरसंज्ञकः ॥

गृहस्थश्चाप्यनासक्तः स मुक्तो योगसाधनात् ॥२५२॥

tasmātkriyāvidhānena kartavyā yogipuṅgavaiḥ /

yadṛcchālābhasanṭuṣṭaḥ santyaktvāntarasajñakaḥ /

gṛhasthaścāpyanāsaktaḥ sa mukto yogasādhanāt /252/

Therefore, the wise yogi should practice yoga according to the prescribed rules. He who is satisfied with what he is endowed with, whose senses are under control, who is also a householder detached to worldly objects, is liberated through the practice of yoga. –252.

गृहस्थानां भवेत्सिद्धिरीश्वराणां जपेन वै ।

योगक्रियाभियुक्तानां तस्मात्संयतते गृही ॥२५३॥

gṛhasthānāṃ bhavetsiddhirīśvarāṇāṃ japena vai /

yogakriyābhiyuktānāṃ tasmātsamyatate gṛhī /253/

By following the practical techniques and rules of yoga correctly, even the noble householders attain perfection through the practice of *japa* (repetition of a *mantra*). Therefore, a householder should also endeavor in the practice of yoga. –253.

Householder's Life – A Noble Opportunity

गेहे स्थित्वा पुत्रदारादिपूर्णः सङ्गं त्यक्त्वा चान्तरे योगमार्गे ।

सिद्धेश्चिह्नं वीक्ष्य पश्चाद् गृहस्थः क्रीडेत्सो वै मम्मतं साधयित्वा ॥२५३॥

gehe sthitvā putradārādipūrṇaḥ

saṅgaṃ tyaktvā cāntare yogamārge /

siddheścinhaṃ vīkṣya paścād gṛhasthaḥ

krīḍetso vai maṃmataṃ sādhayitvā /254/

Leading fully a household life with wife and children, giving up all types of attachments and following the path of internal yoga in the midst of them, a householder eventually sees *siddheścinha* (the signs of success) in his practice. Therefore, by following and practicing yoga according to this *Yogaśāstra* of mine, he lives a blissful happy life. –254.

इति श्रीशिवसंहितायां हरगौरीसम्वादे योग

शास्त्रे पंचमपटलः समाप्तः ॥५॥

iti śrīśivasamhitāyāṃ haragaurīsamvāde

yogaśāstre pañcamapaṭalaḥ samāptaḥ //5//

Thus, the dialogue between Lord *Śiva* and

Pārvatī on the Science of Yoga,

ends the Fifth Chapter

of *Śiva Samhitā.*

ABOUT THE AUTHOR

Swami Vishnuswaroop (Thakur Krishna Uprety), B. A. (Majored in English & Economics), received his Diploma in Yogic Studies (First Class) from Bihar Yoga Bharati, Munger, Bihar, India. He was formally trained under the direct guidance and supervision of Swami Niranjanananda Saraswati in the Guru Kula tradition of the Bihar School of Yoga. He was initiated into the lineage of Swami Satyananda Saraswati, the founder of Bihar School of Yoga and the direct disciple of Swami Sivananda Saraswati of Rishikesh. His guru gave his spiritual name 'Vishnuswaroop' while he was initiated into the sannyasa tradition.

Swami Vishnuswaroop is a Life Member of World Yoga Council, International Yoga Federation. Divine Yoga Institute has published his nine books on classical yoga, meditation and tantra. He is one of the few yoga practitioners registered with Nepal Health Professional Council established by The Government of Nepal. He has been teaching on the theory and practice of traditional yoga and the yogic way of life to Nepalese and foreign nationals for more than twenty-five years.

Swami Vishnuswaroop has designed a comprehensive yoga program called 'Yoga Passport' in order to give a broader theoretical and practical knowledge of yoga which includes various aspects of yogic practice. Many health professionals, yoga practitioners and people from various backgrounds of more than forty-seven countries from various parts of the world have gone through his yoga courses and programs. He currently works as the President of Divine Yoga Institute, Kathmandu, Nepal and travels abroad to provide yogic teaching and training.

11685837R00111

Printed in Great Britain
by Amazon